THE PASSER

C. YVETTE SPENCER

THE PASSER

C. YVETTE SPENCER

Drama Novelist

This is a Busybee Publication

busybee
PUBLICATION

https://www.facebook.com/busybeepublication/

Originally published in the United States May 2015
Revised June 2019
ISBN: 978-0-692-44391-0

To my readers:

‡‡‡‡‡‡

Thanks for choosing:

THE PASSER

You encourage me to continue what I love doing, creating great characters with great stories.

While writing this book, I was blessed mentally and creatively to travel back in time and visit plantations. On one, I got to know this one character by the name of Jesse. He enlightened me by answering my question. "What if a slave was born looking like a White man?" His smile to my question intrigued me. "I am that slave you speak of," he answered. After getting over the shock, I sat with him and listened as he told me his story that was so different than any slave story I'd ever read or saw. Learning of it was such an amazing experience. I hope it affect you the same. If so, tell me how. C.yvettespencer@gmail.com

Let the peace of God operate in your hearts and minds. And remember, the only help God needs from you is faith. Stay prayed up, my friends.

Drama Novelist

C. Yvette Spencer

Author's Reflections

The Passer

This African American historical fiction is intended to be enjoyed and not to offend. It's from my imagination; a "what if" question that came to mind in the year 2000. I wondered and pondered until my pen met my writing tablet and the two began a dance that lasted for fourteen years, finally reaching its ending and taking to the publishing stage in 2015.

Two years later, in 2017, after having written and published eight more books, I began editing for other authors. It was that experience that helped to improve my own writing and led me to revisit my work and marrying my enhanced skills to my published work, to create a beautiful union. This revised version is the seed of that marriage. I am in love with this relationship. I pray that readers appreciate the newly found love as I have.

Author's Sentiments

First and without delay, I thank my Lord and Savior for seeding me with the gift of storytelling. I give Him the glory for the work He has placed in my hands and mind to create words of enjoyment.

I am blessed to be loved and supported by my husband, Ronnie Sr., my son, RJ, and my twin daughters, Sharell and Shauntrell. You all have been the cornerstone of my structure, and it is your belief in me that keeps me believing in myself.

To my daughter, Tiffany Spencer, who sat in on readings and gave essential feedback. You're a gem and I thank you dearly for your support and help.

When composing stories, my memory will always go back to my mother, Gloria, who was my first storyteller. I'm encouraged by your spirit whenever I write. Thank you for what you planted. I will never be uprooted.

I honor the spirits of my siblings who did not witness my first published book: Gwen, Sammie Lee, Angela, and Monica. Your deaths came too soon and left voids that can never be filled.

To my sisters, Devonna, Latachia, and all my nieces and nephews. Continue the fight to be strong. We are a family of strength and faith, and God will continue to hold us up through our saddest times.

To the men whom I call my fathers, Charlie Brown and Willie Grant, I love you. Thank you, Uncle Carroll Brown for always checking on me. Love you, dearly.

To my sister, Thelma Whiting-English, glad to have you in my life.

A special thanks to my editor, Richelle Grann-McFate, who kindly lends her time and expertise to catch every mistake and help to aid in my confidence of producing quality work. You offer pure kindness from the heart.

Prologue

Jesse had been in these woods before, but his reasons are much different this time. Before, he could stop and appreciate the smell of cedar and pine trees. In time past, he was able to get caught up in the beautiful display of wildflowers that created a magnificent array of colors. The serenading of a bird singing in a nearby tree would always draw him into a peaceful place of tranquility. He would allow his mind to drift from his world into a world that only existed in dreams. But that was then...

This time, Jesse couldn't stop and smell the forest's trees. Although the spectacular recital of leaves dancing to nature's orchestration of blowing winds was going on around him, he could not enjoy the performance. And there was definitely no time to welcome a song from a blue jay's sweet, peaceful voice from a nearby tree. No, not this time. Because Jesse was running. He was running hard, running fast, and he was not stopping, FOR NOTHING!

÷÷÷÷÷÷

Jesse and his family were born on the Hartford Plantation. But his life was not like his family's or any other slave for that matter. He was quite different at a glance, and it was that difference that tells his story. And oh, what a story it is to tell. But first, let's start with the Hartford's and Roy, as they all play a pivotal part in Jesse's life.

One

*T*he Hartford's owned a cotton plantation in the southern parts of Georgia. The owner, Massa Ordell Hartford, well, I guess you could say that he was a fair man. He treated his slaves as decent as any master in the southern parts of Georgia. He even allowed his wife, Missis Jewel, a sweet Christian woman, to educate some of their slaves. Now, it wasn't like schooling, of course; that was forbidden. It was simple things like how to spell their names, basic arithmetic to help them with their daily chores, and words from the bible like *obey, master,* and *servant.*

Missis Jewel kept her secret of teaching slaves to herself. Only her immediate family knew of the joy she felt when teaching a simple lesson of arithmetic to a young slave girl.

What would others think, her husband often reminded her. Missis Jewel was stubborn and really didn't care what others thought. However, she did mind her husband's concerns. So, she assured the safety of her secret by only teaching a few slaves whom she knew she could trust.

One evening, after the end of a social dinner with a few lady friends, Missis Jewel was in the dining room with a slave girl teaching her how to properly shine and store her most delicate China.

"Place it this way, always facing up. Now, let's count them. One. Go on, repeat it," she said to the servant girl who took the spoon from her, placed it in the storage box and started counting.

"One."

Missis Jewel passed another spoon to her. "Two. Don't forget, face up."

"Yes, sum. Two..."

"Three..."

"Three—"

"Jewel! What in heaven's name are you doing?" Ann, Jewel's sister, clutched her chest. She was staying for the evening. "Are you teaching that nigger girl to count?"

"Yes, I am. Four—"

"Why would you do that? Teaching slaves is forbidden!"

"Certain chores require arithmetic, Ann." Missis Jewel's southern accent was unmistakable. "And it makes them feel special. It creates a trusting and submissive relationship between the master and the servant. And I'll swear by it that it works. We've never had a slave to run," she proudly boasted.

"You don't break the law to gain their obedience, Jewel. And besides, it's a waste of time. Studies have proven that they have small brains and can only retain a little information. Trying to teach them will render them mentally ill. You have to beat them to gain docile behavior."

"Beat them!" Missis Jewel laid a spoon on the table and turned to the slave girl. "Excuse me, dear." And after patting the twelve-year-old's shoulder, she walked over to her sister and gave her a stern stare. "Our slaves are not in front of the mule, they are behind them. They are not animals. They are humans who don't require a firm slap to get them moving like a mule. A polite asking, sometimes followed by a *please* and follow up with a *thank you* are all they need to get them to comply!" She returned to the slave girl's side and picked up the spoon. "Now, where were we?"

"On four, ma'am."

"Of course, four..."

"Fo-ur," the girl stuttered while Ann stared at her.

"Come on, keep up, dear. Five..."

"Five..."

Ann stormed out of the kitchen. The heels of her shoes clacked away and faded up the staircase.

So you see, Massa Ordell and Missis Jewel Hartford were, by far, more reasonable slave owners compared to many others in their time.

As Missis Jewel and the girl counted, two loud voices came from the hallway. Missis Jewel slightly shook her head when she recognized them. "Sounds like my eldest is in trouble again," she whispered and attempted to ignore the argument with a continuous count. "Six..."

"Six..."

"Seven..."

"Seven..."

"Eight..."

Meanwhile, around the corner in the hallway, two male voices escalated.

"You have a name to uphold, Walter, and if that doesn't mean anything to you, it damn well means a great deal to your mother and me!" Ordell fussed after learning that Walter, the eldest of their three children, had acted up in school again.

"NINE..." Missis Jewel's raised voice did not drown out the argument her husband and son were having. The two had stopped getting along the moment Walter turned nine.

"You'll carry the family's name with honor and dignity or lose all the privileges that being a Hartford provides you, boy! Now, get to your room while I decide what to do with you!"

Walter's rage led him away, and he was glad to be relieved of his father's anger.

A few days later, after fighting with his father a second time in the same week, Walter stubbornly ran off into the woods on their land with the broadening threat of never returning home. He went deeper into the forest, deeper than he'd ever been and in no time, he was lost and left wondering if he could find his way back home. The thought of 'never returning home' suddenly became a regrettable notion when creeping and crackling noises surrounded him.

"What was that?"

In fear, he turned left, right, and around to locate the pouncing of fast-moving feet. *If it is someone, maybe they can direct me home.* Taking a step in the direction of the physical sound, he almost slipped. His feet had landed on dew covered leaves that surrounded him. He carefully placed steady feet on the leaves, cautious not to be their slippery victim. Walter came to a halt when spotting the image of a boy who was kneeling with his back to him. The boy's hands rapidly moved, tossing something aside.

"Hey!" Walter yelled out with shaky nerves.

Still kneeling, the boy glanced at Walter and returned to what he was doing. "Yeah, what can I do for ya'?" He continued pulling and jerking on something.

"What are you doing out here? This is my family's property." Walter masked his fear with authority.

The boy stood and faced him with a skinned rabbit dangling from his hand. "Catching dinner." He raised it to show Walter, whose eyes were fixated on the knife in the boy's other hand.

Noticing Walter's concern, the boy stuck the bloody knife in the waist of his pants. "Don't worry, I'm no threat." Wiping blood from his hand onto his clothes, he moved closer to Walter and stuck it out. "I'm Roy."

Walter looked at Roy's blood smeared hand and rudely passed on the handshake by slipping his hands into his pants' pocket. "I'm Walter Hartford. My father is rich and powerful."

Left hanging, Roy pulled his hand back and put it on the handle of the knife that stuck out the waist of his pants. "And my father is poor, but he's not out here to save me either."

Not knowing what Roy was capable of, Walter stood bravely.

"What you preparing for? A fight?" Roy lifted the rabbit again. "I told you, I'm looking for food, not a fight." He eased the moment with a smile. "You ever had rabbit, rich Walter Hartford?"

"Sure, I've had it many times."

"Hmp...I doubt it. Come on, you'll have your first go of it." He stuffed the rabbit inside a bag that hung on his shoulder. "I had a good hunting day." he said while patting his bag and walking away. "Six catches totaled. Come on, let me introduce you to my parents. My mother's the best rabbit cook in all of Georgia."

With the curiosity of how poor white people lived leading the way, Walter followed Roy.

"Hey, Pa?" Roy motioned behind him with a head nod towards his new-found friend. "This is Walter. He'll be having dinner with us."

"Hey, Walter," Pa said from the rooftop of their cabin.

"Hi, sir."

"Come on up. You boys can help me with the roof."

Roy's mother came outside and after a brief introduction, she took a closer look into Roy's bag. "You made out good this time, son. I'll go start dinner. You welcome to stay and have dinner with us."

"We already offered, Ma. It'll be his first time trying rabbit."

Walter smiled at the short dark-haired woman. "Thank you, ma'am. I would love to stay for dinner."

She smiled. "I'll leave you men to your work."

That day proved to be a revelation of several firsts for Walter while getting to see how poor people lived. It was the first time he did physical manly labor. On top of the roof, he helped Roy and his father patch the roof's latest hole. After filling a pail with water by pumping and priming a well, he carried it to the shack, up the ladder and passed it to Roy, who handed it off to his pa to test the so-called patched job.

The water found every leak unsealed, leaving Roy's father scratching his head. Fixing their broken-down shack was not his greatest skill.

But the leaks did make good for one thing, the smell of sautéed rabbits screaming from the cracks.

"Let's go fill our bellies," Pa said.

Walter slowly followed the two into the small shack. At first, the stuffy smell traumatized his senses, but the initial shock was overtaken when he saw the condition of the shack. It was full of mismatched odds and ends. Perhaps things they'd found, things people had thrown out. Everything was out of place, undusted, old. The collaboration of junk piles minimized the little space they had to move about. The wooden walls were covered with mildew. Some parts of the floorboards had rotted away, leaving the ground's dirt a part of the flooring.

With a raised nose that had been confiscated by the stuffy mixture of the shack's smell and sautéed rabbit, Walter looked up to see the work on the roof they'd just completed. Light from the sky pierced through the cracks of it. He caught himself shaking his head in disbelief at the shack's condition.

"Dinner's ready." Roy's mom placed plates and utensils on the small unleveled table with three chairs in the same condition. The serving dishes that did not match took up much of the space on the little table.

Roy grabbed a crate. "I'll sit here."

Walter sat and had to immediately grab the table to stop the chair that tilted and almost unseated him. They all laughed as he steadied the chair before taking their reaching hands that awaited his for prayer. When he took their hands, in unification, they closed their eyes and the mother said a prayer.

As if they could not wait to hear the word "amen" the moment she uttered it, Roy and Pa dug into the food like it was their first meal in weeks.

"Hey, hey...guest first." Ma nodded toward Walter and smiled.

Walter helped himself to rice, beans, cornbread, and sautéed rabbit. They politely waited until he'd filled his plate before resuming to piling theirs.

Walter's first bite of rabbit was observed with curious stares. They visibly awaited his opinion. "Tastes like chicken."

They laughed and feasted immediately after.

In the months that followed, Walter got to return the experience. "Please, Father. It's just for the night. It's cold in his house," he begged Ordell.

After looking Roy over for a long time as he stood on the porch in old worn, dirty clothes, Ordell finally grunted out to one of the slaves, "Get him cleaned up and put him on some of Walter's clothes. Something he can keep once they touch his body. Hurry up about it! He can have dinner with us. Maybe put some meat on his bones." Never being a man who required a response, Ordell walked away.

Sitting in the mansion, in front of a huge dining table set-up with coordinating real porcelain dinnerware and silver spoons and being served by slaves was another life for Roy. That night in the guest bedroom, he walked around observing its richness. The tall canopy bed, oversized dressers, wall hangings, tall ceiling. "This room damned near bigger than our entire shack."

Roy opened the French doors that led outside and walked out onto the balcony. He looked over the plantation and was mesmerized by the property's spectacular garden. Going home would never be the same, and the moment he opened the door to their shack after returning home, reality met him with a mildew scent.

"Glad to see you, son. The rain came through hard last night, tore right through my last fix. I need a hand on the roof." Pa carried a hammer out the door as he passed by Roy.

Wearing the clothes that Walter had given him, Roy never said a word. He went into the shack and tossed his bag of washed, dried and folded old worn clothes onto the shabby narrow thing he called a bed. Looking around his house in every direction, he was disgusted. He sped to the front door, forcefully slamming it behind him.

"Where you off to? Get up here and give yo' pa a hand."

Roy kept on walking, never looking back as distant words from his father forced a temporary halt. But his moment of thought was quickly followed up by a jog in the woods. It was in the afternoon when Roy returned home the next day. He'd slept in a tree all night, only leaving to go home when urged by his empty stomach. He neared the shack still disgusted by their living condition but stopped when met by his mother.

"He's gone, Roy. Fell from the roof while trying to patch it up. He broke his neck." Looking into her son's eyes, she waited for Roy to run into her open arms for comfort. But Roy stood staring. His mother's look beckoned for him to respond, and he did.

"Stupid white trash!" He ran off, passing by Walter Hartford who'd just walked up to visit.

"Hey, Roy! Where you going?!" Walter jogged to catch up, following him into the woods where they sat on a large tree stump, breaking limbs. "I never had any family members to die," Walter said, trying to interrupt the silence. "How does it feel?"

"I don't care. We were poor before he died, and death ain't gone make no difference." Roy applied pressure to the thick stick that wouldn't break.

Walter glared at his friend, who after bringing his knee up, slammed the stick against it, snapping it into two. He looked at both pieces and frowned. Walter wondered if Roy's feelings were normal. *It doesn't seem right not to cry about his father's death. But we're talking about Roy, he's tough.*

With a dropped head, Roy used the broken stick to crush crawling ants in the ground.

"They're really trying to get away, aren't they?" Walter said.

"Yeah, but I ain't gonna let 'em. If I could find the queen, I'd crush her too."

Yeah, that's Roy. He won't cry.

The boys were as different as night and day, which became the foundation of their friendship. Walter wanted to explore his wild and free side but was prohibited by his father and mother. "They're too proper and strict. ~*I just wanna be free~,*" he attempted to sing.

Roy laughed. "I hear ya'. Ain't nothing like the freedom to do what you want. Having the ability to be free is nice, but there's nothing nice about an empty growling stomach." Roy's family had always been indigently poor.

His unemployed father had gotten work when and wherever he could find it and his mother washed clothes periodically for a few families who couldn't afford to own slaves but could afford to pay help every once in a while. Meals were not always guaranteed, and they often lived off that freedom that Walter so ignorantly wanted. Wild and liberated, Roy was Walter's alter ego, but without the poor attributes, of course.

Over the next few months, Roy would leave home and return days later. He would often be covered in blood but offered no explanations or answers for his appearance or aloof behavior. Other times, rabbit or some other dead animal he'd brought back for supper would substitute for answers.

One day after a long disappearance, Roy's mother came out of the small room she called a bedroom and was happy to see that Roy had stayed the entire night. She stood over his cot looking down at her son, who, after having bathed and changed clothes, looked decent for a change. His behavior worried her. She had no idea what was going on with him. He'd never shed a tear for his father.

"Roy? Roy, wake up, son."

Facing the wall, he rolled over and sat up. "Yes, ma'am," he said with a dropped head, thinking that he was being awakened because of his latest mischievous act.

"Look up, son." His mother wore a smile with one hand behind her back, completely unaware that he'd snapped the neck of their most generous egg-laying hen the night before. "I have something for you, son."

He noticed her smile. *I guess she doesn't know.*

She moved her hand out front. Her smile widened and so did his eyes when he saw it.

"The knife!" He stood to receive it.

"Yes, son, it's yours now. Your father wanted you to have it."

He'd only seen the knife that was promised to him twice. His father had once said, "It's an heirloom. Been in our family for generations." After his father made the announcement, he took the handmade stilted handle blade from a wooden box.

Since Roy's friendship with Walter, his father had begun noticing his resentment for their 'take what you can get' lifestyle. But truth be told, Roy's father lied about the knife. It was given to him in exchange for labor when a man he'd worked for could not afford to pay him. It was a unique object for sure; very detailed, cleverly made to last a lifetime, but it was not a family heirloom. Just a thought to give Roy the sense of pride he needed at the time.

"It comes with a sharpener and sheath to carry it on your side." He pulled it out and showed it to Roy. Turning it from side to side, he explained its value. "You see the blade…see how sharp it is? I can cut through anything. My pa once cut a bear open with one swipe. My grandpa gutted a gator with it."

"What about you, Pa, what did you kill with it?"

His pa looked at the knife, holding it close to his face. Gripping it in his fist, he stabbed it into the crooked table, then looked at his son and lied. "I killed a nigger with it. Stabbed 'em right in the heart and cut 'em down to his stomach. All his guts dropped out."

Roy listened with widening intrigued eyes. "Why?"

"Cause he tried to rape your ma. He was a big black buck, but I cut 'em down to size like the hog he was."

Now holding the knife between his fingers after being given to him by his mother, Roy recalled the knife's heritage. The blood that it had shed…would shed. "Wow! Our family heirloom! Look at it, Ma. The blade's long, ain't it? It can cut through anything."

"Yes, son. Now, I need you to be caref—"

"I will. It'll be the sharpest knife in all of Georgia." He walked away star gazing at the fine object on the proudest day of his life, leaving his mother with the hope that the knife would dismiss his bad behavior. But by nightfall and after he'd sharpened it, she learned that her son was incorrigible.

"It was a stupid, worthless stray cat that would've scratched your eyes out the first chance it got!"

His mother stood in shock with eyes full of tears, some for the gutted cat, but mostly for her son. The knife had been given to him on the day of his birthday, and she'd planned to cook him a birthday cake to celebrate the special day. She headed to the chicken coop to collect eggs to add to the cake's ingredients, but the moment she turned the corner of their shack, her feet came to a halt, her hand went to her mouth, the other to her stomach at the sight of the dead animal. His body completed disemboweled. And she still hadn't learned that there were no eggs to collect from the dead hen. The death of the cat had momentarily stolen that knowledge.

It was a scrawny cat that minded its own business and belonged to no one. It had shown up every now and then, but more so after her husband's death and now it was dead. Its life lost at the hands of her son.

"It was a cat, Roy. A living, breathing animal."

"It gave me a snobbish look…like it was better than me. Like I'm poor white trash. WHO'S POOR NOW, CAT?! YOU ARE! YOU'RE POOR AND DEAD AND TOO DUMB TO KNOW IT!"

The cat lay draining its last few drops of blood.

Roy coughed up a hunk of phlegm and spat on the bloody animal. "I killed you with my knife!" He proudly lifted it, staring it over with villain's eyes and causing an unchangeable fear in his mother's heart. Roy had never been the best kid, but his father's death had brought out the worst in him.

"Walter, y'all have room for Roy in that big house of yours?" she asked her son's friend when he brought Roy a birthday present the next day. "I'm afraid that if he's not saved by someone, he's not gonna make it to his next birthday." A tear fell for every spoken word.

"I'll ask my mother and father."

Two

*O*rdell Hartford allowed Roy to move into one of the small employee shacks. "Maybe our family values will curb the boy's appetite for radical behavior. It definitely can't make him any worse."

Roy immediately tested Ordell's words after he'd sent Walter to awaken him for school. Walter ran back to his father almost out of breath with Roy's response. "Father, he said he's not going. He's going to sleep in today."

Ordell's brows immediately raised. "Not as long as I have anything to say about it. He has to obey my rules if he wants to live under my roof!"

"Actually, Father, he lives in one of the shacks. It's not technically under your roof."

Ordell's raised brow dropped, turning into a sullen stare. "Get out of my way and get off to school. Roy'll be right behind you." Ordell headed for Roy's shack, mumbling and growling along the way. Without knocking, he yanked open the shack's door and scowled at Roy, who was still in bed in his usual position facing the wall, his back to Ordell. Sensing that someone was towering him, he pulled the blanket over his head.

"Get out of bed, boy! Get dressed and run off to school!"

"I decided I don't wanna be schooled no more. I've had enough teaching."

"You'll get out of that bed right now, you will, and get off to school!"

Heavily sighing, Roy yanked the blanket off his head and sat up. "My ma and pa were schooled, and they still ended up poor. I might as well skip those useless years and get to working. Was hoping maybe I could work on the plantation. Earn some money to help my ma now that my pa's not there to help out."

It was an understandable request. "Let me think on it. But for now, you'll be schooled until I decide."

"You don't understand. I'm not returning to school. Ever!"

Realizing Roy was strong-minded, Ordell thought for a moment. He knew that there was no changing his mind. "Stand-up, let me have a look at'cha."

Roy stood.

"Turn around...all around."

Roy obliged.

"You're just a kid. A rawboned one at that. But we could use more help." He didn't need any additional help, but the boy had just lost his father and wanted to help his mother. Ordell respected that. "You'll quickly learn that it's a whole lot easier to be taught in school than in the field on a hot sunny day and during cold winter months. And no more sleep-ins. You'll be up and out of bed before sunrise."

"Yes, sir."

"Well, get dressed! You'll be working with the overseer."

"Help him keep the slaves under control?"

Ordell gave the now thirteen-year-old a narrow look. "My slaves don't need controlling. They're very disciplined. You'll be on hand for the overseer. Whatever he tells you to do, do it or you'll be gone."

"I'm never going back home."

"I don't care where you go. Any bad treatment of my slaves and you'll be gone off this plantation." Ordell huffed away. He wasn't a mean man but detested undisciplined individuals. He would be kind to you as long as you were willing to show the same respect, and his slaves and employees had always done that. On his way out of the shack, Ordell gave the door a hard push behind him that made a loud thud leaving Roy with the sound of authority to ponder.

Roy stared at the closed door. Ordell may have meant to make a statement by slamming it, but if he thought that it made a fearful impression on Roy, he was sadly mistaken.

Roy's desires to "keep the slave under control" went far beyond Ordell's understanding. They were the one race that he was superior to; they were beneath him. Although poor, his family was rich compared to slaves. "I earn a living," his father once compared. "I don't call no man master and come and go as I please." He reminded his son who'd questioned their economic state. "Be proud that you were born white, boy. Any man not born white is worse than animals." The words gave Roy freedom to hate slaves and treat them just as his father had described them, "worse than animals."

With the door closed and Ordell gone from his sight, Roy's smiling lips revealed his thoughts. His evil eyes shared in his thoughts as he reminisced about the cat he'd recently killed. It could not speak of the torture that he applied while taking its life, but slaves could, and the very thought that he had the power to take their lives, made him feel superior. "Time to get to work." Rushing to put on his clothes, he stuck his knife into the sheaf on his side and reported to the overseer.

÷÷÷÷÷÷

"Is that him?" the overseer asked one of his men as Roy made his way to the field.

The man turned to see. "Yeah, that's him."

"Come here, boy. I was told to teach you everything I know. You do as I say and maybe one day, you'll get a job as an overseer on another plantation. Do you know what an overseer means to a plantation?"

"Yeah, to rule over the slaves. To beat 'em and punish 'em when they get out of order. Make 'em mind you."

The men laughed.

"Rule right and you won't have to beat 'em. You see this lot of slaves? Only a few of 'em have been whipped."

Roy looked around at the field hands. Disdain subconsciously took over. He'd never interacted with slaves but couldn't stand the sight of them. Their dark skin habitually drew a frown on his face. His intention of ruling and having power over them had no similarities to how Massa Ordell and the overseer ran the plantation.

A slave boy about his age walked by carrying a pail of water got his attention. Roy watched as the boy passed by a slave girl about the same age. Suddenly his contempt changed.

"Roy! Roy, get over here," the overseer yelled.

"Yeah, I'm coming." Roy could hardly move forward from looking back.

Three

At sixteen-years-old, Roy had turned into a tall thin young man. Although he and Walter didn't hang out as much as they used to, every now and then they would spend time together in Roy's cabin talking about life's experiences and drinking whiskey.

Bad jokes, secrets, and laughter filled this particular evening in Roy's shack. After drinking his share, Roy wiped drippings of whiskey from his mouth with the back of his arm and passed the jar to Walter.

"You ever tried it?" Walter asked, then took a swig of whiskey and gently frowned. He'd gotten quite used to the strong drink by then.

Roy grew a proud grin. "You betcha. As often as I can. I grabbed one a year back. It was my first time. I talked another one into joining me in my cabin, but she was already broken in. There's no comparison. Nothin' like breaking one in, being the first. They'll never forget it and neither will you. The fear in their eyes, crying shit scared. There's nothing like it. How 'bout you, Walt, you still a virgin?"

No need to answer, laughter from the two freed Walter from what seemed to be an embarrassing question.

"Come by my shack tonight, I'll have something waiting for you."

On that night, as he'd done before, Roy snatched a young girl who was returning to her family's shack.

When Walter entered Roy's shack, he was stunned. "She's about eight."

"No, they look younger than they are. All of 'em do until the field tarnished 'em."

"Let's ask her."

"They don't know their ages. They don't know how to count years. They don't know how to count anything. Their dumb, brainless." He knocked on the side of the girl's head. "Hello? Is anybody in there?" He he-heed out loud. "See, I told ya'. Can't count. Brainless."

Walter gave him a *matter of fact* look. "They can count. My mother teaches some of our slaves."

"But that's against the law."

"Only a few people know it. I don't like it either, but it's how they run their plantation. But that doesn't change the fact that she's a child."

"The younger the better."

"I thought you said, 'the blacker the better'."

"Same rule applies, trust me."

Walter looked at the dark-skinned child. Her face was drenched in tears. "I wanna go home." The girl's silent tears increased to sobs.

"I can't. Not with her, she's a child. Send her home."

Roy looked at the girl. "You sure? Younger the better."

"Let her go, Roy!"

They let the child go, and a few nights later, they were standing in Roy's shack again.

"I can't promise you that she's not broken in, but I can guarantee you that you'll become addicted after tonight." Roy stood behind a twelve-year-old slave girl, his hands gripping her shoulders.

She silently stood in fear, tears dripping like melting ice.

That night, Walter lost his virginity and became a habitual slave rapist.

Four

 News of Roy's nightly activities spread in the ears of slaves. Parents stopped allowing their girls out at night. Only on rare occasions that left them no other choice would they be caught out in the thick of the dark and this night was one.

"Mama, you need water, I have to go fetch it." A girl's mother lay frail; body thin, gravely ill, barely clinging to life.

"No, baby. You, you...can—(*cough*)... You can't. It's not—(*cough*)...safe."

"I'll be careful." Kissing her mother's warm forehead, she looked around their small shack in hopes of finding any stored water, but only found an empty pail. Returning to her mother's side, she put the back of her hand to her forehead. The warmth confirmed the fever. She was burning up.

From the window behind her, a gust of wind crept in like an immature spirit, its presence barely felt, and doing nothing to extinguish her mother's burning fever. Turning around, the girl looked at the pail on the floor, and with fear, she knew what she had to do. "I'll be right back, Mama. I'll be caref—"

Her mother's eyes softly closed.

"Mama..."

"Um...um'ma be alright, baby." Her mother could barely lift her eyes to see her child. She was too weak to stop her from leaving. Gravely ill, the mother understood the danger that lay in the dark on the

Hartford's Plantation. A single tear raced down the side of her face. She gripped her daughter's wrist with little might.

"Don't worry. Just rest."

"Baby, please, please don't leave—(*cough*)... Um'ma be alri—" Her inaudible words cease to a whisper; her head eased to the side. Her grip released.

The girl felt her mother's head again. "Still warm." One last kiss on her forehead and the child picked up the pail and left.

The path to the well was dark. Everything out that night was dark. The cabins, the grass, the path; even dark clouds had hidden the stars. She had to rely on familiarity to find her way to the well. Her little feet moved rapidly, as fast as they could to safely get the water and return home to her mother.

"Where you going?" Coming from behind a large tree, Roy's words caused the girl to stumble sideways in fear. That late in the night a slave could be accused of trying to run. But seeing that the mild-mannered child carried a pail and knowing that she'd been caring for her mother, he knew she was of no threat of running.

"My...mmy mama, she be sick, sar'. Um goin' to the well to fetch her wa'dar."

"To the well, are ya'? What you got in your hand, a weapon?"

"No, sar'. It's a pail for wa'dar." Already clinched with fear, it grew when she noticed him looking around, assuring that there was no one in sight. "I gotta go. I gotta gets my mama sum wa'dar."

He stepped in front of her. "You gone just take my good water and run, gal, is that it? You think my water is free to slaves? You think slaves don't have to pay bills like us good white folks? Is that what you're saying to me, gal?"

"No, sar'. I gotta go take care of my mama." She stepped to the side, trying to go around him, but he followed her movements.

"You can go take care of your ma after you pay for that water."

"But I don't have money, sar'. I promise to work for it in the fields. I need to go tend to my mama. She sick, sar'."

"I know your ma sick. What?! You saying I don't know what's going on-on my plantation?"

"No, sar'. I gotta go, sar'. My mama needs wa'dar. She be burning up wit' a fever."

He took a step closer, stopping in front of the child. She tried to go around him, but his hand went to her chest. Dropping his head sideways, his hand moved in a circular motion over her chest. *Young, dark, and ripe for the picking.* "Yeah, you'll do just fine. It's been a while." He squatted in front of her. "You see my cabin over there?" He pointed. "You and me going in. You'll get to see your mama again, but only if you don't scream. You let me do what I want to do to you, and I'll let you go on to the well. You understand?"

"Yeaa, yea...yes, sar'."

He stood, wiped his drooling mouth and after looking around, he pushed the child in the direction of his cabin, walking behind her.

Roy had to be careful now that his sexual exploitations had gotten back to Ordell who warned him that if he ever touched another slave girl, he would be banished from the plantation forever. A warning that fell on deaf ears. You see, Roy's behavior was not that of a mischievous sixteen-year-old; he was a serial slave rapist.

Although being led by his push, the child wasn't moving fast enough. He grabbed her arm and tugged, causing her to drop the pail. Once he had her in the shack, he ripped every piece of garment from her small body, down to her underwear. After slinging her on the bed, he roughly relieved himself, and once finished, he uncaringly yelled, "Get out!"

The pain he had inflicted forced her damaged body to move slowly from the bed. Every footstep felt dramatic. The dark, unfamiliar room blinded her steps. She bumped into a chair, forcing it to scrape against the floor. Light from around the door frame guided her teary eyes. Finally, she made it to the door, and as soon as she opened it, a hard kick to her butt forced her face down on the dirt. Her hands rushed to brace the fall, but a soft pop to her right wrist made the save unsuccessful.

Roy eased the door closed and left the poor child to care for herself. She made it to her feet, cradled her broken wrist and looked around until she located the pail. With the purpose of her journey still on her mind, she continued on to the well, filled the pail with water and headed home.

It was late in the evening, and the plantation slaves had settled in by that time. There was no one out that late to observe her naked, abused, broken body as she made it home while carrying a heavy pail of water and nursing a broken wrist.

She pushed the door to their shack, and after going in and placing the pail on the table, she rushed to her mother's side. Feeling her mother's forehead, she smiled. "You ain't hot no mo'." She quickly dipped a cup in the water, turned her mother's head face up, and putting the cup to her mouth, she urged, "Come on, Mama, wake up. You need to drink."

Her mother's head tilted to the left, falling from the palm of her daughter's hand. She set the cup aside and picked up her mother's head. "Mama! Mama, I need you to wake up and drank this here wa'dar...Mama...Mm...Ma-ma?" Slowly laying her mother's head on the bed, her hand went to her mother's chest, hoping to feel a heartbeat, but she only felt a stillness. Suddenly, all the pain from her abused body rushed to her heart, causing fear to encamp there. Falling over on her mother's still chest, she cried.

No, it can't be. She rose up and placed an ear on her mother's chest, hoping to hear even a weakened heartbeat, but it had rested. Being careful of her broken wrist, she wrapped her arms around her mother's body and rested. Her sorrows turned to moans. She fought to find peace with the loss but to no avail.

She lay still beside her mother with a dead stare, completely naked, Roy's latest victim. Sniffles, tears, and pain had full control of her being. "At least you didn't see." The only peace that comforted her little soul was the thought that her mother had died not knowing what

Roy had done. She snuggled in close to her mother and stayed there all night.

When morning arrived, the light from the window glared in the child's face. Hoping it was all a bad dream, she quickly rose to check her mother but stopped when she felt wetness. She reached between her legs and came up with a hand full of red gooey substance. She jumped out of bed and saw the widespread red spot left behind while blood racing down her legs tingled. The bed, her hands, legs, the floor were all clear reminders...it was not a nightmare. Roy had taken her innocence in the most violent way.

Feeling no concern for herself, she quickly cleaned her body but took her time caring for her mother. Meticulously cleaning and dressing her in the only decent clothes she owned; an old worn smoky white dress with an antique lace collar.

She reported to the appointed slave assigned to tend to the arrangements of deceased slaves. That afternoon, her mother was laid to rest. Nine months later, the child turned twelve-years-old and, on her birthday, she gave birth to a baby girl who she named Willa.

The girl was a black slave with dark skin, who when raped by Roy, gave birth to Willa, a half white and half black daughter. When Willa was thirteen, she was raped by Massa Walter Hartford. The rape left Willa pregnant and nine months later, she gave birth to a baby boy who she named, Jesse.

Jesse was born 3/4 white and 1/4 black. He looked white from the top of his head to the sole of his feet. With dark wavy hair and hazel eyes, any black in the child was from within because on the outside, he'd been drained of his African pigmentation. But no matter how white he appeared, when they looked at him, they saw one thing only. A nigger.

Five

Years prior to Jesse's birth, after Roy had turned eighteen, the head overseer's dead body was discovered dangling from the ceiling of his cabin. The slave that he'd had the most trouble with was accused of killing him.

Roy gladly whipped the slave until he screamed out his final breath. As the beneficiary of the whooping staff, Roy took the reigning throne and became the head overseer.

Roy had a different approach to slave control than his predecessor. "Fear and pain," he said, was the key to produce obedient slaves, but he went beyond cruelty to prove it. On several occasions, Ordell Hartford had to reprimand him because of his venomous physical and verbal abuse toward the slaves. Arguing his case, Roy said, "If I don't, they'll take over. Then you'll be begging me to put them back in line. It might be too late by then. There's more of them than us. A revolt can easily break out."

"No more abuse, Roy, or you'll be gone!"

"But—"

"No more, and that's final!"

Roy stormed away in anger, dragging the whip behind him with his tucked, knife rubbing up against his side. Roy was a tall, thin man who was void of hygienic cleanliness. He had grimy salt and pepper hair. His leathery skin had been darkened by the sun and a lack of bathing. Lengthy, wild sideburns stuck out on the sides of his face, giving him a rough and rugged look. And although warned to never touch another slave girl, he could never *just stop.*

One evening, just before dark, a stout slave girl was headed to her family's shack. Roy grabbed the girl from behind and pulled her into the woods, but he quickly learned that she was a fighter. One hard deep bite and he was forced to release her. She attempted to run, but he grabbed her by the hair and slung her to the ground. When she tried to scream, he climbed on top of her and with a hand pressed to her mouth, her screams were muzzled. After disabling her ability to fight back, he pulled out his knife and threatened, "You move, you die. You scream, you die!"

He mistook her wide-eyed stare of anger for fear and released her. Laying the knife on the ground, he came up to his knees and tried to unleash his pants. With one good drawback of her foot—POW! Came a hard-powerful plow to his testicles. She rushed to scoop back, he tried to reach for her and another—POW! Went to his nose. Cupping it, the burning numbing pain and blood was a clear sign that she'd broken it real good.

He looked at her, she at him...they both turned to the knife and made a wild dash for it, but he was faster.

With a tight grip, Roy lifted it high above his head and plunged it into the girl's stomach. Pulling it out, he stabbed repeatedly. Every penetrating stab in anger to the girl's helpless body increased his malicious desire. With a sadistic smile plastered on his face, he pierced unfathomable strokes of his long blade deep into the girl. Finally, her fighting came to an end. Her body only moved with the stabbing motions of the thick, long, sharp blade as he continued stabbing long after she'd ceased the painful resistance and stopping only after his vindictive emotion had been thoroughly rewarded.

Roy stood up, breathing hard, knife in hand, dripping blood. His face and clothes were completely drenched in his and the girl's blood. She was dead, but the evidence of the fight she'd put up gave him a lasting memory. The attack left his nose forever altered, misaligned, and flattened. It became his trademark, and she'd become another victim of his reprobate mind.

He looked at his blood-stained knife and then at the girl's nearly decapitated body and smiled. That day changed his life forever. There was no going back and no one—not anyone—could stop him.

"Pleasure" was the name he gave his knife after that day, named for the feeling he got while stabbing the sixteen-year-old to death.

News of the girl got back to Ordell after dogs were led by Roy to catch the girl who was said to have run away. But Ordell knew better. And the excuse Roy gave of an attack by an animal didn't convince him otherwise. He just couldn't prove it. He asked Roy outright after viewing the girl's brutalized dead body. "Roy, did you do this?"

"I keep slaves in order, I don't kill 'em."

Ordell took a few steps forward, stopping in Roy's face, looking him over, the scratches, his broken swollen nose. He spoke with narrowed eyes. "If I EVER find out otherwise, you're as good as gone." Not needing a response, Ordell turned to the other men who worked for him. "Take her to be buried." Now on a cane, he limped away.

Six

"Seems you have quite the appetite for the darkies," Ordell's houseguest said. The two men stood out on the veranda, overlooking the plantation.

"I've tried a few in my younger days, but I've never touched another woman since I wedded my dear sweet Jewel."

The man held a glass of wine and puffed on a cigar. Taking it from his long-bearded lips, the houseguest looked at the cigar that was given to him by Ordell and smiled while releasing smoke. "That's a mighty tasty smoke."

"I pride myself on collecting only the finest."

The man turned back to the property. "It is quite noticeable that your employees are having a grand ole time with your female slaves. I would advise you, my dear friend, to put a stop to it or your entire lot of slaves will be filled with children running around looking like...what's the boy's name?"

"Jesse."

"Yes...Jesse. You wouldn't want a whole stock of them running around, would you?"

As soon as the man departed, Ordell called for a meeting with what was left of his four employees. "From this day forward, none of you are to touch a slave with pale skin. That includes you, Roy. And you too, Walter." Ordell looked at the two, knowing they alone were responsible for the increase in the population of the light skinned slaves. He had to undo what they had done.

After everyone had left, he spoke with Walter, giving him strict orders. "You are to go to the slave trading block and purchase the darkest male slave you can find."

A week later, Walter returned with a tall, strong dark man who looked to be in his early twenties. Because of Jesse's pale skin, his mother, Willa, was the first to be paired up. "Willa, this is your new mate. May the two of you enjoy each other and be very fruitful." And that was it, Walter's unofficial officiating of the two. No wedding ceremony to take place, they were coupled up with a few words while he and Roy walked away laughing.

The Hartford's purchased several more very dark-skinned men and paired them with the lightest female slaves that were of childbearing age. They later purchased very dark female slaves and matched them up with very fair-skinned men.

There was no use of fooling himself that the slave girls would go untouched. Ordell had done what he could to assure that the impaired skin color on his plantation was diminished. And his unforbidden light-skin slave raping rule remained in place until his death.

With Ordell Hartford dead, the Hartford Plantation had a new Massa, Walter Hartford. He quickly put new policies in place and abolished others. Educating slaves was the first to go. "Anyone caught teaching or even showing any knowledge or interest in learning will immediately be put to death!"

His new rules drew his mother to illness. No longer able to teach the slaves, and with her son's new bride, named Anna Bell, who took the role of the plantation's first lady, Missis Jewel stayed locked away in her room until she joined her husband in death.

Seven

*Y*ears forward...

"Come along, Jesse," Missis Anna Bell, Walter's wife called while headed to the woods. Little Jesse ran behind her carrying a basket. Whenever she went into the woods to pick wildflowers from their property, she always brought Jesse along to accompany her. Then the day came when she sent him to pick flowers alone when he was just ten.

"Now, I'm trusting you to go in the direction where we picked dandelions and daisies. You're a good child, Jesse, and I know you won't run off. That would cause me to trust no other slaves, and I do trust you. Do you understand?"

"Yes, sum."

"I would go, but I have to get everything ready for the social and I need those flowers to dress my arrangements for my tea party this afternoon."

Jesse stood waiting for any other special instructions.

"What are you waiting for? Go on, run along. Go."

"Yes, sum." Jesse hurried off with a basket in hand. It was the first of many times that he would visit the woods alone, and he loved it.

Jesse was a well-mannered child who never gave Massa Walter Hartford or Roy, the overseer, any problems. But his behavior did not spare him from being badly treated. It was in the woods where he was able to escape the cruelty. He would retreat into its rich greenness in the midst of tall, towering trees while birds sang him sweet songs. Jesse enjoyed the wind's kisses and the smell of nature that offered its pleasant aroma. He felt safe and free in the woods and hated to return to his tortured life as a slave.

As a young child, Jesse didn't understand why he was slapped when he dropped one of the several heavy logs he was made to carry. He never understood why they called the other male slaves "boy" but referred to him as "nigger". It made no sense to him that the twisted, flat nose overseer would leave him standing out in the scorching sun in an attempt to darken his skin. Jesse learned early on to never stare a white man in the face after being beaten down and kicked in the stomach by Roy because he gawked at his deformed nose.

No matter how badly they treated him, Jesse tried his best to please them. He hoped his humble demeanor would bring him mercy, but years would pass before he was forgiven for being born a white slave.

One day, they realized that there was no need to call him names, beat or subject him to abuse to remind him that although he looked like them, he was the complete opposite. Jesse had always submissively done everything that was instructed of him, the way they instructed him to do it, and when he was told to do it. And as time passed, they came to trust him more so than any other male slave on the plantation and often praised his pleasing work ethics.

At thirteen-years-old, Jesse became one of the plantation's 'strong men'. His job required a lot of heavy lifting, pushing, and pulling. The physical labor toned his tiny muscles into a muscular masterpiece.

A few more years went by and Jesse graduated to the position of a house porter and the personal butler to the houseguests. He tended to all of their needs in the wee hours of the night. At first sight, some houseguests would quickly turn away and go about their business. But others would stare, finding him to be quite intriguing.

One particular evening when Massa Hartford was hosting friends, Jesse was called to carry the bags of one of the guests who would be staying overnight.

Massa Hartford, his friends, and an overnight guest named Harry greeted one another in the foyer.

"Jesse, get here boy. Carry Harry's bags to the guest room. He'll be staying overnight," Massa Hartford ordered.

Jesse, who'd been standing with the other slaves waiting for their orders, rushed over, head bowed, body bent, like a submissive dog to its owner.

When Jesse came forth, Harry laughed. "Walter, surely you have a slave who can perform this duty. Why use your son as a servant? Is the child in trouble and this is your method of discipline?"

The other guests who knew about Jesse laughed. "Harry, my dear friend, Jesse is a slave," one of the men explained.

"But he's—"

"White, we know. He's the product of a man enjoying his property," another guest said.

They all laughed and retreated to Massa Hartford's cigar room where they shared light conversations about women, business, political debates and discussions about wine and where to buy the best cigars. But Harry's mind could not escape what his eyes had seen. "A white slave who's a nigger. Ree-markable," he said.

"I guess he's the example of how we would look if we were slaves," Massa Hartford said.

"He is quite astonishing, isn't he? Do you think we would be endowed with his muscular features? I mean, if we were slaves," one man asked.

"I'm uncertain. Nevertheless, being created with such a body structure has its purpose. I think it's that very reason God endowed them that way. Being a slave requires an awful amount of physical labor. And there is only one place I enjoy physical labor." Massa Hartford snickered and nodded towards a beautiful light skin slave woman who entered the room.

Feeling their eyes on her, she nervously poured four glasses of wine and with shaky hands, served them on a platter.

The men took the glasses and raised them up. "To you, my dear," Massa Hartford said.

The slave curtsied and turned to place the platter back on the table, but hearing the smirking laughter from behind, she felt uncomfortable and quickly changed her direction towards the door. The louder their laughter became, the faster she walked, running right into Jesse who came around the corner. Their meeting eyes stopped them both, but only hers were full of tears.

Jesse could hear the men laughing and supposed that was the cause of her sadness. Holding both her arms, he let her go and approached the doorway where he stopped and dropped his head. "Is 'dare anything else, sar'?"

"No, Jesse. You are excused for the evening," Massa Hartford answered.

Jesse stepped back and took hold of the door to slide it close.

"Hold on," Harry said, "come here, boy."

Jesse took a few steps forward, stopping between the doorway.

Harry pointed to the door. "Close it."

Jesse walked to the outside of the door and began closing it.

"No. You come in and close the door behind you."

After closing the door, Jesse turned around with a bowed head, his back slumped.

The other men stood silently, waiting to learn of Harry's intentions.

With an inward wave, Harry called for Jesse to come closer. Putting his drink on a table, he met Jesse, who was moving towards him. Jesse stopped the moment Harry started circling him and finally stopped. Facing Jesse with his finger on his chin, he crossed his chest with the other. "Take off your clothes." He pointed.

Jesse's head sprung up. His eyes rushed to Massa Hartford hoping he would rebuke the indecent command. But Massa Hartford head went up and down, nodding for Jesse to obey. Jesse's head dropped to his chest. Obediently, he slowly removed every piece of garment as the men in the room looked on. After lifting his leg to remove that last of his clothing, he stood butt naked in front of four sets of eyes that were all on him, shamefully displaying his bareness, trying his best to cover his private parts.

Still standing in front of him, Harry shook his head. "No, put your hands to your side."

With a stiffened body, Jesse uncovered his manly parts, nervously placing his hands at his sides.

Harry twirled his finger. "Turn around."

Jesse complied and stopped when facing Harry.

Harry touched him.

Responding with a shivering jerk, Jesse's obvious fear did not curtail the examination. Harry's hand continued on its expedition, rubbing Jesse's hair, his face, neck, shoulders, traveling downward, he didn't stop until his hand was gripping Jesse's...

Jesse's stomach and chest sunk in. His jaw bones protruded when his genitals were lifted, separated, squeezed, pulled, growing in thickness, rising to the occasion while shamefully responding to a man's touch.

Harry's pupils found their way to Jesse's eyes. Putting his hand to his nose, he smelled it with a slight smile. With the same hand, he lifted Jesse's chin with a single finger. "Hmm..." Grabbing his face, he turned it left and right. "Open your mouth."

Jesse's lips tightened. Harry's hand was covered with the musk of his private parts. The same hand that was now touching his face.

Harry gave him a stern look. "Open-your-mouth!"

Jesse's mouth flew open, completely afraid that Harry's hand was going in and in a panicky reaction, he would clamp down on it.

Harry bent and leaned forward to take a closer look. Satisfied, he took a few steps back before walking over to his glass of wine that he picked up from the table and sipped.

The other men in the room stood silent, unsure of what had just happened, or perhaps not wanting to learn of his reasons.

With a dropped head, Jesse cupped his private parts.

"No matter how white he appears, he's still a nigger." Harry turned to Jesse. "You may leave now... *boy*!"

Jesse rushed to put his clothes on and ran out of the room determined not to drop a tear. He ran right into a dark male dressed in a black and white servant's uniform. Their eyes met. Looking at the man, Jesse fought against warring tears, but he lost the battle.

Eight

*E*veryone in the big house liked Jesse, from the slaves to the master's family, especially Miss Delilah, the Massa's daughter. She'd taken an intriguing interest in him because he looked so much like them...white.

Miss Delilah was two years younger than Jesse, but she enjoyed being around him. She always found ways for him to be in the big house. Some days, she called for him to bring her fresh-picked flowers and other days she requested that he fetch fruits or fresh water from the well. "It tastes sweet and cold," she would say, "when it's freshly drawn from the well." Anything and any reason she could think of, she used as an excuse to have him in her presence.

Miss Delilah didn't know that Jesse was her half-brother, but with the mind of a curious child, she did wonder how he got that way. Her family shunned her questions to the side, so she took them to her nursemaid. "How did he get that way, Mable?"

"Skin color don't make a slave, birth does, child."

But no explanation satisfied Delilah's curiosity. *If he looks like us, then surely, he has more of our attributes than those of slaves.* And with that notion, she privately set out to affirm her theory.

"Come here, Jesse," Miss Delilah called.

"Yes, sum."

"Yes, ma'am. Jesse, it's yes ma'am."

He nodded in agreement.

"No, you must say it."

Confused and nervous, Jesse obeyed. "Yes, ma'am."

"That's it. Now, is it hot out today?"

Not understanding why or what she was doing, Jesse was slow to answer. "Yeees...ma'am."

"Wonderful." She continued asking questions and teaching him the proper way to answer. And in no time, her theory was proven. Not only did Jesse look like white folks, but he also possessed their qualities, their ability to learn. And learn he did.

Jesse caught on very quickly, which excited Delilah. And from there, she decided that he would become her pupil, and she would be his teacher. One day, she asked him to tell her what fruits were in the storage house.

"War'damelon an pee-just, an—"

She promptly signaled for him to discontinue with a waved hand. "No, Jesse. It's, wa-ter-mel-lons an-d pea-ch-ch-ch-es-, peaches." She led him to a desk in the parlor where she wrote the words out, carefully explaining and pronouncing each syllable while pointing to the letters.

On many days, Miss Delilah strategically planned for them to be alone. She would pretend that she was giving him chores to do, but she used the time to teach him. Going from one room to the next, various objects around the house were her instruments for practice.

Thinking there was no real harm to teach Jesse to read and write because he was forbidden to ever take one foot off the plantation, Miss Delilah made it her mission to continue educating him.

Day after day, week after week, months and years passed. Jesse got older and wiser, excelling in all that was taught to him. Everything Miss Delilah learned in school, she secretly taught it to Jesse. It was their well-kept secret that they shared for years to come.

Jesse had become quite proficient in language, but he found math to be his favorite subject. He loved all the ways that numbers could be formulated to solve problems. Miss Delilah couldn't keep up with how fast he was grasping math, so she secretly brought books to him to learn on his own. There were even occasions when he had to help her with her math homework.

Jesse's thirst to learn always left him wanting to accumulate more knowledge, so he gratified his quest by stealing books from Massa Hartford's library. Books on agriculture, finance, investment, and fiction. Any literature that was available and could be quickly grabbed before anyone saw him. Jesse read various novels and learned about different cultures, the lives of characters, some books inspired by true stories.

Miss Delilah's teachings went beyond the books. She taught her novice the proper way to walk, eat, and stand. He'd become her obsession, and she could not control her need to instruct him when noticing anything he did or said that needed correcting. "Not like that... Don't say it that way... Stand up straight... No, no, no, close your mouth and try not to chew like a mule. Chew slowly, properly." He was increasingly engrossed and welcomed her corrections.

For years, Jesse monitored every behavior of the white people as Miss Delilah had directed for his homework assignments. How they sat, made hand gestures, the way they laughed, even how they crossed their legs.

Circling him one day to admire his straight posture, relaxed shoulders, head upright, stomach tight, Miss Delilah was pleased with her accomplishment. He was nineteen, she was seventeen. She'd taught him everything she knew, except one thing.

"What can you teach me about the north?"

Nine

Weeks before Jesse questioned Miss Delilah about the north, he was charged with serving drinks during Massa Hartford business meeting with three other slave owners.

"We have to put a stop to it. We can't stand by and allow this sort of behavior to go on. It must be stopped at once!" A slave owner pounded his fist on a table.

Jesse eased back and stood against a wall, waiting for the next glass that needed filling while the conversation continued. He'd taken over the position as drink attendant left by an elderly slave who'd recently died until they found someone they trusted to take on the position permanently. Not just any slave could fill the position. Information shared during those conversations required a trusted ear that would not act upon or repeat what was said amongst the owners. Conversations that surprised Jesse, who stood still, trying to be invisible.

A slave owner suspiciously looked over at him.

Noticing the man's attention on Jesse, Massa Hartford spoke up, "Jesse is very loyal. Been that way since he was a child. We can speak candidly in his presence. Rest assured, he will take our words to his grave."

"Traitors! That's what they are. To think of all I've done for them. I feed them, clothe them, take care of their families and ask for only loyalty in return. They are a bunch of lazy traitors!" A fat owner shouted, forcing the attention back to the subject at hand.

A blonde-headed owner spoke, "I've lost two of my strongest bucks to the North. They up and ran off overnight."

"Did you send the search dogs after them?" a man with a mustache curled on each end asked.

"Useless. Their trails grew cold. I had to hire bounties."

"We're going to lose our most profitable investments to the north."

"Of course. The north offers them hope," a calmer owner explained. "Work for wages, freedom to go and come as they please. I've lost one to the north as well. When I learned that he'd run off, I knew he would be a loss. He had the stamina, strength, and endurance. And good heavens he was fast. In a night's time, his trail was cold as ice."

"Probably had help," the bearded man suggested.

"Possibly, but who?"

"Well, I'm not going to standby idly and lose all the time and money I've invested to the north. We have to put a stop to this, and we have to do it now!" the blonde slave owner fussed.

"We can beat fear into them," the fat owner recommended and held up his glass for Jesse to fill with bourbon. He looked up directly into Jesse's eyes while he poured. "Beat every speck of black off them until their entire bodies are bloody red."

"That's one way. But there are other ways to garner their loyalty," Massa Hartford said.

The men carried on their conversation as if Jesse was not a slave who would never desire freedom. As if he was content to remain a slave. And he had. His obedience had taken him from years of abuse to the big house. He was now one of their most trusted slaves, and he was proud of that. But that was before he'd heard their conversation.

Never had Jesse heard of such things. *Blacks living free and working for wages?* He had heard of the shopping stores and even places where people could sit and dine for a price, but not black people living free. *Does such a place exist? How could this be?*

All Jesse knew about and had ever seen was slavery. He had never heard of a slave being free. He knew that some had tried to run to be free, but no one he knew had ever made it to freedom.

He was complacent with life. A slave in the big house. Not working in the fields. No longer being beaten because of his skin color. But there he was, standing with listening ears, learning that freedom could belong to a slave and why slaves were running to pursue that freedom. The news excited Jesse like nothing had ever excited him before.

He wanted to learn more about this freedom and on the following day, he took his inquisitive thoughts to Willa, his mother. "Boy, don't you ever speak 'dem words from your lips again!"

Just like that, she had turned his possibility into 'never.' From the word 'never,' he learned to never share his thoughts with another. But the word 'never' didn't remove the thought. He wanted to hear as much about the north as he could.

When they permanently put another servant in Jesse's temporary position, his time in the big house was once again limited to bringing things in, helping to move things out and to be on hand when company visited. But visitations grew few and far between. He needed to find another avenue to learn more, and there was only one person who he trusted to share his questions about the north.

"What can you teach me about the north?" he asked Delilah, leaving her dumbfounded.

Ten

A few years later...

Fastening the last of the accessories, Missis Anna Bell stepped back and adored her daughter.

Delilah caressed the antique pearl necklace that had been handed down two generations. They made the occasion all the more special for the bride.

"You're beautiful, my butterfly."

Delilah was not a pretty girl when growing up, but she'd blossomed into a beautiful young woman. With shaking lips, Missis Anna Bell tried to hold onto her smile as she stood behind her daughter, viewing her image in the mirror.

Wearing a cream-colored beautiful wedding dress with a train that was the length of her height, Delilah turned from the cheval mirror and looked into the tearing eyes of her mother. Softly smiling, she reached for a handkerchief that was on a nearby table and cleaned her mother's face. "The ceremony hasn't even started, Mother, and you are already full of tears."

Chuckling, she took the handkerchief from Delilah, looked into the mirror and dabbed, assuring that her makeup was still perfect. "If I cry now, maybe my tears will be all dried out when I see you walk down the aisle."

The months leading up to the special day had been emotionally bearing on Missis Anna Bell. One minute she was giving orders, the next she was inconsolable. While planning for the wedding, Jesse had become her greatest help. Most women in her position required the help of a maiden slave, but after her maiden broke a unique porcelain candle holder she'd ordered for the wedding, Missis Anna Bell trusted no one to carry the precious wedding items but Jesse. Years of being beaten for dropping items had trained him well.

Now, that the special day had finally arrived, Missis Anna Bell was a nervous wreck. The recent graduate, Delilah would soon be a wife and her mother was agonizing over her only daughter leaving the nest. "She's so young, too young to become a wife and mother." In her mother's heart, Delilah would never be old enough.

Delilah was eighteen and madly in love with the thirty-year-old handsome man she'd been promised to marry.

Jesse was having mixed feelings about Delilah leaving the mansion. A couple of years back, he was moved into the big house and living in the servants' quarters with a few other house servants.

All his life, he'd grown up as a loner, unable to fit in between the dark and light skin kids. He'd been groomed to one day work in the big house and had only spent time with his family. Delilah had become more than a friend; she was his teacher, his mentor, and the only person he ever really talked to.

Her marriage would end his lessons and their friendship that had once been threatened by one question. "What can you teach me about the north?"

"Jesse, I could have you strapped up and beaten for that question. Get out! Get out at once while I decide if I should take your question to Father!" She didn't, but she seriously considered ending their lessons...but she couldn't. Like her grandmother, Missis Jewel, she loved teaching. If the role of becoming a wife and mother was not in her near future, she would have become a teacher. Teaching Jesse was her passion, and she understood that a teacher had to be their student's confidant.

Days later, Jesse apologized, and the subject was never mentioned again. She forgave him and continued teaching him until her engagement. Preparing for the wedding left her no time for him.

÷÷÷÷÷÷

Delilah's wedding day was everything she'd ever dreamt of. The guest, the decorations, the cake, the music, ceremony, and reception were magical. But like any magic trick, what was once there, disappeared. And in a few days, the house had returned to normality.

By that time, Jesse was able to read, write, and speak as proper as any Caucasian, but the secret remained between the teacher and pupil. He continued with his servitude mentality. A lowered head, slouchy walk, and broken grammar that sometimes required repeating for clarification. Never hinting that behind the outer appearance of an obedient servant was a young Caucasian man, who sat up straight, walked with proper body alignment and spoke perfect grammar. When they saw and heard him, he made sure they always saw Jesse, the slave...the nigger.

Delilah's departure left Missis Anna Bell with an empty nest. To help brighten her days, her maiden would send Jesse to the woods to pick her favorite flowers in hope that they would lift her spirit.

Jesse left one early morning to spend as many hours as possible in the woods. He sat in between two tree stumps. Leaning on one, his feet propped on the other. He looked up into the heavens and listened to birds chirping, allowing his mind to take him on a long journey away from the Hartford Plantation, drifting into a world with no limitations. A world where he was able to speak whatever he thought and go wherever he wanted.

Freedom! Jesse had thought of it each and every time he visited the woods. He could not think of anything else. It was so enticing, so alluring and had begun to obsess his thoughts more and more. And because he had no one to share his thoughts with, there was no one to talk him out of it, so he talked himself into it. He would do it. He would run and he would be free!

Eleven

A couple of years after Delilah was married, Massa Hartford became ill. His body just gave out on him. Seems his bad habits had finally caught up and put an end to his excessive lifestyle. He'd over-enjoyed everything from food, cigars, and alcohol to slave women and whores.

Massa Hartford was a tall, very heavy man who had become bedridden. His illness required someone with a strong back and the strength to be able to change his clothes, lift, bathe and move him. He specifically asked for Jesse. "Not only is he faithful, he doesn't require supervision to provide quality care," he told his wife. And Jesse was very strong. He was everything Massa Hartford needed after coming to grips with the fact that his days were numbered. And at that stage in his life, he just wanted to die with dignity.

With Massa Hartford sick, Missis Anna Bell's social parties had become obsolete, which meant her need to send Jesse in the woods to pick flowers were few and far between. And the fewer visits he had to the woods, the fewer thoughts he had about running. He was now twenty-two-years-old, and the plantation's newest overseer told him that it was time to be coupled up.

"Yes, sar'. I hear you, sar'. But 'dis not be a good time to lees' Massa Hartford. He not feelin' too good 'dees days."

The overseer looked at Jesse, clearly trying to read his unenthused response. He wondered if he was that committed to taking care of Massa Hartford, or did he lack interest in the opposite sex? Jesse was a prime candidate to produce strong valuable offspring. His loyalty to Massa Hartford could not interfere with the needs of the plantation.

While Jesse went about the room doing things for Massa Hartford, the overseer watched and realized that taking care of him was a twenty-four-hour, seven days a week job. He looked around the room and was reminded that Jesse lived in that room, slept on a cot, and only left when ordered by Missis Anna Bell or for Massa Hartford's needs. He had to devise a plan that would allow Jesse to socialize without leaving Massa Hartford unattended. "I got it."

"Sar'?"

"Never mind." He left.

That evening, Jesse sat by the window. His eyes went back and forth between the window's view and Massa Hartford who was asleep. It was cool that night. The wind so easily invited itself in and filled the room with its coolness. Jesse listened for any disturbances. There were none. It was the perfect time to practice. He made a quick check on Massa Hartford to assure that he was sound asleep. "He is." Jesse returned to his chair where his imagination took over.

He wore the latest men's suit, stylish shoes and carried a finely crafted cane like the ones he'd seen Massa Hartford's friend carry. Walking into an upscale restaurant, he was seated, and his order taken.

A tall, thin Caucasian fellow in his mid-40s came over. "If I may permit myself?" His question revealed his French origin. He gripped the back of a chair at Jesse's table. It was the only seat left in the crowded restaurant.

"Be my guest, friend," Jesse replied.

The waiter returned and poured a glass of wine. He turned to the gentlemen. "How about you, sir?"

The man held up his glass. The waiter filled it and left the two. The man put the glass to his mouth but stopped when noticing Jesse, who lifted his glass, smelt, and twirled it. The action intrigued him. It was an etiquette Jesse had borrowed from watching Massa Hartford and his guest.

The man turned to the cane and admired it. "Exquisite. What a finely crafted object." Jesse imagined him saying. *Looking at the cane, he examined its details.*

"Thank you."

"May I?" He reached for the cane in the midst of Jesse's "Yes."

Spinning it around, the man said, "It's quite unique. I've never laid eyes on anything like it. It's stunning."

"Thank you. It's the craftsmanship of a friend—"

The door to Massa's Hartford's bedroom opened, breaking Jesse's daydream. In walked the overseer but he was not alone.

Jesse popped up from his seat with a dropped head.

The overseer stopped in the center of the room. Reaching behind him, he grabbed an arm and a girl came forward. "Jesse, this here is Nina. She gone keep you company while you tend to Massa Hartford. I'll be back to get her after a spell."

"Yes, sar'." Jesse's head slowly elevated at the same slow speed of his broadening eyes. She was the most beautiful girl he'd ever seen. Her perfect dark skin shined as if it had been freshly dipped in dark chocolate. When she raised her head, the brightness of her shiny eyes appeared to have never seen a sad day. On her shoulders rested thick, crinkled hair from recently loosened braids.

With locked eyes, there were no words spoken to release their stares. Seconds passed, and he was still at a gaze. Her mesmerizing beauty had snared him. A quick jerk and the room came into view. He rushed to retrieve a chair from across the room. "You welcome to sit if you has a mine to."

Nina smiled, thinking that he had the same dialect as the other slaves on the plantation. "Thank, ya'."

He wondered how she could be more beautiful until the little smile she offered allowed him to see her depthless dimples. As taught by Delilah, Jesse held the chair for Nina and waited patiently for her to sit. Once seated, he checked on Massa Hartford. *Still asleep, I mean 'sleep.'* He returned and sat in the chair next to her.

Always being a loner, the company of his kind was rare for Jesse. In silence, he tried to sit comfortably, but it was a wrestle, more so in his mind. *Would it be an affront to her graceful presence to sit as a slave? Would she notice if I sat like the whites*? His thoughts made his self-imposed battle more complicated than they had to be.

A deep sigh, and finally he was still. Not comfortable, but still. Sitting straight up, head stiff, looking forward, a space between his back and the chair, legs L-shaped, feet solidly on the floor, hands settled on his thighs. It was uncomfortable indeed, but it had to do. He didn't want her to think he was nervous. *Break the silence, Jesse. Say something.* "It be hot out today."

"It's been hot most days. Rain would help, but we haven't seen rain for a while. Nothing but the heat."

That was stupid to say. Selfish. You work in the big house. She works in the heat. Now you have her thinking about how hot it is in the field.

Their eyes never left what was in front of them, Massa Hartford laying on the bed, his chest moving up and down. Several minutes passed quietly.

Suddenly the sound of a roaring bear broke their silence and gave way to laughter. And the discomfort of unspoken words was removed.

With a shushing finger to his lips, their laughter lowered.

"I never heard nobody sound like that before," Nina said between giggles. Her hand covered her smile. But when she removed it, she turned to him with open lips, displaying a beautiful smile.

He was hypnotized all over again, but only for a second. Everything about her seemed so perfect. "How ole is you?" To him, she looked to be about fifteen.

"Seventeen. How old are you?"

"Um twenty-two."

"I know your family. You don't get to see 'em that much since you be taking care of Massa, do you?"

"I visits 'dem an evening out the week. Massa 'quires a lot of lookin' after, so I mostly be here wit' him. I don't member seeing you on the plantation. I miss a lot since 'um seeing after Massa."

"I been here for a few months. My ole Massa, he lost his plantation to gambling and paid the bill with us. We came—"

A ghastly sound emanated from Massa Hartford. Jesse ran to his bedside. "Go fetch Miss Anna Bell."

Nina rushed out of the room.

Jesse poured a glass of water from the pitcher that always sat on the table beside Massa's bed. Lifting his head, he helped him take a drink of water and gently returned his head to the pillow.

Missis Anna Bell entered the room with concern covering her face. Her little, petite body glided effortlessly across the room to Massa's bedside. "How's he doing, Jesse?" she asked in her strong southern accent while placing the back of her hand on his forehead checking for a fever. An illness that had been present more often than not.

With closed eyes, Massa peacefully laid as if the dreadful cough had never occurred.

"He fine now, ma'am." After placing the glass on the table, Jesse took a few steps back toward the wall, close enough to hear Massa's distress should it happen again. He lowered his head.

Missis Anna Bell turned to Jesse. "You may leave to visit your family, Jesse."

"Yes, sum."

She waited until the door closed before turning to her husband. "You look so weak, my dear. Oh, how I missed you so. The slaves miss you as well. Not much has happened since your absence. Everything is productively running along with only a few minor hiccups. Nothing too serious that would require your attention.

Oh, yes. Celcie finally had her baby. It was a strong baby boy. Dark as the night's skies. Her sister will soon follow her lead. Her stomach looks like it's about to burst open in a day's minute... And Bayell passed away two days ago. Dellbee asked about you. He misses you so much, my dear. I know he's your favorite slave... They all miss you, dear. We all do." She dropped her head and silently cried.

The door opened.

Missis Anna Bell quickly turned and rushed to wipe her face with her embroidered handkerchief.

"Jesse, how was your visit with your family?"

He'd visited his family a few evenings ago and although he was always delighted to see them, not much had happened since his last visit. "Good, ma'am. Thank you."

During his visit with his family, he wanted to inquire about Nina, but he had learned early on in life to be self-reserved. A thousand things could be going on in his mind, but he would be the only keeper of his thoughts. Besides, he had decided that the overseer's plans would not work.

He was planning to run as soon as he could figure out how it could be done without getting caught. Ignorant of how to do so did not stop his desire. It was the most important thing in his life, and he had no intention of allowing his heart to distract his plans. While on his way back from his family, he vowed that he would show no interest in Nina. *No matter how beautiful she is, freedom is more attractive.*

"Good. That's good." Missis Anna Bell kissed her husband goodnight, and glided across the floor, leaving to retire for the evening.

The following evening, there was a knock on Massa Hartford's door. Only the servants would knock before entering, and Jesse didn't expect their visit. The usual task of changing out his pitcher of drinking water had already been taken care of.

"Who could that be?" He opened the door.

"Hi, Jesse."

"Hi…ah."

"Nina?"

He knew her name, but her presence clouded his memory. "Yea, Nina." *Stay focus.* "You needs some 'em."

"No, I don't need anything. The overseer sent me to keep you comp'nee."

"Ah. Okay. Come in." Jesse watched as Nina walked to the chair and made herself comfortable. He took a deep breath and slightly shook his head. *A woman like her is dangerous to a man's plans.* He knew the overseer had especially handpicked Nina to do what no other female slave would be able to do. Make him think of something other than Massa. After all, Jesse was a man, and no matter how dedicated a man is, at some point, he will feel the need of a woman, especially if she looked anything like Nina.

Nina had all the makings of a woman of seduction. She was young, beautiful, curved in the right places, and yet, she had an appeal of innocence. And because her prior Massa prohibited the raping of his slaves, she'd escaped being touched by any man. As a slave, she was prime property. She was strong, obedient, a hard worker, and at a young age, she could give the plantation more human property.

With Jesse, the two of them could procreate children that would grow up to be valuable assets for the plantation. The kind that understood their value and knew they were created to serve their master.

After Nina sat, Jesse went over to check on Massa Hartford. Nina found herself enjoying his attendance to the Massa with such details and waited patiently for him to complete his duties. Jesse brought a chair over and placed it near her.

"How's he doing?"

He sat before answering. "He be alright. He just lay there, mostly. He not much trouble to take care of, just needs some tending to like normal things."

"How long he be like that? I never seen him on the plantation."

"He be sick for a while, now, but he got worse a few months back. Some days he opens his eyes and some days he don't."

Not long into Nina's visit, the two of them were sharing smiles and laughter about nothing. They were making fun of the three-legged, one-eyed dog that ran head-on into trees while trying to catch the cat that always got stuck in the trees to escape the three-legged, one-eyed dog. Before she knew it, she was enjoying his company. Before he knew it, he loved hers.

Without warning, Jesse abruptly stood. "You gotta leave."

"Huh?"

"I needs you to leave. Now!"

She jumped. Confused and not inquiring why or what had happened, Nina immediately got up and ran out of the room.

Jesse fell back into the chair, blinded his eyes with his hands and continued moving them until they stopped on his temples. *I can't believe it.* He was getting drawn in like a twirling tornado, sucked right into the overseer's trap. He stood and walked the few steps to the window and watched Nina, who was briskly walking across the yard.

It was evening, and the only light that shined was from the moon. Still watching her, he saw when her steps increased to a slight jog. Soon she was out of his sight, but not out of his thoughts. *This cannot be happening.*

He was losing and the overseer was winning. It was as if he had taken a peep into the plans of Jesse's heart and vowed a bet that he could change his plans of running by ripping them out and replacing them with love. Love...a word he had never pondered.

Twelve

*T*alks had begun amongst the field slaves about Nina's and Jesse's visits. The coupling was not new. It was well-known that the overseer would pair up a strong field hand with a well-mannered slave in an effort to produce model slaves. Jesse and Nina were perfect for such a breeding.

"Nina," the overseer called her from the field. "You dismissed for yo' visit."

Words Nina looked forward to. They didn't come every day and mostly came towards the fields cut off time, but they were a joy to hear. She hurried to have her cotton sack weighed and rushed off.

Knock, knock, knock–came soft beats on the door drawing a smile from Jesse. One he couldn't let her see. He refused to encourage what would never be. *It wouldn't be fair to her.*

"Hey, Nina." He stepped to the side so she could enter. As usual, he set a chair next to her, held her seat while she sat, checked on Massa and joined her. They mostly talked about life. All they knew of it was slavery, so it steered their every conversation. But on this day, it changed.

With Massa Hartford in her view, Nina leaned over to Jesse and whispered in his ear. "Ever thought about running?"

He pulled back and turned to her. His face completely distressed, in shock, in disbelief. "Don't ever say 'dem words again. You can be hung." He stood. "I think it's best 'dat you lees', now."

"But, Jesse, I was—"

He walked to the door, opened it and stood to the side.

With a lowered head, she walked to the center of the door and looked at him once more before leaving.

What 'um gone do with that thought. He walked over to Massa Hartford, tightly tucked the covers underneath him and went to his chair by the window. He could see her walking across the lawn. She turned and looked up at him, but never stopped walking.

"Nina, you can go for your visit," the overseer said the very next evening. It was rare that she was allowed to go back-to-back days. And after last night, she wasn't sure if she was welcome. Dragging her cotton bag from the field, she waited for it to be weighed and not long after, she was on her way to the big house.

Walking towards it, the house appeared to be larger than normal. She couldn't get her mind off Jesse and the night before. Her words had caused a look on his face that she'd never seen. "I can't." She saw a space under the back stairs that led to the house and consider climbing under them for the length of time she would have spent with Jesse. Looking around once more, she went towards that 'space' just as the back door opened.

Two older slave women came out talking and laughing. Recognizing Nina and knowing the reason for her visit, one held the door for her. "Come on, child, I don't have the rest of my life to be holding 'dis here door for you."

"Yes, sum." She went in and headed up the stairs but stopped at the door with many thoughts going through her mind. She stared at the door before knocking. Fear increased the moment it opened.

"What you doing here?" Jesse asked.

"The overseer...he sent me...to visit...I...I should go—"

"No, come on in. I'll be right back. I gotta get some fresh towels."

He left and she entered. Taking the empty chair that was always near the wall, she set it next to his and waited. Sitting up straight, Nina felt uncomfortable. She leaned back, hands in lap, crossed her legs, and uncrossed them just as the door open. Watching as Jesse put up the towels and tended to Massa Hartford, she could feel her heartbeat louder every time she thought he was headed her way. Finally, his footsteps found a sure direction toward her.

As soon as Jesse sat, he turned and grabbed her hands. Looking at her trembling hands, he knew her pain. "Nina, um sorry. It's what I was taught. It's all I know. To be so sca'ed to run 'dat you can't even talk about it."

"I understand." Looking at him, a smile grew.

There it is. So lovely. I have to say more to continue receiving it.

Their evening was fun and pleasant. They laughed harder than ever before.

"Hey, let me teach you a game," she said.

"A game." Jesse had never played a game. "Okay."

She put her hand out front, palm up. "Try to grab it before I pull back."

"Okay." He was slow moving as she pulled her hand away causing him to miss it.

"Oh, okay. I gotta catch it 'foe you pull back."

"Yes."

"Okay, but you know 'um good at this?"

"You never played it buh'fo."

"Don't matter, I is good at everything."

"We'll see."

He quickly proved it. Catching her hand every time, and she kept failing to catch his. By the fourth round, Nina was determined to win at least one game. She slowly extended her hand and with tightened eyes, she glared at Jesse's hand and waited for him to make his move.

Not taking her eyes off his hand, she stared with total concentration. He reached but failed.

"I won!"

"Shhh."

Giggling, she whispered, "I beat you."

"One more time."

"Okay."

Her hand was out front, face up, waiting.

He stared and grabbed. "Got it!" Pulling her into him. The two locked eyes. Twinkles of butterflies traveled down his spine. Their hypnotic gaze magnetized their bodies.

Jesse delicately placed his lips on her plush lips. Releasing her hand, he took her shoulders and pulled her in. His mind battled with his heart, telling it to stop, move away, release her, and ask her to leave; but his heart disputed and won the fight.

The kiss was intense, it was long, and yes, it was moist.

A light knock on the door broke the passionate moment. Lips separating, they quickly turned forward in their seats.

Not waiting for permission to enter, the door opened and in walked a young slave girl. She'd been sent by her mother to change out the pitcher of water. Carrying the container with two hands, her little brown bare feet briskly moved towards the table. She sat one pitcher on it, took the other and left without saying a word or looking their way.

Nina had turned forward in her seat and kept her head down. As soon as the door was closed, her fingers went to her lips, caressing them, wondering if the young girl saw the impressions of Jesse's lips on them. She turned to Jesse, who got up and walked to the window, obviously nervous.

Standing in silence, he looked out into the yard, hoping no one had seen their moment of intimacy.

Slaves were returning to their shacks from a long day of work. No one had stopped to look up to the second floor, peeped in the window, and witnessed the private moment between the two.

In a soft, calm voice, he said, "I needs you to lees'." He kept his eyes facing the yard, unwilling to even look at her.

Saddened, Nina got up and walked out without looking back. She felt a strange feeling in her chest. By the time she made it to the servant's door, she understood that feeling. It was pain. The feeling that came from a broken heart. Something she'd never felt before and the unwanted tears that fell from her eyes confirmed the introduced emotion.

Once outside, she wanted to run home, but the few slaves who were still going about their chores would notice. She kept her head down until making it inside the shack that she and her mother shared. And there, she embraced the tears that would not stop running.

Thirteen

Hi. How you doing? I been waitin' fo' you to wake up.

A few days later, just as it had each morning, pain patiently sat on the side of Nina's bed waiting to spend its day with her. The only release she got from its whispering words was in the field. She was glad to get dressed and head to the field that morning.

By noon, she'd picked more cotton than any woman in the field and some men. But her relentless labor caught the attention of the other field hands and the observation of the overseer. "NINA!"

Snatching cotton from their boll, her fingers ran counter to almost every bristle that continued slicing her tips, leaving stinging pain that she ignored, along with the overseer's voice. "NINA!"

"Nina...Nina...you hear 'dah overseer callin' fo' you?" a nearby slave asked.

But Nina ignored him too.

Now walking towards the field, the overseer yelled again, this time, building a wall around his mouth with cupped hands to enhance the yell. "NINA!"

She stopped. Not caring if she was in trouble, she took her time catching her breath. Placing a hand on her waist, she wiped the sweat from her forehead and took one last deep breath before walking to the overseer. Stopping in front of him, the sun was blinding. She shielded her eyes. "Yes, sar'?"

"You didn't hear me calling you, gal?"

"No, sar'. Was working, sar'."

He looked at her for a moment, figuring she was lying but it was the first time. Something had to be wrong. "How's yo' visit goin' wit' Jesse?"

"Fine, sar'." Droplets of sweat ran down her face.

He wondered if she was speaking truthfully. It was hard to discern.

"You two ready to couple up?"

"No, sar'."

He took a step back and walked around her, admiring her shape, her dark beautiful face. Even with field clothes on and the scent of work, she was still attractive. He stood silently, wondering what to do and considered whether Jesse liked girls at all.

"It's that all, sar'?"

"No... No. Go get cleaned up. Put on your best dress, fix your hair, and then go visit Jesse."

Nina had never been given the opportunity to clean up and change before visiting Jesse. She'd been sent directly from a hot, sweaty day of fieldwork.

Seeing the slave huts a distance away, she walked in their direction feeling forced to pursue someone who wanted no part of her. She'd never shed a tear before meeting Jesse. Since he'd last dismissed her, she couldn't stop crying. *What if I clean up, will that make him want me?* Her private thoughts broke free and leaning over, she burst into tears.

Raising up, she looked into the mirror that sat on a table leaning up against a wall. It had been given to her by her old Massa's daughter. She cleaned her face, erasing all visible tears, and started unloosening her braids with stinging freshly lacerated fingers from that morning's work. Tears fell again. As she wiped them away, anger grew. *What did I do to make him send me away?* "Kissed him!"

Suddenly, the need to know dominated all of her thoughts and actions as her finger moved rapidly, unlooping every twist of her hair. Finally, she was done. An angry image stared back at her in the mirror. A whole new emotion she'd never experienced.

Fourteen

Walking to the window, Jesse looked out. From a distance, he could see the slaves laboring in the hot sun. He wasn't able to make out any faces but seeing them working hard from sunup to sundown did something to his heart. Only spending a few years in the field, the old overseer, Roy, had made sure he worked harder than most.

When Missis Anna Bell learned that he was being used as a field hand, she was very upset. "Does he look like other slaves?" she questioned Roy, her husband's childhood friend. She'd disliked him since the day they first met.

"No, ma'am, but the boy needs the sun to darken him up."

"The sun is not darkening him, it's blistering him. The child is as ripe as a dark Georgia peach. I'm sure you can find other tasks for one as unique as him." She knelt down in front of Jesse, who stood with arms away from his body, trying his darnedest to not touch his topless sunburned skin. "When you're all better, you'll accompany me in the woods to pick flowers. Would you like that?"

"Yes, sum," his sweet, innocent little voice answered.

Standing up, Missis Anna Bell looked at the overseer, her demeanor quickly changed, assuring him of her anger. "Send him to Addie to be healed this instant! And if I ever hear of any further abuse to this child by your hands or orders, I'll have you removed."

With squinting eyes, he dared her threat with a stare. "Come on, nigger." He turned and briskly walked away, making Jesse run to keep up with him.

A month later, Roy was up to his old stunts again. This time, crippling a young man for life, leaving him of no use to the plantation.

"You have got to put a stop to him, Walter. If he stays, I leave."

Walter was not about to lose his wife whose ultimatum came as a clear serious threat.

Roy left the Hartford Plantation that evening, never to return again.

÷÷÷÷÷÷

(*Cough-cough-cough*)

Jesse's mind returned from the past, taken away by Massa Hartford's cough. His eyes were still closed. Jesse had shaved him that morning and given him a good wash. He swooped his hair across his head to hide as much of the large bald spot on top as possible. He rubbed the wild stray hairs of his eyebrows before returning to his seat.

Jesse thought about Nina. He hadn't been able to get his mind off her since the night he had dismissed her so harshly.

She was special. He wanted her to know that and tried in every way to show her. Holding the chair before she sat, stroking away stray hairs, and laughing at her corny jokes. Maybe his actions had confused her. They were definitely confusing him. Where was the thin line between being nice and flirting? Whenever he touched her, it felt right. When he stared into her big beautiful eyes, they never failed to draw him further in, "...and THAT, I cannot allow to happen."

Shaking his head, Jesse sat up straight. He had to get his mind off Nina. *I'll practice. I haven't done so since she was planted to infiltrate my plans.* He looked at Massa Hartford and continued past him, looking over the room. The same room he'd sat in day-in and night. *Taking care of fat Massa Hartford.* He laughed and looked at the bureau. The last time Missis Anna Bell had visited her husband, she had left behind the newspaper she'd brought to read to him.

Sitting in a corner, hiding it from the view of anyone who would walk into the room, Jesse read the paper silently. It felt good to have something new to read, something to take his mind off Nina.

÷÷÷÷÷÷

After assuring that she looked her best, Nina walked across the plantation slightly holding up the front of her long simple floral pattern dress that barely touched the ground. Her going towards the big house that early in the afternoon had caused the female slaves to take notice.

"Where she goin'?" someone asked.

"Spinnin' a lot of time in the big house," another mentioned.

"Maybe she finely gone 'dare for good," the other answered.

"I heard she been spinnin' time wit' Willa's boy. Overseer wants 'em to couple up."

The house slaves were going about their daily duties. Only a few took notice of Nina going up the stairs. Most of them knew that the overseer was pairing the two up, so they paid her no mind.

Standing in front of the door, Nina was frozen stiff. She tried to get her nerves under control by taking in a deep breath, straightening her posture and catching fallen tears. Looking down, she swiped away unseen particles from her dress. One last breath and she balled up her fist and knocked three taps. After a brief wait, three more taps followed, but still no answer. Taking in a deep breath, she tapped three more times.

Fifteen

On the same day the overseer sent Nina to visit Jesse, Missis Anna Bell entered her husband's room earlier that morning while Jesse bathed him. "Jesse, as soon as you're done here, I need some freshly picked flowers. And make sure to include some Maypop in the batch." After turning to leave, she stopped. "Oh, and give them to Althea. Have her place them in vases throughout the house."

"Yes, sum." The order suited him just fine. He sped up the chore of cleaning Massa Hartford, eager to visit the woods - to reunite with his beloved plans to run. With Nina in the picture, his dreams of running had become an endangered species.

Before entering the pastures, the smell of pine brought on a smile. He wanted to go in deep that morning, but Missis Anna Bell had stressed a timeline. He could only take in the moment for a short time.

Jesse set the large basket next to a wide, thick tree, sat beside it and thought of his plans to run. *Wait until everyone is asleep. The season matters. Winter will be too cold, summer too hot, maybe spring—* Nina's face appeared. Her beautiful eyes, calming smile, "and she has the cutest nose—"

Speaking aloud, he hoped that spoken words would keep him focused. "Maybe fall is the best time. October. Yeah, wet leaves might help to cover my scent." He chuckled and remembered when Nina smelt underneath her arms. "Do I stink?" she asked. He laughed again, *she's always so blunt.*

He picked up a twig and threw it. His mind was clearly possessed by that woman. *Why did I allow that to happen?* The overseer's plans were coming together, and his plans were falling apart. Even in his place of serenity, he couldn't shake her from his thoughts.

He didn't ask for this, but it came. He didn't want to get close to her, but it'd happened. He didn't want to love her, but he did. He did. It had happened. "I've fallen madly in love with her." *Goodness, this was not supposed to happen.*

Her face came into view, her crinkled hair, her big beautiful eyes, her lips. *What soft, juicy lips that's full of sweetness.* He could see them, coming closer to his and without thinking, he puckered. Jesse jumped at the sound of a fallen limb. *Just in time.* He had to get her out of his mind.

"I have to get those flowers." He stood, but the thought of her refused to vacate. His back went against the tree, sliding down, and seconds later, he was sitting again.

After several self-pep talks, Jesse was finally able to get his mind on track. He found those flowers and left. "Here, Miss Althea." He gave her the flowers and went outside to clean up before heading to Massa Hartford's room.

Missis Anna Bell had left for town to prepare for her sisters who were coming to visit for the weekend. It was in the afternoon when Jesse fed Massa Hartford and was returning from the kitchen.

As soon as Nina heard him enter, she turned. The wind rushed through the window and blew her hair just as she turned to face him. The sunlight must have known the precise moment to rest upon her face.

Enchanting. "Nina?" He couldn't take his eyes off her, although he wanted to. The self-pep talk had coached him to not be caught by her beauty, but there she stood in front of him wearing the type of attire that slave girls wore for their wedding unions. But with Nina's shape, the long hanging dress captured every curve of her body. "What you doing here?"

"Um, sorry. I let myself in. I knocked, but there was no answer." Her visits would always be just before nighttime and the darkness didn't detail Jesse's life in that room. But the daylight gave her a tour of what life meant for him to take care of Massa Hartford.

The cot he slept on was in the corner of the room and all that he owned was neatly rolled up and placed at the foot of the very narrow bed. The very idea of it made her mad for him.

While she visited the room with her eyes, Jesse got her a chair, but this time, he dusted it off to remove any dust that had gotten on it since the last time she had sat in it. He carefully placed it by the window to assure that she could feel any blowing wind.

"Thank you."

Sitting next to her, Jesse kept his eyes on his hands that rested on his lap. He remembered that pep talk. *If you keep your eyes off her, you can keep your heart off her.* But the fight to not look at her was proving to be easier said than done. "Overseer let you lees' the field 'dis time of day?"

"Yes. To come keep you comp'nee."

They sat in silence, not knowing what to say with the thought of their last meeting that required questions from her and being ignored by him.

Nina's hands went to her lap. She sat up straight like she'd seen the white ladies do.

Jesse tended to his slave's attire. Her fine clothes made him aware of what he was wearing. He looked down and brushed away every speck that looked like dirt.

She looked at him from the corners of her eyes. "Sure is cool in here this time of day. Who would've thought?"

"Yeah, it is." He could find no words to continue the conversation. Minutes of silent thoughts circled with not one word. "That sure is a pretty dress you wearing, Nina."

"My last misses gave me the cloth to make me a dress for our annual social gathering." She looked down at the dress while explaining. "Wasn't but a little material. Not enough to make somethin' fancy, so

I settled on this." She brushed it off. "It be a bit small since I last wore it. Fitting tighter than I would like."

"Well, it sure is pretty and fits you mighty fine. Wish I could see you in it all the time."

"Wish I could wear it all the time."

"What the name of the plantation you come from?" Their conversation continued until Jesse said, "I gotta check on Massa."

"Okay." *Go right ahead, 'cause I ain't going nowhere.* Although it was the overseer's plans that had brought them that far, she would not let it be all for nothing.

Sixteen

$\underline{S}$ome plantations allow their slaves to gather for annual festivities. Others allow union ceremonies between couples, although slave marriages were not a binding contract or a recognized marriage. The Hartford Plantation was quite the contrary. They were about business and the cares of the plantation and its owners were a top priority. Their all work and no play enforcement didn't allow time for celebratory events or festival gatherings.

If a couple was permitted to be paired up, right after leaving the fields at the end of the workday, they would get cleaned up and put on their best clothes. An appointed slave officiator would unify the couple. After which, the couple would retreat to an available slave shack to consummate the union. If a vacant shack was not available, the couple had to share a shack with their family. The next day would be work as usual. There were no times for preparations, parties, congratulatory celebrations or honeymoons on the Hartford plantation. It was always about expanding their property, and slaves were a part of that expansion.

Seventeen

"*I* need you to keep an eye on Jesse and Nina." The overseer didn't have to go into details. The Big House Snoop had been given the quid-pro-quo duty before.

"What I get for tellin'?"

"What you want?"

"I want a night with Thomas. 'Dis time a whole night."

"That ole fool? He's a lady's man. Pick somebody else."

"No. Can't no man satisfy me like Thomas."

"Alright, then. But after I get what I want."

"As soon as I know, you'll know."

The overseer sent Nina to visit Jesse three days straight and on the third day...

"Oops. I sorry, wrong doe'. Gotta mind where I go." The Big House Snoop rushed the news to the overseer.

"What you got?" he asked.

"A kiss. And it wasn't no peck on the cheek. 'Dey was slobbin' all over each other."

"Okay. I'll let Thomas know you'll be visiting tonight. You sure you don't wanna pick somebody else? He's a sixty-five-year-old lady's man."

"And 'dares a reason why he's still a lady's man at sixty-five and it's 'dat reason I don't want nobody else but him. Just say to 'em, it's numba three's turn."

"Number three?"

"Yes." She laughed and scurried off.

Shaking his head, the overseer walked off. First, he spoke to Thomas. "Number three will see you tonight." He left a happy grin on Thomas' face and went to see the assigned slave officiator. "Nina and Jesse ready to be paired up. They'll be coming to you tomorrow after work." Leaving the field, he went to the big house straight to Massa Hartford's room. His stomping boots sounded the alarm and warned of his nearing presence.

When he opened the door, Jesse was tending to Massa Hartford. Nina was turned forward in her seat looking down, her hands in her lap. The warning on his stumping shoes had prepared them.

"Good evening, sar'," Jesse greeted.

"You two getting coupled up tomorrow."

Nina's head sprung up. Her big beautiful eyes were as noticeable as a shiny sun that quickly disappear when she dropped her head to assure she was not staring.

Jesse turned, locking eyes with the overseer, but minding his manners, he quickly dropped his head as well.

The overseer turned to Nina. "Nina, get going. You gotta long day ahead of you tomorrow. You need to prepare for it. Jesse'll be staying with you and your ma. Right after work tomorrow, you two will see the officiator. I'll send Jesse over when the field work's done."

Nina sat quietly, unsure of how she should feel; how Jesse felt about being forced.

"Get now!"

She jumped up and rushed out of the room.

With tightened lips and even tighter eyes, Jesse barely shook his head. He had no freedom to protest, no power to reject, no position to take a stand. No strength to be a man. He was theirs to order as they pleased. To instruct as if he was a horse, going in every direction signaled by the rider. He felt demeaned. It was the only time he appreciated the order of 'not looking into a white man's face because his eyes were full of tears.

"Jesse, Miss Anna Bell likes you. She gave the order for you to live with Nina and her ma. You'll visit Sunday night at nine and come back to your duties before daylight on Monday morning. Tomorrow after y'all coupling, you get to stay the whole night, but you be back here the next morning like it's Monday morning. You understand?"

He had never disobeyed their strict rules before and knew the penalty for disobeying it, but he didn't care. For the first time, Jesse was quiet, refusing to answer a white man who had the authority to whip him.

"Jesse! You sleep or something? You heard my orders?"

Jesse looked up directly into the overseer's eyes. With tense jaws, his nostrils flared, his angry eyes spoke loudly. "Yes, sar'!" he said sharply like a soldier. "Whatever I ordered to do, I do it, sar'!" His strong muscular statue and the look on his face as he stared into the eyes of the overseer were menacing. Out of nowhere, his face softened. Growing a smile, he dropped his head, cuffed his hands behind his back, causing the man who'd just given him orders to have unsure thoughts of what to make of Jesse's demeanor.

Staring at Jesse, the overseer wanted to say other things, give other instructions, but he was careful. He could tell that Jesse was not happy about the order he'd been given. Feeling somewhat intimidated, he left the room.

The closed-door relieved Jesse of his servitude stance. Tears quickly rushed down his face. He hurried to wipe them. Turning to Massa Hartford, he pulled the covers up and neatly folded them back.

Massa Hartford and his family had treated him well, but his value to them said how much they really cared. Jesse walked to the window to see if Nina was in sight. She wasn't. He wondered what she was thinking about them...about him.

He loved her, but she'd been forced on him. A scheme to trick him to fall in love. And he had, madly. A weakened heart that went astray. His heart had gotten caught up, drawn in by this warm, caring, and beautiful, wonderful soul. Even standing there, his heart softened for her. He could not imagine being apart from her. But it was not the life he wanted to live. Not as a slave. He wanted to be free. Free to ask her to marry him, free to make love to her because she was his wife, not for the purpose of producing more slaves. "I won't do it, and they can't make me. I won't be forced to marry anyone!"

Eighteen

*H*is strong arms squeezed tighter.

She opened her eyes with a smile. Her back to his front, snuggling closer, lying next to the man she loved. She turned to face him. "How you know how to do those things?"

"Love directs you." He smiled while caressing her face, adoring it. Jesse couldn't believe that freedom could come in the form of love. He'd learned that nothing could compare to the fusion of making love. The two had spent the entire night allowing their bodies to learn from each other. Harmonizing a beautiful love song as if it were the last song they would ever hear. And every time they awakened, they made a brand new song.

Staring at each other, they shared unspoken thoughts that made them giggle.

Looking at his beautiful wife, he wanted to take her again.

Being so close to him, she felt his desire rising to the occasion. Although it was morning, it was still dark outside and in less than an hour, their perfect first night together would be interrupted by work details for an entire week. The very thought made him dread the sun's arrival.

Nina would no longer be allowed to visit him in the big house. They couldn't bear even the thought of being apart that long. But it was the way of the plantation that offered them no options.

His arms squeezed her. He pressed his firmness against her, and looking at her, he climbed on top and the music started playing again.

Slowly, then increased, creating a delightful song, a romantic duet that hit high and low notes. An orchestrated masterpiece that ended with an admiration of applauds that woke up Nina's mother, who was just a room away in the small shack. She smiled, rolled over, and went back to sleep.

Nineteen

"*I* need water," the rusty voice said.

In shock, Jesse jumped up from his seat and rushed to Massa Hartford's side.

His illness had forced nearly two years of hibernation. Most of that time he lay in silence, barely opening his eyes, only offering a little help to assist Jesse. They suspected that his life would soon draw to an end. But a few days earlier, he found a reason to live.

It came early one morning when Missis Anna Bell rushed into his room. "Walter, great news. Delilah, our only daughter is pregnant. She is adding a new addition to the Hartford family. Delilah is expecting a baby. Isn't that wonderful?"

Her husband didn't move a muscle. But the news had awakened his neurons.

Six months later, she was back in his room. "Walter, I'm thrilled to pieces. Delilah will be coming next month. She wants to have her delivery here. Isn't that wonderful news, my love? I can't explain how happy and excited I am. Oh, my baby is going to deliver a baby. Our child is going to be a mother, Walter. Isn't that grand? Oh, I have so much to do. I have to prepare a room. I have to shop. I need to assign one of the girls to take care of Delilah and one for the baby. Whom will I choose? Oh, I'll figure it out." She patted her husband's chest. "You rest now, dear, I'll visit you this evening." Kissing him on the forehead, she left mumbling about the task before her.

It was as if the news had charged Massa Hartford to get up and get to living. Privileged thoughts moved about in his mind. His heart clamored with cautious excitement. For the first time in a long time, Massa Hartford felt he had a reason to live, a reason to fight the unknown illness that confined his body and restricted it to bed. He wanted to see his first grandchild, to hold it in his arms. And that day was the beginning of his quest.

"I need water." Massa Hartford was barely audible.

Jesse rushed over in shock as if he'd seen a ghost.

"Gggive...me some water?" The hard, throaty words sounded painful. "Boy. You...youuu hear me, gggive me some water."

Jesse grasped the pitcher of water and poured some in a glass. Holding up his head, he steadied it while Massa Hartford took big gulps.

"You alright, sar'?" Jesse was slow to ask, with a look of concern on his face and surprise in his voice. He didn't know what to do. Massa Hartford had always been a man of authority who only allowed his slaves to move and speak upon his orders. In habitual obedience, Jesse waited for his orders before moving.

"Help me...hoouu—(*cough*) Hoouuu...help me sit...help me sit up." He took deep heaving breaths in between each word while flimsily trying to force his weakened muscles to obey his will.

Jesse was unsure of what he needed. Gripping beneath his underarms, he lifted him. The attempt was difficult. Massa Hartford's muscles were in a great stage of atrophy, offering no assistance to Jesse.

Massa Hartford had infrequently drifted in and out of alertness from time to time. The strain and inability to move by mental command surprised the once strong man that he used to be.

After a while of struggling, the straining effort depleted Jesse's back. He propped Massa Hartford in an upright position and stuffed pillows around him.

Out of breath, Massa Hartford scratched at his throat.

Jesse looked confused. *Perhaps he's asphyxiating. Should I run for help*? At that point, there was no need to wait for the verbal order from Massa Hartford. It was not coming. "You needs me to fetch help, sar'?"

Massa Hartford tried to lift his hand that felt weighed down by a twenty-five pound of sugar. Half extending one finger, he pointed towards the water.

Jesse poured another glass and helped him drink.

"Mmmy wife...and son. Ggget 'em."

His son, Massa Ordell, was away on business as usual, but Jesse figured he would let Missis Anna Bell explain that. "Yes, sar'." He hurried off.

Missis Anna Bell rushed into the room and found her husband tilting over.

Jesse rushed over and re-stuffed the pillows in place to support him.

"Walter darling, how are you feeling? Jesse confused me so. I couldn't understand a word of what he was saying and thought him to be out of his mind claiming that you had awakened. Oh, darling, how do you feel? Are you alright? Do you need anything?"

Massa Hartford felt too bad to answer.

"Walter?" Concerned, Missis Anna Bell reached for his shoulders. She turned to Jesse, who pushed him back into a sitting position.

The fight had removed his will to sit. He just wanted to lie down, but his fatiguing efforts to hold himself up had depleted his ability to let them know what he needed. He sat looking miserable.

Missis Anna Bell could tell when something was wrong with her husband but didn't know how to help him. She began fussing over him, fluffing pillows, pulling his large, heavy frame toward her to prop him up further. He frowned, depicting clear discomfort, but she didn't notice. She was too busy trying to reverse the look on his face that she was worsening.

No longer able to endure her exacerbating care, Massa Hartford summoned up his inner strength. "Stoppp. Haaaa. Stop, please stop— (*cough*)."

"Hold on, ma'am. Let me straighten his pillows." Jesse removed the pillows. He always kept a folded sheet under Massa Hartford that he tugged and pulled, easing Massa Hartford to a lying position. Lifting his head, he slid a pillow under it and straightened out his clothes with a few body shifting techniques. Finally, Massa Hartford was at peace. Exhausted, but resting.

Missis Anna Bell didn't know what to make of his recovery and sudden alertness. She summoned for the overseer to get the doctor.

A couple of hours later, the doctor was examining Massa Hartford. He removed his stethoscope earpieces and turned to Missis Anna Bell. "I've seen this before. A sudden turn around with no explanation to help us understand why. I need you to understand that moving too fast could reverse the recovery, and he could become worse just as suddenly as his recuperation," he warned. "You cannot allow him to overexert himself. The recovery must happen slowly, in moderation, and it's very important that he has round the clock monitoring." He looked at Jesse. "You have to be here every second of the day. Completely aware of his every movement."

Every second? But what about my time with my wife?

"He will, doctor. Jesse cares greatly for Walter and will do everything in his will to assure that he heals properly. We all will," Missis Anna Bell said.

The doctor gave some physical therapy practice and left.

In the days that followed, they all put in the time to help Massa Hartford recuperate. But more effort went towards keeping him from pushing himself too hard. And when Delilah came, her visit evoked him to push even harder, going against the doctor's orders. No matter how much they argued, they didn't understand. He had to get better, for the birth of his grandchild.

Twenty

*T*he hour was late in the night when the baby finally arrived. Bundling up the little one, Missis Anna Bell walked out of Delilah's room holding the newest member of their family. "Walter," she whispered. Leaning over his bed, she laid the tiny child in her husband's arms and witnessed the wet love dripping from his eyes. Wiping his tears with her, she smiled.

Scooting to sit up, the simple movement brought on tiredness. Walter had fought and pushed his body to experience that one moment of joy that had finally arrived. It meant more to him than any of them knew. "She's so beautiful." Walter looked at his precious granddaughter and knew that she wouldn't carry the family name, but her birth meant that the family would continue on after his death.

He'd seen tendencies in his son, Ordell. Propensities that told him that he and his wife would not be getting any grandchildren from their son. At least, the only son he recognized as carrying his blood. The others were just property. Ordell, on the other hand, was his blood, his heir who had never shown even a bit of curiosity in women. And he'd tried hard to hide his desire for men. But such behavior could never be hidden from a father, even if he denied it otherwise. After trying to force several women on his son, Ordell's lack of interest left no doubt. Walter gave up and accepted it, but never talked about it.

Ordell walked into the room and joined his mother, putting his arm around her neck. They both watched as his father cradled his granddaughter.

Sitting up, still holding the baby, Walter looked as exhausted as Delilah who'd just given birth. They knew he needed to lay down, but they wouldn't dare rob him of the hard-fought moment. When they were finally able to get him to give up the baby and return to bed, he rested well that night.

The morning following Delilah's delivery, Nina asked the overseer if she could visit Jesse, who was still tending to Massa Hartford every second of the day. Although he was doing better, he was still incapable of doing for himself and required a lot of assistance.

With the overseer's permission, Nina visited her husband. Gently knocking on Massa Hartford's bedroom door, Jesse opened it and was surprised to see her. She was no longer allowed to visit him since they'd been coupled up. She stood in the doorway staring at him. The look on her face concerned Jesse. "Nina, what's wrong?"

"Jesse." She dropped her head.

He grabbed her shoulders. Standing a couple of inches over her, he bent down to face her. "Nina, you be alright?"

"Yes. I just wanna let you know that we 'specting a child."

Jesse's eyes widened. "Oh my God." He lifted her.

"Get somewhere with all that racket!" Massa Hartford shouted.

Jesse pushed her in the hallway and closed the door behind him. Still holding her shoulders, he looked left and right to make sure no one saw them. "It's so good to see you. I miss you so much. 'Um sorry 'dey won't let me see you. Massa, he be needing looking after all day and night. But I see you now and 'um so happy. And you come wit' this kinda news." He wrapped his arms around her and held tight. "You make me a happy man."

"Jesse, I'm scared. I don't know how to be a mama."

He took her hands and smiled. "Shh...you gone be a wonderful ma. And 'um gone be a' great pa."

"How can you when you spen' all your nights and days here but one? And since Massa wake, sometimes I don't see you for weeks. You ain't but a walk away from me, but I don't hardly see you."

He couldn't answer. She was right. How could he be a great father as a slave? The baby wouldn't belong to him, it would belong to the Hartford's and there was nothing he could do about it. The overseer had won. Jesse reached for his wife and held her once more. He kissed her, and she left not feeling any better than before coming.

The news of Nina's pregnancy didn't change their course of work or allowed more time for the young expecting couple to be together. Nina still worked long hours in the hot field and Jesse still attended to Massa's needs with hardly any days off.

Missis Anna Bell walked into Massa Hartford's room one evening. "Jesse, I'm allowing you time with your wife. It's not right that you're not with her during her state. Get Master Hartford ready for bed, and I'll send a girl up to relieve you. You be back here early in the morning and I'll see about letting you visit her every so often." The smile on her face was caring.

Life wasn't fair, but every so often it gave mercy. And it was those times as a slave that he appreciated. "Yes, sum. Thank you."

In six months since learning of Nina's pregnancy, it was Jesse's fifth visit. He eagerly waited for his relief person.

"'Um sorry 'um late," the large, tall woman said. "I had to finish up the kitchen. Had a lot of cleaning to do. Betsy wouldn't let me leave until I was finished. I tell you—"

Jesse walked out in the middle of her rant and rushed to be with his wife. He tip-toed to the back room to avoid disturbing his mother-in-law who was snoring.

Nina always left him a basin of water, soap, and sleeping pants to change into just in case he came. Lately, those times had been unpredictable. After washing his body, Jesse lit the lantern and lay beside his wife. The light never bothered her. It was their only time together and they always slept with the lantern lit. He loved seeing her face.

That evening was abnormally hot. Nina lay completely nude with the window shutter cracked. Jesse smiled. Pregnancy complimented her beauty. He didn't want to disturb her, but it was killing him not to touch her. The desire to make passionate love to his wife made "it" self-known. He pressed "it" against her. *That made it worse.*

He placed his hand on her stomach. Rubbing it, hoping to feel the baby move but her stomach only moved when she breathed. Applying pressure, he felt around, stopping on the spot where the baby would normally kick. But still, there were no movements.

Jesse sat up and touched her stomach again. Pressing his ear against it, suddenly felt a kick. Relieved, he cuddled up close to her, rested his hand on her stomach and slept that way the remaining three and a half-hours he had left. He'd lost his desire to make love to his wife for the first time. Concern was on his mind.

Before sunlight, Nina rolled over and felt Jesse's leg. Her eyes opened. "Jesse, when you get here?"

Concerned for her, he'd barely slept a wink. He smiled. "I been here fo' hours."

She smiled and laid on his lap. "I miss you so much."

"I miss you too."

She snuggled in closer as he rubbed her back. "Nina, how you been doing?"

"I been good."

"I just want you and the baby to be alright. I hate I can't be here every night wit' you."

"We be fine. But..."

"But what?"

"Well, the baby...it don't move sometimes. So, Mama, she takes me to see the birthing mother."

"And what she say? The birthing mother, what she say 'bout the baby?"

"She said it's not what to expect, and it's not 'sposed to happen a lot. But as long as the baby moves most time, it's alright."

Jesse was sure that the birthing mother was well experienced, but her experience did nothing to rest his anxieties. That morning, he walked to the fields before daylight with Nina, her mother, and the other slaves. As they went to the field, he went to the overseer.

"What you doin' out here, Jesse, and not with Master Hartford?"

"Miss Anna Bell, sar', she let me have a night wit' my wife. I 'bout to go to my duties now, sar', but I was thinkin' 'dat maybe...well, it's Nina, sar'. She and the baby ain't doin' too good. The baby, it hardly moves. I was wondering if maybe she should rest a spell. Maybe just till the baby—"

"Rest?" The overseer was sitting on his horse. He never looked Jesse's way. "I think you need to get back to your duties of looking after Master Hartford and leave the field hands for me to mind."

"But, sar'. Nina—"

"Our slaves work, they don't rest." He turned to Jesse. "And when they can't, we put them down like wounded animals. Now gone, get back to your duties."

"But, sar'?"

"I tell you what, Jesse. I think it'll be best if you tend to Massa Hartford without leave."

"Without lees', sar'? But Miss Anna Bell, she said—"

"Without leave. We'll fetch you when that wench of yours birth the Hartford's property. Now, I won't tell you again. Get back to your duties."

"But Miss Anna Bell, she said I could have some nights with Nina."

"I'll talk with Miss Anna Bell. Won't take much to convince her that the plantation's needs are more important than a slave."

Jesse rose his head and looked the overseer directly in the eyes.

"Boy, you threatening me with that look?"

Jesse never said a word. He didn't have to; his eyes spoke loud and clear.

"Control that mule! Get it under control now!" one of the overseer's men yelled.

"Get back to the big house, Jesse!" The overseer turned to the sound of the loud shouts and summoned his horse to ride to the commotion.

Jesse looked around, trying to spot Nina in the field. The cotton was tall, hiding her in its thrones. He dropped his head and returned to his duties.

÷÷÷÷÷÷

Jesse got the news one morning when Missis Anna Bell sent him out for fresh flowers.

"Jesse, did you hear?" one of the older slave men asked as Jesse passed him by on his way to the woods.

"Hear what?"

"Nina, she done lost that baby."

"When?"

"A month back. I figure you didn't know 'cause she was back in the field two days after and I ain't never seen you. She cries out 'dare in the field. It ain't right. It just ain't right." The man walked away.

Two months prior, Jesse had seen Nina from a distance. Her mother was helping her walk as she slumped over.

After freeing the grip his eyes had on the man, Jesse continued on his way to the woods where he released his anguish. He dropped to his knees and wept. He had no idea how much time had passed when he got back up. Snatching the flower basket, he stood paralyzed by thoughts.

"It's time."

Twenty-one

*I*t was as if his body suddenly attacked itself. He came down with a fever and from there, he was never the same. Massa Hartford took a turn for the worst.

"What's the matter, Jesse? Is he alright?" Missis Anna Bell asked frantically.

Holding Massa's head, Jesse held the glass of water to his mouth. He put it on the table and carefully eased Massa's head on the pillow. "He fine now, ma'am."

"Oh, thank heaven." Her hand rested on her chest.

Jesse dabbed Massa's forehead with a cool moist cloth. Now, Jesse had washed Massa's forehead before. He'd bathed him many times. But it wasn't until that moment when he noticed Massa's eyebrows, his nose, his cheekbones. They were identical to his.

He'd known that Massa was his daddy, his mama never tried to conceal that from him. He never thought much of it, didn't make sense to. Massa had fathered many of the children on the plantation and although their daddy was the owner, they had no legitimate rights. Jesse reached back into the basin and dipped the cloth again. But he didn't dab the Massa's forehead, instead, he dipped it again, rinse and dipped again. He'd lost his sense of purpose.

Missis Anna Bell reached over her husband and stuck out her hand. "I'll take it from here, Jesse."

"Um sorry, ma'am. It's just—"

"I know. It's hard to see him like this. He really loves you, you know. And I know you love him."

A head shake in agreement. He dipped the cloth again, squeezed and passed it to her.

Folding it, she patted her husband's forehead and hummed a song.

Jesse took a few steps back near the wall, stopping where he would often stand when Missis Anna Bell was in the room. Cupping his hands behind him, he stared blankly. Thoughts came to mind, filling every ticking second. His eyes found their way on Massa Hartford. He made a mental effort to refrain his facial expression from revealing what he was thinking, *and it has nothing to do with love.*

The man lying in that bed had raped his ma. And because of his sexual attack on her and the sexual assault on his grandmother by his friend, Roy, another white man, Jesse had been abused for coming out wearing their skin color. There were many days when the overseer had him stand in the sun and Massa Hartford walked right past him, ignoring the abuse that his dear friend, Roy, was doing to his son. When he did take notice, the two made bets on the abuse.

"Two cents for each darker shade," the overseer said about how dark the sun would turn Jesse. Massa Hartford's bet was on redder. Each time, Massa Hartford would win, but only after the overseer was forced into defeat by the time Jesse was burnt.

"Look at him, he's blistered. He's not getting any darker, Roy. From the looks of 'em, you owe me about eight cents." Walter laughed, stuck a cigar in his mouth and walked away yelling out, "You can pay in other ways. Have me one ready to go tonight. Make sure she's a darkie. The blacker the better, you know."

Missis Anna Bell became his savior when she learned what they were doing.

Jesse's thoughts caused his eyes to tighten. He recalled the next overseer's pressure of pairing him up with Nina. If not her, then with another. As a man, he had no control over his life. He was theirs to order, to serve, to breed. His lips tightened. Becoming anxious, he slightly rocked from side to side, thinking about how he was not there for Nina when she lost their only child. *Delilah is celebrating her child, while Nina is crying for hers.*

How can life be so unfair? He and Delilah had the same daddy, but different lives; one free, the other a slave, nearly the same age, the same skin color and if cut, they both bled red.

The overseer had told him just a few days back that it was time for him and Nina to try again.

"Yes, sar'." He hated the purpose, but it would permit him to be with his wife again. "To produce more property."

"Say what?" Missis Anna Bell asked.

"Ma'am?"

"You just mumbled something."

"Yes, sum. I said it's sad 'bout Massa."

"Yes, it is, Jesse." She turned to her husband. "It's very sad."

I won't do it. It's not right. Tucking in his lips, his eyes tightened even more. His head involuntarily shook defiantly from side to side. He was deep in thought, trapped in every known deed of Massa Hartford, his father, and Roy, his grandfather who had caused his mother, grandmother, and so many other women pain. But no matter how angry he got, because he was a slave, he could never avenge their assaults against their abusers, whose blood was the fault of his anguish.

Jesse stood in that room, standing close to that wall with increasing hatred.

"Jesse?" Missis Anna Bell called.

He could not hear her. He only heard his thoughts that angered him, deafening in his ears, validating his reason to run.

"Jesse?"

Still, no answer while making plans to run. The day, the time, the hour, and how.

"Jesse?!"

You've waited long enough. The time is now! The overseer hasn't won. You can't let anything or anyone stop you.

"JESSE?!"

"Yes, sum?" Jesse snapped out of it and found Missis Anna Bell standing right in front of him with her hands on her hips. Her face cherry red from anger, her thin lips now just a horizontal tense line, her squinting eyes barely visible. "I have been calling you for a while. Boy, where is your mind! Now, I need you to go tell the overseer to fetch the doctor. Then you come right back here! Go now and hurry along. Massa Hartford's not looking too good."

Jesse rushed out of the room, found the overseer, and gave him the message. When he returned, he found Missis Anna Bell wiping Massa's forehead. "Ma'am, the overseer's off. The doctor'll be here in a spell. Is 'dare anythang else you needs me to do?" His head was bowed as usual.

"No. Thank you, Jesse. I'm going to stay here with him until the doctor comes."

"Yes, sum." Jesse took his place near the wall.

Not long after, the doctor entered the room with his medical bag and immediately started working on Massa Hartford.

Missis Anna Bell stood at the side of her husband's bed, her arms wrapped around her small frame, nervously rubbing her waist in an up and down motion.

Jesse stood dutifully in his usual spot, waiting for any command.

After contacting the doctor, the overseer took the news to Massa Ordell, who was in town on business. Since Massa Hartford took ill, he was always away on some kind of *business*. He immediately returned home as soon as he learned of the news. Upon entering the room, his mother rushed into his arms. "Son, it doesn't look good."

As the two stood embracing the other, the doctor turned to them and sighed. "I'm afraid you're right, Anna Bell, it doesn't look well at all.

His pupils are dilated. I'm not sure if he will make it through the night."

"Oh, God, no!" Missis Anna Bell buried her face in her son's chest.

"I'm sorry, I can't do anything else for him. It's in God's hands now." They were the only comforting words the doctor could leave with them.

"Thank you, doctor." Massa Ordell walked the doctor to the door.

"Please let me know the moment anything changes or when the time comes." The doctor exited the room.

"We will and thank you again." Massa Ordell closed the door behind the doctor and went back in the room to be at his mother's side.

Jesse was still standing in the corner with a lowered head. Slightly looking up, Missis Anna Bell and Massa Ordell were in his view. He lowered his head but stopped. His eyes did not leave Massa Ordell. He was about the same size as Jesse. Something he'd never noticed before. There was no reason to do so until now and the reason was good. The same size meant they could wear the same clothes! He would need a clean pair of clothes to change into when he ran in order to remove the appearance of a runaway slave.

He lowered his head and thought. For his plan to work, time would have to be on his side. And while he stood in the corner, he methodically planned his escape.

He had to act fast, while Massa Ordell, Missis Anna Bell, and the overseer were occupied with Massa Hartford's condition. With death on their minds, they were not thinking about a slave running. It was the perfect time. Massa Hartford's death would make Jesse's plans all come together.

"Scuse me, Massa Ordell, Miss Anna Bell, if ya'll don't needs me right now, I sure gotta let myself out." With his legs squeezed together, he looked as though he was about to urinate on himself.

"Of course, Jesse. You may be excused," Missis Anna Bell granted.

Jesse exited the room and hurried down the hallway. He had to urinate, but it had to wait until after his plans were executed. Taking a sharp left at the end of the hallway, he continued until he was in front of Massa Ordell's doorway. He looked over his shoulder, twisted the knob and hurried in. Rushing to the back of the closet, he selected trousers, a shirt, and shoes, items he figured Massa Ordell had long since worn and would not miss. Backing out of the closet, he rushed to find the sock drawer where he took a pair, rolled them up in the trousers along with the other items and stuffed everything underneath his arm and quickly left.

Rushing down the stairs, Jesse was off to hide the items. He dared not go outside to face the crowd of slaves who were socializing about the news of Massa Hartford's condition. Knowing that he was Massa's caretaker, they would surely confront him with questions. He had to find somewhere inside to hide the things.

Considering how long he'd been gone, he figured it was time to check in to make sure he wasn't needed for anything. He stashed the clothes in a space under the stairway and rushed to the room. Head dropped, hands cupped behind his back, he went to his regular spot. "How he doin', sar'?"

"The same, Jesse." Massa Ordell thanked him for his attentiveness. "We'll sit with Father for a while. You may be excused to go visit your family."

"Thank ya', sar'." Jesse turned to walk away.

"Jesse?" Massa Ordell stopped him.

The very sound of his voice caused Jesse to become nervous. He turned submissively with a lowered head as always. "Yes, sar'."

"Don't forget how important your family is to you and how much you love them."

Those words bound Jesse in a standstill as Ordell turned back to his father, ignoring any response from Jesse. *Cursed words,* Jesse thought. He didn't need to hear them. Not while in the midst of preparing to run.

Jesse stood, trapped in his thoughts. *Of course, I love my family, and wife but I can no longer be bound by limitations, ruled by authority, and mentally programmed by those who want me to be no more than a slave. I am unable to make a move unless YOU give me permission. I can only fall in love when decreed by YOU. My life is not my own to control because YOU own me. You control my every will. Now YOU are ordering me to love my family. It will be the last time YOU command me to love another.*

"Jesse, do you need something?" Ordell asked.

"No, sar. I just hate it for Massa is all."

"I know." Ordell turned to his father. "I hate it too."

Jesse left.

Twenty-two

*J*esse ran down the stairs. The moment he saw the overseer coming up, he slowed down. As the two men passed each other, the overseer looked at Jesse, nodded and continued ascending the staircase, mute of any words.

Jesse headed to his family's shack, but not before being mobbed by a dozen slaves. Some were family members. Others were natives of the plantation and a few had been sold to the Hartford's. But they all wanted to know the same thing. "What's going on wit' Massa?"

"I hear he dead already. That be true, Jesse?" a female slave asked.

Jesse opened his mouth to answer but was curtailed by a shout.

"I heard death gone catch him fo' sunup."

"Well, good for 'em. I hope he die sufferin'." A slave named Gretta who had two children by Massa Hartford left no doubt about her feelings.

"Gretta, that not be nice to say," someone said.

"He ain't nice. Serves 'em right," Gretta argued. "You get what you give!"

"That be the truth," a different slave yelled out.

There were whispers and shouts in the background, some sad, some glad.

After hearing Jesse explain what he knew, they crowded around each other and talked amongst themselves, allowing him to squeeze through and continue on to his family's shack.

Jesse walked in and found the shack empty. Just as he turned to leave, he smiled when his mother entered. Buried in the thick of the crowd, she saw when he left and had followed him.

"Jesse, you be alright?" Seeing the shine of his eyes from growing tears, she wondered if Massa Hartford's condition concerned him. "Son, it's just life, that be all. You gone be alright?"

"Yes, sum."

"It be good to see you, son."

Jesse tried to hold back the welling tears, but the thought that he may not ever see her again weighed heavily. He looked into her eyes, stared at her face, wanting to memorialize it, to etch it into his memory. The long observation brought attention to her many distinctive features.

The look of tiredness from the stresses of laboring years in the cotton fields told of her life as a slave. A woman of mixed race, her hazel eyes were framed by dark rings. Deep facial lines outlined her suppressed pain. She was but a hundred pounds, with silky long dark wavy hair divided by two large plaits that hung below her shoulders. She smiled, and years of neglected teeth instantly robbed the moment.

Tears that Jesse had been fighting escaped, sloping down his face like a runaway herd that was too powerful to stop.

Knowing that Jesse had been in that room with Massa Hartford for so long, *surely his heart for his white daddy must've got caught,* she pondered with open her arms that went over to console him.

Jesse's head fell onto his mother's shoulder. He wept.

"Son, it be alright. He was a very *sick man.* His ways done caught up wit' 'em. 'Dat be all."

Leaving her arms, Jesse looked at her. "Mama, I not cryin' for him."

With concerned eyes, Willa stared at her son. She knew he was heavily burdened about something, but she didn't dare ask. A part of her didn't want to know out of fear of what he might say. She pulled her eldest son into her bosom and held him tightly, afraid to let him go. Believing that if she did, it could mean his death.

He remained in her cuddle but needed every second he was losing to her embrace. "Mama, I loves you and I always will. I'll never forget yo' face." He was afraid to look her in the eyes while hinting his plans, so he squeezed tighter. But what he said begged for attention.

She released him and took a step back. Studying his eyes, she tried to figure out the thoughts behind his words. The look on his face filled her with worry. She slowly and carefully spoke every word. "Jesse, what you thinkin'? You not planning on doing somethang stupid like running is you?"

Jesse dropped his head.

"You answer me, boy!"

"I got to, Mama."

"Jesse, you can't do—"

"Mama, I not changing muh'mind. I'll be fine. I won't get caught!"

"Son, you can't. They kills slaves for even thinking that way. You—you gone run?! What you gone do 'bout Nina? She runnin' wit' you?"

"No, 'um going by muh'self. Nina'll only slow me down. I needs you to help her get through this. Let her know that I loves her."

"You ain't tell her'. You just gone run oft wit'out her and ain't gone say nothang to her? Son, this gone break her heart. She done lost a child, now you gone runoff and lees' her. Jesse, you can't do this. You can't do her like that. It ain't right."

"Mama, listen. I can't be no slave no mo'. 'Dis ain't no way for a man to live. Do what they say, when they say do it. Now, I know what 'um doing ain't right by Nina, that's why I needs you to mine her fo' me."

With time wasted, he fell into his mother's arm and gripped her tightly. One last look into her eyes and he left. His rapid feet were mindful of their purpose as he walked behind shacks and around trees to avoid any possibility of seeing Nina. He knew that no matter what he said to her, she would never understand why he was leaving her. He was too much of a coward to face her tears.

How could he explain to her that he had to leave in order to truly live? He didn't want the task of convincing her that leaving didn't mean he didn't love her. There was no time to explain that his reasons for not sharing his plans of running were for her protection.

The hardest thought that came to him was the possibility of Nina being punished for him running. The overseer would assume that she knew of his plans and any resistance to share them would be beaten out of her.

To remove self-guilt, Jesse relied on the overseer's instincts of having the ability to know when a slave was telling the truth. He used certain levels of punishments to get the truth out of slaves who were holding back information, and his efforts didn't go unwarranted. The less Nina knew, the less she would be punished. At least he hoped.

Massa didn't allow brutal punishment to the older slaves because he had learned that the health of many of them would decline quickly after a bad beating. He would punish them by stripping them naked and stringing them up by their arms from a tree that stood in the midst of the slave quarters for however long the punishment fit the crime. While there, they weren't allowed to be fed and was given only enough water to live. And they could not be freed to relieve their body's waste but had to soil on themselves. With the punishments embedding into the slaves' consciousness every day, and the punished slaves crying out all night, others became dispirited to run or misbehave.

Jesse knew that there was a possibility that his family could face the brutal cruelty, a regret that had held him back too long. The malice punishment had been put in place to cause guilt and to self-imprison slaves on the Hartford Plantation for the rest of their lives. But that evening, he would break their mental manipulation regardless of the sacrifices that had to be made and those who would be punished because he'd ran.

Twenty-three

As soon as Jesse was back in the house, he saw the overseer coming down the stairs. *Go sit down somewhere, man.* Fortunately, the overseer continued to the front door without saying anything to Jesse, who stopped outside of Massa's door in a servitude fashion.

Looking down the hallway, he saw Missis Anna Bell's handmaiden standing in front of her door. Jesse turned and looked straight ahead. *Why are we standing here? For the sole purpose of waiting to be ordered.* The very thought sealed any cracks of reconsideration that might had change his mind.

Massa Hartford's door opened and out came Massa Ordell holding his mother's arm, wrapping her in a hug, he helped her walk. "Jesse, I'm going to lay Mother to rest. Father is sleeping now, please keep a close watch over him. I have to go into town and finish some business. I shall return shortly."

"Yes, sar'."

As he walked her towards her room, the handmaiden rushed to Missis Anna Bell's side and assisted.

Jesse watched as they took Missis Anna Bell, who looked to be mentally weakened into her room. He didn't move a muscle until they were no longer in sight. He entered Massa's room to wait for Massa to give him the opportunity to escape. To find that doorway to that freedom he'd heard about, dreamed about, and that he had put off for far too long. He sat and waited for Massa Hartford to die.

A few hours passed, and Jesse's elbows were resting on his knees, his eyes focused on Massa Hartford who was still breathing. He started to lean back in his seat but heard someone approaching. Quickly rising, Jesse stood in his regular manner at his regular post. The door opened and in walked the overseer.

"How's he doing, Jesse?"

"He fine, sar'. No change doe."

"Where's Miss Anna Bell and Massa Ordell?"

"Massa Ordell, he done gone into town, said he had sum' business to see after. And Miss Anna Bell, sar', she gots tired. 'Cided to take a rest."

"Okay, I'm going to my cabin. When Massa Ordell gets back and needs me or if Miss Anna Bell has need of me, you come fetch me there."

"Yes, sar'. I sure will, sar'."

On his way out, the overseer met Massa Ordell. The two conversed and after speaking about Massa Hartford, the overseer left.

Ordell closed the door behind him and walked over to his father's side. Massa Hartford had been a horrible master who had used abuse as lessons more often than not. A slave rapist, who after fathering many of the kids on the plantation, treated them all as if they did not bear his blood. Yet, he was a wonderful father to the children he shared with his wife...his heirs.

Massa Ordell looked down at his father emotionally devastated and unprepared to let him go. Almost an hour of holding his father's hand with tears streaming down, he dried his eyes and kissed his father goodnight.

He was finally gone, and Jesse was thankful for his exit. Massa Ordell's visit meant Jesse had to stand during his entire time there. His body felt its exhaustion. He walked over to the chair, sat, and before he knew it, he was sound asleep.

About thirty minutes later, he was awakened by the opening door. It was Delilah.

Jesse immediately rose and went to his post. He was still sleepy, but that could never show in his duties. Sucking up his sluggishness, he stood dutifully while Delilah visited with her father.

She didn't pay him any attention as she rushed to her Father's side. Her husband came in behind her. She turned to him, buried her face in his chest and cried. Rubbing her back, he patiently waited before walking her out of the room and closed the door behind them.

Thank God. Now I can rest.

÷÷÷÷÷÷

Jesse's plans were set into place; as soon as Massa Hartford died, he would run. His only concern was the lack of rest he'd gotten due to the constant visitors that came in and out of the room, not allowing him a moment of peace. He had to be well-rested for the journey that awaited him. A lack of rest would put his run in jeopardy.

After being awakened by Delilah and her husband, Missis Anna Bell came back into the room. Her visit was long and solemn. Not long after her visit, Delilah returned to the room and joined her.

Jesse would jump up and stand in his usual spot in his usual mannerism whenever someone entered the room. Most of the time they would ignore him and other times they would ask for updates.

Not long after the two ladies left the room, Jesse stood for a moment. *Why try to sit and rest?* It made no sense when visitors kept coming and going.

About thirty minutes passed without a visitor. Feeling assured, Jesse walked over to his chair, and just as he bent to sit, the door opened. Massa Ordell entered the room. He wanted to visit his father one final time before he went to bed.

Finally, everyone had said their goodnights to Massa Hartford as if it would be the last time while breath was in his body. In their hearts, they had made peace with him and that peace helped them all fall asleep. And their peace made room for Jesse to fall asleep as well.

Twenty-four

Did he have the guts to do it? He was trying to, but it wasn't as easy as he wanted it to be. Something was keeping him from carrying out that final action? Surely it wasn't love, so why was he hesitating?

Jesse was searching for the determination to muster up the courage to smother Massa Hartford. He had gotten up in the middle of the night, lit the room and found that he was still breathing. He stood over his bed looking down, watching his chest slowly ascend and then hesitating to drop. And regardless of the delay, it wouldn't stop moving. It just kept right on pumping and putting Jesse's plans at risk.

He's almost dead anyway, it would only be putting him out of his misery. You old goat! Jesse tried to convince himself to take Massa's life. *Will you just die already?!* Massa Hartford had always been so stubborn and unwilling. *You know something, you have to change, Massa. Just die before I find enough nerves to help you out!*

That was it! Jesse couldn't take it anymore! This man had ruined his life long enough, he wasn't going to let him ruin his plans of running too. Dying in the daylight would give everyone time to settle down from the news. And come nightfall, they would be more aware of what was going on, like a slave running. *No! He has to die right now! He has to die tonight!*

Jesse slowly reached across Massa. Pulling the pillow from beneath his head, he held it up over his face. Heavy breaths exuded; sweat grew, fearful nerves caused trembles. *God forgive me.* The pillow slowly lowered, closer and closer to Massa's face. Stopping in mid-air, he hesitated and cowardly pulled away. *Oh, God! I can't do it. I can't.*

Jesse laid the pillow next to Massa Hartford and walked away with a moistened face. Desolation weighing heavily. Disappointment taunted him. Hope urged him to finish the job. *It may be your only chance to run. To escape unnoticed and be miles away before the morning hours arise.*

Jesse turned around, took a few steps forward and glared down at the breathing old man. He grabbed the pillow and squeezed with tightened lips while tense lines formed on his forehead. Seconds ticked away while he tried to find the courage. *You have to do it!*

The pillow went down and raised up. Once again, Jesse snatched it away. Succumbing to his conscience, he lifted Massa's head and placed the pillow in its proper place. Jesse walked to the other side of the bed and carefully fluffed the covers, tucking Massa in tightly, leaving no clue of his attempt to kill him. He made sure that he looked peaceful, a comforting memory to leave with his family.

He stood looking at Massa. A tear fell. Lowering his head, he extinguished the lantern, walked to the corner of the room near his cot and sat on the floor. Bending his knees, he wrapped his arms around his legs and rested his forehead on the top of his knees. Sadness engulfed him, realizing that life would never grant him another perfect opportunity for freedom.

He heard footsteps followed by an open door. It was Delilah carrying a lantern. She looked over and saw Jesse seated on the floor, starting to get up. "Please, remain sitting. I'm sure you're tired. How are you, Jesse?"

Void of interest, he answered, "I fine, ma'am." He stood anyway. Slavery forced it.

"Jesse, you don't have to pretend with me. Now you answer me as I taught you."

Jesse gave her his full attention. Since Delilah's departure, his verbal abilities had remained a secret to him alone. Her demand was very welcomed. "Yes ma'am, I'm fine. And how have you been?" His whispered words were barely audible, but she understood his discretion.

"I've had better days, of course. Isn't it awful about Father?" She walked over to his bed, but before she could rest her feet, a strange noise came from Massa Hartford that drew her to frown. His chest went up for a long time, then slowly went back down. She watched and hoped to see the return of his breath. Her eyes blinked rapidly. Tears came quickly. His chest lay still.

Crying out, she dashed out the room with the lantern still in hand. In the midst of the huge hallway, she called out for her mother, her husband, and her brother.

Her husband was the first to come. As he took hold of her, her entire body dropped into his arms and he eased her to the floor. Her head fell back, her tears were many, her voice sung of her pain. He took the lantern from her and placed it on the floor.

Missis Anna Bell and her handmaiden came into the hallway, then Massa Ordell.

Jesse stood quietly in the room with a lowered head. There was nothing he could do for the dead man who was his father. His death brought him no tears but had yielded him the opportunity he'd been waiting for. Soon, they would all be in the room, and he had to be ready. He stood in the corner waiting.

The door opened and in walked the entire family. The females in tears, the men supporting them, they all gathered around Massa's bed. About ten minutes later, Massa Ordell instructed Jesse to tell the overseer to fetch the doctor. "And Jesse, your service is no longer required for the remainder of the evening. You may go spend time with your wife. You've taken care of Father well. I know how much you loved him. I'm sure you need time to grieve as well. You have permission to do so. Return tomorrow at noon."

"But what about Massa, sar'?"

"The doctor will send someone out to prepare his body for burial. You need not be present at that time. They normally bring their own help."

"Yes, sar'." He nodded and left the room. A part of him wanted to celebrate, but he couldn't. A smile wanted to form, but he had to resist. He moved as fast as he could, passing by the linen closet, grabbing a blanket and continuing to the stairway. With the rolled-up blanket tucked underneath his arm, he noticed Missis Anna Bell's handmaiden standing outside of Missis Anna Bell's door. She never looked up to notice him. He could hear her sniffles and knew that she was crying.

Jesse ran down the stairs and went to the small compartment where he'd hidden the clothing items and shoes. He wrapped them all in the blanket and ran out of the big house and into the cooking house located outside behind the house. He took a couple of loaves of bread and rolled everything into the blanket that he hid behind a tree near the overseer's cabin.

Jesse lightly knocked on the overseer's door trying not to wake up any of the slaves whose shacks were only a short distance away. With no answer, he continued knocking. Suddenly it opened. The overseer stuck his head out. "It's over. Massa Hartford's dead, ain't he?"

Jesse answered with a nodding head. "Massa Ordell, sar', he wants you to fetch the doctor. He said I done for the night. To go be wit' my family."

With no response, the overseer spat on the ground, closed the door, and minutes later, he was on a horse headed down the dirt road to fetch the doctor.

Jesse returned to the big house to inform Massa Ordell that the overseer was on his way to get the doctor.

"Okay, Jesse, you're dismissed. We would like to be alone with Father."

"Yes, sar'." He backed out of the room, went down the stairs, and rushed out the back door.

÷÷÷÷÷÷

That was it. Jesse couldn't believe it. He was nervous, scared, but he had no time to cave into fears. He went behind the tree, got the blanket, looked around to make sure that the coast was clear, and then ran. He was running hard and fast, so hard that he could hear every pound of his heart that violently beat against his chest wall as if it was trying to tear through. With fearful excitement, Jesse didn't look back. He kept his eyes and mind on the journey ahead.

In no time, he was past his familiar woods, deeper than he had ever been. He was tired, but there was no time for resting. Soon the overseer would be back on the plantation and even though Massa Ordell told him to go be with Nina, for whatever the reason, he may need him for something. No, there was no time to rest, he had to keep moving.

After a while, he was tired and had to slow down, but he wasn't stopping...he wasn't stopping for anything. Whether they were after him, he didn't know. The sounds of his beating heart and the fight with the bushes and leaves drown out all other noises. No time to care, no time to worry, he just ran. Fighting through fatigue, he only slowed down long enough to recover.

Could he look back? Would he dare?

The further he got, the more encouraged he felt. If dogs were near, he would have heard them by now. *No, don't look back. Keep running.* He sped up.

The woods got thicker and darker, wetter. Limbs, stems, and bushes stretched wider, higher, farther out. Some noticeable, others surprised him, causing tripping, flipping, and falling. He ducked, dodged, and crossed over long thick branches, logs, and tree stumps that poked out everywhere, slowing him down. At a slower pace, he was able to hear the woods' strange sounds. Some familiar, others not. Growls and hissing, crackling and creepy noises. He wondered if he heard human voices. But he continued to run. There was no time to waste investigating. Besides, he was afraid.

Jesse's pace decreased dramatically. He was tired, nearly out of breath. Sweat running down his face, stinging his eyes. He reached up to wipe and BOOM! He collided head-on into a thick tree branch that knocked him out cold. It was just as well because his heart had begun running a faster pace than him.

Twenty-five

*J*esse woke up to birds chirping and the forest's mild misty wind. He was barely able to open his eyes and research his surroundings, so he lay there for just a moment to collect his thoughts. At first, he couldn't quite remember where he was or how he had gotten there, but it all came back when he felt the pulsating head pain as he tried to raise up from the ground.

Touching the achy spot on this forehead, he discovered a large lump. He attempted to stand but was too dizzy to do so. He took hold of the tree branch that had victimized him and used it to get up. Looking around, he searched for his belongings. "There you are." His things were a few feet away. He slowly walked over, but when he bent over to pick them up, his pain became greater.

He had to get moving but was somewhat limited by the unwanted pain. Maybe food and rest would help the pain subside and give him the strength to move on. He'd run all night without hearing dogs, but surely, they had to know by now that he had run. After consuming a few pieces of bread and sucking water from the leaves, a resource he'd learned from one of the many books he'd read, he was on his feet and running again.

÷÷÷÷÷÷

Jesse's panting heart was beating back and forth against his chest as he lay flat on his back in a bed of dew-covered leaves. His face pointed towards the tall scaly oak trees, bearing long dark green leaves that shielded the rising sun from his eyes. He was deep in the woods and was hardly able to catch his breath. The darkness of the night had turned into daylight and was causing Jesse's nerves to get the better of him.

He had been running all day and night, only making very brief intermittent stops to catch his breath. No matter how tired he'd felt, he collected all the inner strength he had inside to keep going.

A new morning had risen and so did Jesse. After eating a few pieces of bread and drinking water from a flowing river, he was running again. His mind drifted to his family, onto his mother's words. *"Son, you can't. They kill slaves for even thinking that way."*

He shook his head to free his mind, but it landed on Nina. *Nina...how can I bear it? No.* He couldn't dwell on thoughts of Nina and his family; he had to keep running forward and stop thinking backward. But her face had overtaken his mind, leaving it without a clear focus.

All of a sudden, Jesse felt a painful tight pull in his leg. Rubbing it didn't release the tension. He hopped on one foot, reached down and grabbed the tensed area. It was a muscle cramp. He sat on a large branch and massaged until the pain was gone. The break gave him the well-needed rest that he used to regain his focus and strength.

He was tired, confused, fighting to be guilt-free. The attention to the pain had helped, but there she was, back on his mind. Loving her was greater than loving his dream. He couldn't deny the pain she must be feeling knowing that he'd run and left without saying a word.

Resting became complicated with thoughts of guilt. Jesse grabbed his things and started walking. With a dropped head, he walked in the opposite direction of freedom, towards the Hartford Plantation. Headed back to be in his lover's arms, to take the lash for her love, facing the possibility of being beaten to the point of death for his disloyalty.

"Maybe they haven't noticed." *Surely, they have.* An entire night and day had passed. The pain he'd caused and that which she had received could no longer be undone. He turned and ran towards his future without another guilty thought.

The night came and went again, and Jesse still hadn't heard any dogs. He smiled, but without slowing down. He was still a runaway slave and considered a valuable asset. They would surely come after him.

The sun had risen high in the sky, peeking down through the trees that surrounded him. Although he was far away from where he started, he was clueless about where he was.

Jesse was exhausted. The unrelenting run had taken its toll. He tried to move as fast as he could, but his feet had reduced to brisk walking. The pain returned to his head. Maybe it was from the bump on his head or perhaps because he hadn't eaten. Regardless of the pain he was feeling, stopping was not an option. At least that's what his mind said. His body had other plans. A few sluggish steps and he fell over.

His body was completely worn out and forced him to rest. Unwrapping the blanket, he pulled out the last of the bread and ate it. He looked around in search of a secure and discrete location. A spot where he could see others before they saw him. A place to lay his head and nap *for just a moment.*

Kneeling, he noticed bushes near a dirt road. Jesse crawled underneath the bushes, closed his eyes and the daylight world around him disappeared into the darkness of sleep.

Twenty-six

The settling sunlight shined on Jesse's face. He'd only slept for an hour and awakened to sore stiff muscles. At least his headache was gone and so was the time. He quickly got up and began gathering his belongings when he heard a sound. Ducking down, he carefully pulled the bushes back and saw a horse and wagon.

"Whoaaa," said the driver, as he pulled the horses' straps.

Jesse watched the man step down and walk towards the bushes near him. He swatted at a wasp. Angered, the pesky insect attacked him, buzzing around his head, eyeing a place to land and sting.

Jesse waved it off, trying to keep his attention on the man, but the bug was not to be ignored. It bumped against his head. Aggravated, Jesse swung and fanned, causing the bug to feel under attack. The aggressive creature fought back, missioned to destroy its attacker, but one hard swing shooed the nuisance pest away.

Jesse turned his attention to the man who was loosening his pants. Afar was the vengeful flying creature, its beaming compound eyes focused on Jesse's ear. Flapping its thin wings, the wasp stream through the air, its venomous stinger aimed at its target. A turn too late and Jesse bellowed, grabbing his inflaming painful ear, giving away his hidden location.

The man's hands rapidly moved, fastening his pants as quickly as possible. Once done, he bent and looked into the bushes in the direction of the loud scream. "Who goes there?!"

Still holding his ear, Jesse dropped to the ground.

The bushes shook, the man turned and caught a glimpse of him. He walked over and parted the shrubs, finding Jesse, who was on his back, staring at the seven-foot, two-inch, dark black man who stared back.

Jesse reached out for his belongings. Rolling over to collect them, he tried to run, but his foot slipped.

"Sar', you alright?"

Scuffling to get up, Jesse dropped his blanket that he knew he had to leave behind.

"Sar', you needs help?"

Jesse made it to his feet and tried to run again but tripped over the blanket he was trying to leave behind.

The man went to the blanket and picked it up. "You leavin' yo' thangs." He reached out the items to Jesse.

Jesse flipped over on his back, snatched his things from the man and stared at him.

"Young man, you be alright? You needs help?"

"Yes, sar'. I is fine, sar'." Jesse answered nervously.

Startled, the man's eyes narrowed in disbelief. He moved in for a closer look. "It can't be." He thought Jesse was white, but after hearing his dialect, he knew he was as black as him. Maybe not in skin color, but by the definition of slavery standards.

"You runnin'?"

"Yes, sar'." Jesse replied reluctantly and wondered what the man would do with that information. He squeezed his things closer to his chest, picked himself up and stood up tall and brave.

"Well, I guess you be goin' North then?"

Jesse didn't know what to make of the man's question, so he continued with the simplest answer. "Yes, sar'."

"Well, I be going in that direction, but I not running doe. You welcome to ride wit' me for a spell, but then my direction gone change. This ride'll help takes the scent off yo' trail. You'll have a better chance at getting away. Don't know how far you'll get doe." The man headed back to the wagon and grunted as he got on.

Slowly walking to the opposite side, Jesse's eyes remained fixated on the man. He held onto his belongings, pressing them against his chest like he was protecting them.

"Come on now if you coming. I don't have all day. I'on my way to pick up some 'plies for muh' Massa. I makes 'dis here trip fo' times a year. Never been late and never had no troubles." He turned to Jesse. "And I don't plan on being late or having no troubles 'dis time either. You understand?" Not waiting for a response, he turned forward, sat up tall, and grabbed the horses' straps. Looking ahead, he waited as Jesse got on. He made a commanding sound that the horses understood and with a slight snap of the straps, the horses were on their way. The man drove a little faster to make up for the lost time.

"I sure thank you, sar'. And I don't wanna be no trouble for you."

"I see the same thangs and the same folks every time I makes 'dis here trip. 'Dey used to seeing me, but 'dey ain't used to seeing you. Somebody new might thank that you muh' Massa on the count of yo' color. If 'dey do stop us, yo' clothes might give us away cause 'dey don't look like nothang muh' Massa would wear."

Jesse looked in his lap at the blanket. "I got changing clothes." He lifted the blanket to show the man.

"Well, get in 'em. It'll surely help."

The man stopped the wagon. Jesse jumped down and stripped butt naked. Using the blanket, he dusted his entire body as best he could, giving special attention to his face, hands and arms before changing into Massa Ordell's clothes. He took the clothes he had just changed from, looked at them one final time, rolled them up in the blanket, and tossed them as far into the bushes as he could.

While they continued on their way, Jesse looked back to see if he could see the slave clothes from the road. He couldn't. He turned around in his seat. A peaceful looked dressed his face. It felt like freedom before freedom had come. He leaned back and looked forward.

"How far north you be goin', sar'?"

"As close as 'dis here trip gone take us. I said my direction was north, but I not goin' north. Now if you wanna make it to the northern states, son, you gotta ways to go. But I gone get you in the right direction. How long you been runnin'?"

"Been runnin' for four days."

"Yeah, yo' trail be hot. A young, strong buck like you and on the count of you looks like them. Yeah, yo' trail be burnin' sum'em hot. We gots to get a move on." He made a clicking sound, and a snap against the horses' backs sped them up.

They continued down the road as the man educated Jesse on all he knew about running. He had tried it a few times himself and had gotten as far north as anyone he'd ever known.

"Don't thank it be smart fo' me to pick up a run-away, but I been 'dare. 'Dis be my way of helpin' one of us be free. We just gotta see 'dem fo' dey see us and we'll be alright. And if dey do catch us, on the count of how you look, I'll say I thought you to be a white man catchin' a ride."

"You thank maybe I should get in the back?"

"No. If 'day catch you back 'dare, dey'll know fo' sho' 'um helping you. Up here, it looks innocent. Like I gave a white man a ride. And, buh'sides, I sure glad for the comp'nee. First time too since Massa stop riding wit' me. Doctor said he too sick to make 'dis kind of trip. He just gives me my traveling papers and sends me on my way. Only been stopped one time. I just show my papers and 'dey let me go 'bout muh' Massa's business. Nobody else stop me 'cause 'dey know I make 'dis trip for muh' Massa. Massa can't afford 'dah help of a white overseer. Our whole plantation ran and worked by us slaves. But muh' Massa don't trust nobody else to make 'dis trip but me.

"Since my last run, he told me if I try again, he gone strap up my family and lees' everyone of 'em in 'dah hot sun to burn till dey dead. So 'dat 'dare did it for me. I stop tryin' after 'dat. Massa said I was smart, and he would treat me good if I treat him good. And he kept his word. Been on 'dat same plantation all my life and I gots mo' freedom 'dan anybody 'dare. I sorry, where's muh 'manners. 'Dah name's Ben from the Mayfield Plantation. What's yo' name, son?"

"I is' John." Jesse couldn't reveal his name to the stranger. He was thankful for the ride and the help, but he had always kept things to himself and wasn't about to change his ways. "I sure 'preciate the help, sar'."

"Glads to help." Ben kept right on talking.

Jesse just sat there listening, only answering questions when Ben asked.

Ben didn't mind Jesse not talking too much. He figured he was tired, worried, and scared. He thought his talking might help relieve the mental struggles that his new riding companion was probably having. So, he continued talking and soon he had talked Jesse to sleep.

Twenty-seven

*J*esse sat with his head swaying from side to side while he half slept. When the ride stopped, he woke and turned to see that Ben was not in his seat. Suspiciously, he looked around until he spotted him. Jumping off the wagon, Jesse walked to the back and watched as Ben moved things around, unfolded a large blanket, and spread it out. He reached into a wooden box and took out a jug of water.

"Here. We goin' through a town. I figur' it's best to hide you 'stead of riskin' it."

Jesse drank the water and climbed into the back of the wagon. While doing so, Ben got a closer look at him just before pulling the blanket over his head. "You know, son, I seen a lot of slave mix wit' white, but you the whitest I ever seen. You gots 'dey hair, 'dey eyes, and skin. You gots more of 'dem in you 'dan us. If it wasn't fo' yo talkin', you could easily pass as one of 'dem." Ben tugged on the blanket as Jesse laid down and made one final reference. "Passer, 'dats what you be. You can pass as one of 'dem. Now when I needs for you to be still, I'll start singin'."

Jesse shook his head.

Ben tucked him under and got back on the wagon. "Yonder 'dare." A snap of the straps across the horses' back and the wagon was moving again, rocking from side to side.

It was bumpier in the back than in the front. To get his mind off the uncomfortable ride, Jesse dwelt on what Ben had said about him passing for white. Jesse hated everything about the stain of his skin color. He shuffled his thoughts like a deck of cards, trying to deal himself a good hand with his new circumstance. Finally, a hand came that might be worth playing. Maybe it would turn what he deemed as a curse into a blessing that would benefit him. *Live as a passer.*

To live as a *passer* put more fear in him than to live as a runaway slave. What would the cost be if he was ever found out? They would surely make an example of his deception for others like him. Yet, he wondered if he could pull it off.

What Ben had said was true, he did have their looks. But what Ben didn't know was that he also had their speech and mannerisms too.

It was all Jesse thought about as he lay alone beneath the blanket. "It is very risky—"

"Lord, you gone help us.
Lord, you gone keep us.
Through our hurts and pains,
Lord, you gone see us through.
All 'dis rain," Ben sang the mid-tempo cotton field song.

Hearing Ben's signal, Jesse stiffened. As the wagon drove through town, he tried to keep calm, but he couldn't help thinking the worst. Ben was a stranger. Jesse wondered if he would give him up out of unexpected fear if he was approached. The devastating thoughts unnerved him. He trembled. Luckily, the vibrating wagon provided cover for his shivering body.

The drive through town seemed to take forever. Periodically, Jesse heard voices close by, unraveling what was left of his nerves.

Ben yelled something and the wagon stopped. The leaning wagon made him aware that Ben was stepping down.

Every muscle in Jesse's body restricted.

Is Ben coming this way? Is he alone? Is he turning me in? Is it smart to lay here and wait to be discovered? To be made an example of, to wait to die. Jesse felt around for a weapon, trying to be as still as possible. *Nothing! I'm a lying target. I have to get away. I have to run.*

He gripped the blanket and pulled it off of himself just as the wagon shook and leaned sideways. Ben climbed back on. Luckily, the walls around the back of the wagon shielded his raised head from the townspeople walking by. Ben yelled at the horses and the wagon resumed.

After leaving the town some distance behind, Ben went to the back and snatched the covers off Jesse. "Come on, son. You can get back up front."

Jesse learned that when Ben had stopped, he was allowing the horses a drink of water. As they rode along on the pleasant day, Ben kept Jesse company with long-winded conversations while Jesse contemplated his journey that would continue long after the wagon ride ended.

After a while, Ben's conversation turned into a whistled song that stopped when he noticed another wagon coming in their direction. It was far ahead, but too close for Jesse to get in the back without being noticed. He leaned over to Jesse. "Just nod at 'em when 'dey pass us. If 'dey ask a question, just say *yes sar* or *no sar*."

"Okay." Jesse anxiously prepared himself, sitting up straight and checking his clothes as the approaching wagon came closer. In minutes, the wagons were parallel to one another. A young Caucasian couple that sat on board stopped.

Jesse's unsettling nerves caused him to sweat when Ben stopped.

Looking past Ben, who was closest to them, the young man directed his attention to Jesse. "Hello, my dear fellow. My lady and I seemed to have lost our way. Can you tell me if this road leads to Palmerville?"

"Yes." Jesse's unsure answer was sharp, and he barely returned the man's stare. The beatings he'd received as a boy taught him to never stare a white man in the face. The unusual behavior was noticed by the man who suspiciously continued with his questions.

Ben became nervous.

"I see. I see. You look familiar, have our paths past before?"

"No."

"How do you know? You've barely looked my way?"

Nervously, Jesse turned and forced himself to look the man straight in the eyes. "No, sssir."

"There you are! Grand! We're trying to find the Hartford's Plantation," the man said, wondering if the name would get any special attention from Jesse. "We're hoping that this road will lead us there."

Jesse's heart leaped. He dared not look down at his chest to witness his most vital organ visibly fluttering. "Pardon...me?"

Simple enough, Ben thought. *Don't say too much.*

"My uncle, who is the proprietor of the plantation recently passed away. We would have otherwise taken the train, except for the nerves of my dear Margaret here who is dreadfully afraid of them."

Jesse urgently needed to get out of their presence, and although Ben had instructed him otherwise, just saying *yes* or *no* did not start them back on their way. He had to do something, say the right thing that would stop the questions from coming. He opened his mouth and words flew out. "I'm awfully sorry to hear of your loss. Please accept my condolence to you and your family. But I'm afraid I can't be of much assistance to you. You see, I don't know of a Hartford Plantation or the path to Palmerville. Nor do I know whether this road will lead you to your destination because I am not of these parts. I'm passing through myself. I do hope you find your way safely." He nodded to the young lady, "Madam," and then to the young man, "Good day, sir."

Ben summoned the horses to resume the journey and so did the young couple after thanking Jesse.

There! He had done it. For the very first time, Jesse had engaged an intellectual conversation with a white person that was not Delilah, and he was rather impressed with himself. A tiny grin escaped as they moved on, but one did not come from Ben. He was frowning.

Twenty-eight

Ben and Jesse continued down the road.

Ben turned around to confirm that the young couple was no longer in their view. He had been very talkative up until that point, but he'd become oddly quiet. He kept his eyes on the road, his head stiffened, his body straight, his mouth sealed. Thoughts, questions, and the word "trickery" filled his mind. "You black right? I mean you a slave on 'dah run, right?"

"Yes, sar'."

"Well, where you learn to talk like you white?" Ben asked while inquisitively giving Jesse the side eye.

Jesse kept looking forward but could sense the suspicion in Ben's voice. "I rather not say, sar'."

Ben didn't say anything after that, and the uncomfortable silence followed them for miles, straining their peaceful ride.

Jesse felt bad, but he couldn't tell Ben everything about himself. He knew that a slave like Ben was more dedicated to his master than to his own kind. The Big House Snoop had educated him well in that aspect and Ben could possibly be that type of slave. Still, Jesse felt bad about deceiving Ben, who was still sitting there not saying anything.

He knew he had better break the silence and try to make things right. Who knows what was going on in Ben's mind? Prior to learning Jesse's secret, Ben had been very kind to him. He felt he owed him at least the partial truth. Jesse took a deep breath and opened his mouth.

"Son, I understand why you don't lets me know all about you. That's smart thankin'. You know at first, I wonder if you gone make it, lookin' white, but soundin' black. I thought yo' talkin' surely gone give you away. But 'dare's no doubt in muh' mine now 'dat you'll make it. On the count of you not only looks white, but you dress white and talk white. Yo' trail be cold now for the dogs to catch you, but they'll still try to fine you by horses. Send one of 'dem hunters after you. 'Dey probably thankin' you headed north, cause all 'dah slaves run 'dat way cause 'dat's be the only chance 'dey has to be free. But you different. You can fit in wit' 'dey kine', and nobody 'spect no difference. Yo' best chance, son, is to thank different from what 'dey thank. Maybe north be not for you...maybe west suit you better."

Ben kept right on talking. Before when he chatted, Jesse had grown tired of listening. But not this time. Ben was wise, giving Jesse something to consider. He'd chosen the north to run to because it's where he had heard freedom was. But he'd never heard anyone say anything about running west.

Twenty-nine

*T*he wagon came to a stop on a crossroad just before the night became too dark to see. There were no houses in sight, only trees, dirt roads, fields, and miles and miles of the same thing.

"Well, boy—I mean, sar'. 'Dis be it. The place I headed to is just up 'dis road." Ben nodded his head in the direction of his journey. "Now you see 'dis road here..." he pointed behind them. "...dat 'dare be yo' south road. 'Dat's where we just come from. The road I take, it go east. But where I go, it not be far, just up the road here, and 'dat road where I go be nothang out 'dare but slavery." Ben pointed ahead of them. "Now 'dat's yo' north road. Some say it be hard for us black folks up dare, but at least 'dey be free. 'Dat's if 'dem hunters don't hunts 'em down. 'Den it be harder for 'dem 'dan it was befo' 'dey ran. But you, well it be easy. 'Dat's if 'dose hunters don't come after you.' 'Dat's why I told you maybe west be good for you. Can't say I knows anythang 'bout it, doe. But I can say 'dat's where I'll go if I be like you.

"Well, son, you just thank on it. I gots to go and pick up Massa's goods. 'Dey let me stay overnight in the barn, 'den I lees' in the afternoon after I pick up my load and heads back fo' the plantation."

Jesse looked at Ben and smiled for the first time since he'd run. He didn't say anything, he just gave a full smile. He looked in the directions of the crossroads, then back to Ben with that same grin on his face.

"What be 'dah matter, boy? Why you smilin' like 'dat?"

Jesse's smile was replaced with a serious look. "Come with me, Ben."

"What!" Ben wanted to make sure he heard that sentence right. "What you talkin' 'bout?"

"Come with me."

Ben stared for a moment, quiet as kept. He looked in the direction of his journey, then north and west. When he turned to the south, he stared for a moment. His lips raised and his eyes told of his contemplating thoughts. *It sure sounds good.* So good that he just wanted to meditate on it a bit. His eyes grew sad, full of water, and his lips trembled. The chance he'd always wanted was standing right there staring him in the face. The right opportunity, but the wrong time. He thought of his family. His Massa had gotten kinder to the slaves in his old age, but only when the slaves were faithful to him. If any turned, so would his master. And that he knew for sure.

He sniffed, grabbed a handkerchief from his pocket and dried his tears. "No, son, I too old for 'dat now. I want you to have the chance I didn't. You be free for all of us who can't be. And don't worry yo'self none, yo' secret will always be safe wit' Ben." He turned in his seat, faced the horses and signaled them to move forward.

Jesse watched as Ben traveled on the east road, then he turned south, west, and north. With no bag, no food, no water, nothing but the clothes on his back, he headed west. He didn't know how far west he needed to go or if he would make it out of the state of Georgia, but he would continue on his journey, searching for the place where he felt safe enough to set up his new life.

For several months he drifted, getting food and water where he could find it, sleeping near rivers in well-hidden areas, and seeing all sorts of things and people while hiding in bushes and behind trees and large rocks.

One day, he saw a couple of runaway slaves being hunted down and beaten by hunters. Following the brutality, they were made to walk behind their captures, who led them away by ropes that bound their hands together and were pulled by horses.

On another day, Jesse nearly walked into a young Caucasian couple making love in the woods. They were so immersed in their moment of passion that they never laid eyes on the white-looking runaway slave who was only a few feet away.

A different day he stumbled upon a slave graveyard. Standing on the sacred ground, the haunting spirits buried beneath held him captive. He could not move a foot, a leg, a hip, not one limb. He felt their spirits crying out from the grassy soil, haunting his mind. Blanketing their pain around his still frame. Their spirits gravitated like thick fog, so thick that he could not see past it. So many cries, a melting pot of voices, those of men, women, and children from graves with no stones, framed by rocks, sticks, and logs.

A warm wind blew, discharging him, but their cries were forever attached to his heart.

Often, Jesse would wonder if he could stop when passing by towns, small cities, and countryside. But no place felt safe enough to test his presence. Hot, miserable days, clammy nights, murky rivers, and deep dark woods overcome with condensation made his run challenging, to say the least. Yet, he wasn't far enough, safe enough, or secure enough to stop.

After a long time of walking and moving about in the woods and sometimes on the road, Jesse became weary of traveling with no place to travel to. A year had passed, and he was still on his quest to find a place that would remove all his worries. Summers were hot, and winter had been freezing cold. Mornings, afternoons, evenings, days and nights came and went. His hair grew longer, his body became thinner.

Worrying that his bones would decay in the woods, he had a decision to make. "I can't continue this never-ending search. I cannot live the life of a fugitive slave, nor will I live the life of a free black man. To survive, I have to live the life of a white man. I must become *The Passer.*"

With his decision, Jesse stripped naked. Stepping onto large rocks, he washed the clothes he'd taken from Massa Ordell and spread them on the rocks to dry. Going back to the river, he stood beneath the flowing waters, allowing it to drench him with its purities. The bath wasn't a normal task, it was a ritual, a baptism of his new birth. He took his time cleaning every strand of hair, rubbing every part of his skin, digging every particle of dirt from his hand and toenails. Every hole, every crack, every gap, every pore was scrubbed as if he was washing away the old and bringing in the new.

Walking away from the waters completely bare, Jesse stopped in an open field. He stretched out his arms and looked up to the heavens with closed eyes. As the wind dried his body, he took in a long, deep breath and blew out all that remained of Jesse Hartford. Freeing himself of the old soul, he made room for his new life. He opened his eyes to the heavens and prayed, "Dear God, I submit to you, the new me. From this day forward, I shall and will forever be known as Cooper Edwards." And in that moment, Cooper Edwards was born, and he marked that day as the day of his birth.

Picking up his clothes, he fanned them out to remove any wrinkles. He took his time getting dressed. Sitting on one of the large rocks, he looked around the place of his baptism. The waters fell over the rocks into rushing waters that zoomed down a clear stream. The scenery was beautiful to see, but it was time to move on.

He traveled alongside the riverbanks, completely shedding Jesse, the white looking slave, and becoming Cooper Edwards, the white man. And as he moved on, he created the story behind the man by combining stories he'd gotten from the books he'd read.

Thirty

Cooper Edwards was a tall, handsome man. With a very light hint of darkness to his skin, he looked to forever have a mild tan. His wavy hair was dark brown, his eyes hazel. He had medium sized lips, and his symmetrically shaped face was blessed with a beautiful smile and a perfect set of teeth. Although he'd lost a lot of weight from nearly two years of running and living off nature, his body was still sculpted with hard muscles.

Cooper was once the heir of a very successful wine connoisseur from Virginia by the name of Corpel De Luca, who had originated from Italy. He was the only child of Corpel De Luca and Elizabeth Edwards, a frail, sickly Virginia woman, who had succumbed to pneumonia when Cooper was just five years old.

Corpel was a very stern father, who reared Cooper with strict rules to steer him into the family's business. But after learning his father was a deceitful and dishonest businessman, Cooper came to despise him and the family business. When Cooper told his father that he did not wish to work in the family's trade and that it was because of his father's corrupt practice, the tense argument pushed Corpel to banish his only heir from the home and remove him from his will.

"I regret your birth, boy. You can no longer bear my family' name!" Cooper imagined him saying.

Cooper left the family's home and business to make his own way in life, starting with the change of his last name. Taking his mother's surname, he became Cooper Edwards.

A few years later, Cooper received the news of his father's illness, and he returned home. Two months later, his father died.

After the funeral, Cooper learned that his father had willed the family's property and business to his new young wife who saw Cooper as a threat to her new fortune. She ran him off and forbade him from returning to the property.

He left the family home for good and never looked back, taking only the clothes on his back and a horse that later died of its injuries. With little to his name, Cooper Edwards was now on the journey of his life, and his path had led him to the banks of the river. But there, he was not alone.

Thirty-one

Dreadful, horrific screams stopped Cooper in his tracks.

The awful sounds came from nearby. Cooper bent low to the height of the bushes just as the loud noise came again. It seemed to come from the direction ahead of him. He squatted lower, his buttocks nearly touching his ankles as he listened for the sound.

After almost two years of traveling, he had gotten accustomed to the sounds of people and the various noises that came from the woods. He was no longer nervous when he heard something strange or unfamiliar. But that sound, those screams, were quite different. Taking no chances, he remained low to the ground as he looked around.

Seconds of quiet went by, then suddenly it was back, but altered, filled with fits of anger. As a drifter, he'd used several survival techniques he'd learned from books and experiences he'd learned on his journey. Like closing his eyes to enhance his hearing. And he did so to identify the sound's origin. He listened quietly, waiting for the sound to come again. He opened his eyes and turned in its direction.

The screams of a woman got louder, became more violent. Although a female, the purpose of her screams was unknown and could be very dangerous. But he had to learn why she was crying in the wilderness for his own welfare.

Still knelt low, Jesse moved forward, stopping behind bushes as he quietly edged forward. He finally saw a Caucasian woman sitting alone beneath a tree near the banks of the river, screaming out as if she was yelling at God.

A few feet away from him was a large tree. He rushed behind it for cover and with his back to it, toiled over his choices. Cooper wanted to help her, but as a runaway slave, being concerned could cost him his freedom or his life. *Yes, she might be a damsel in distress, but I'm no fool. This could very well be a trap.*

He took an inventory of himself. He had been drifting for some time, bathing and washing his clothes in the river. His hair had grown past his shoulders and was in dire need of a wash, cut, and comb. He hadn't shaved since his run. Even if he was mistaken as a white man, his appearance might cause defensive fear.

She's a woman, how could she be a threat? A quick peek around the tree gave him courage. *A woman, Jesse. Cooper...a woman, Cooper. I have to remember that.* His need to help her became a need to help himself. She would be the test that would inform him of how people would respond to him. And she made for the perfect experiment because she *was* a woman. It was better to be revealed in the woods to one defenseless woman than in town surrounded by several angry white men.

Taking a deep breath, he coerced his foot to move. Looking down at his clothes, he dusted them off, combed his locks with his fingers, prepared the proper words to speak, and while still hidden behind the tree, he whispered, "Okay, here we go... Madam, I do not wish to frighten you and will only present myself upon your permission. I wish to make sure that you are well. I heard your cries from afar and wondered if you needed my assistance."

His heart raced, his breathing heightened, but he tried to settle both to hear her response. All he heard was unnerving silence.

"That was a mistake. Now I've allowed someone to know of my existence and it has backfired," he said softly. His eyes quickly searched for a direction to run.

"Who's there?"

Breathing heavily, mind full, Jesse looked down to control his breaths and calm his nerves. He looked back up to continue testing his subject that had spoken just before he ran off. "Madam...I...I am Cooper Edwards and I only need to know if I can be of assistance to you. Are you in distress?" With his hands, back, and head against the tree, he held himself as still as possible.

"Please, show yourself."

"Yes, madam, I shall. But I must warn you, I have been traveling for some time now, and I am in dire need of a bath and to be groomed. As I come forward, please do not be alarmed by my appearance." He dusted himself again and laid his hair down as best he could. His heart turned his test into a pop quiz as he appeared from behind the tree, pushing bushes aside and walking into the open grassy field with her eyes beholding a bum.

Rising up, she took notice of him as he carefully prepared to run while taking steps toward her. Holding an object behind her back, she made a swift movement and tossed it.

Cooper noticed the fast motion of her hand. "Madam, I promise I mean you no harm. I know my image might frighten you, but you have no need to fear me. I heard your cries from afar and wanted to assure that you were not in any distress. I could not rest after hearing such awful screams and continued on my way without attempting to assist my lady." His volume lowered the closer he got. Finally, he was standing only a few feet away from the short, stout red-headed young woman whose dull face bore freckles and dried tears.

Jesse hadn't seen too many white women in his lifetime, and of all that he'd seen with red hair, hers was the reddest. "Madam, are you alright?"

"I'm fine, thank you for your concern." She looked him over. His condition, his clothes, and hair. Briefly taking her eyes off him, she surveyed her surroundings. The bum-looking stranger made her uncomfortable, yet she was inquisitive. "How long have you been drifting?"

"For some time now. Mind if I ask what saddens you?"

"My husband..." She dropped her head. "...he recently passed away, and I am beside myself with grief over his death."

"You have my deepest sympathy. It must have toiled him so to have left you alone."

"His death came suddenly by way of a horrible tragedy that didn't permit me to bid him farewell. I do miss him so." She threw her face into her hands and cried.

"Madam, I'm awfully sorry for your loss, but I am afraid that I cannot offer the comfort of a shoulder to cry on as I'm in much need of a bath and clean clothing. I can only offer words of comfort as a man. I can tell that you are a lovely woman. Oh, how he must have loved you so. However, you must find a way to be strong. I am sure he would not want you out here crying all alone with only sorrows to comfort you. You must find a way to live so that he can be at peace knowing that you will be alright in his absence."

With a few words and a few minutes of his time, he'd comforted her, and she wished to return the favor. She smiled. "Thank you. Thank you so much for your kind words." She smirked aloud. "I bet a hot meal, a warm bath and a restful night would feel great. I'm so grateful to you for taking the time to aid me. Please let me return the favor. My home is nearby, you're welcome to stay the evening while you decide your next move."

His smile showed how very pleased he was with the offer. The two walked back to her home while she shared her story with him.

Suzanna was the daughter of a wealthy businessman who wanted her to marry well. But all the suitors who were interested in her seemed to be more attracted to her father's wealth and the status it would create for them than they were to her.

"Money never mattered much to me. I've always sought the company of genuine friendship." Which had been hard for her to find. All the other girls her age in the same economic status spoke only of marrying wealthy, becoming socialites and attending dinner parties. "That type of life and those kinds of people never interested me."

Suzanna found true friendship in a young fellow, whose family was just the opposite of her wealthy family. The young man's family owned a farm and couldn't afford to purchase slaves. They had to till their own land and raise their own cattle. They sold the fruits of their labor at local markets, which is where Suzanna had met and become fast friends with the youngest son, who was a few years older than her.

She made many trips to the market without her father and was always given extra attention and free produce by the young man. Soon, his kindness included conversations and frequent walks in the woods. Visits that her father knew nothing about.

Once the news got back to her father about the company she was keeping, he was infuriated. "I forbid you to return or speak to that fellow ever again! What are you thinking? They are beneath you!"

His attitude and orders caused Suzanna to rebel against his demands. She secretly visited the young man, got to know his family very well and when she became of age, he asked her to marry him. Suzanna's small private wedding went on without her father's blessing or her family's presence.

Her father felt betrayed. "You have stained the family's name!"

As he shouted, she carried her expensive things out of their mansion into the broken-down wagon that awaited her.

"After the wedding, I moved in with my new husband and in-laws, who welcomed me into their loving family. My husband's parents treated me like the daughter they always wanted, and to my brother-in-law, I was the sister he never had. I loved my new family and life as a farm girl. It was nice to sit together at dinner, laughing and enjoying each other's company. I never dreamed that living so modestly, compared to my upbringing, would be so fulfilling, but it was. My life was perfect. Until that tornado came through and destroyed everything valuable in my life. When it left, it took with it their lives. Every one of them. Leaving me only memories of what life used to feel like to be happy. My husband and in-laws were all killed by the storm."

"And you survived it?"

"With the pain that accompanies me daily, I'm not sure I did. When the storm came, I was attending my sister's engagement party that my husband was not welcome to attend. I kept thinking that I should have forced the issue. Made them accept him and perhaps he would be alive today. I was told that they didn't have a chance. That the storm came suddenly and unexpectedly in the night as they slept."

"What's the nature of your family relationship today?"

"After the storm, my family invited me to return home. But I couldn't abandon the place that had brought me so much joy and taught me what love was all about. After turning down my father's offer, he helped me rebuild the farm."

"So, you had to start over. Alone?"

"No...my father gave me three slaves to help maintain the property. He made other offers, but you would have to know my father. You only accept from him what you need. Nothing more. That was two years ago, and although the land is self-sufficient, it hasn't rendered any income. From time to time, my father tries to help out for his own selfish motives. But my mother-in-law would always say that tough times create tough people and that the value of something depends on how much dedication is put into it. Although they were poor, she was so rich with wisdom. I learned a lot from her. So, the helpers and I are doing the best we can. But to be honest, I have no idea what I'm doing."

"Helpers?"

She grinned. "Oh, yes. That's what I call the slaves Father leased to me. No need to refer to them using a degrading label. They're helping me. Helpers are what they are."

"So, you have to pay your father for their services?"

"Yes, Father still owns them, and he often reminds me of that. I would have to purchase them from him to take ownership. But I must admit, these three individuals, I'm not sure I would want to own."

"Why not?"

"Well, let's say that Father didn't do me any favors by leasing these three particular helpers."

"What do you mean?"

"Well...they're all in their forties. I'm sure you know that in a slave's working body, that makes them very old. One is a female by the name of Remy. Her family was sold from her some years back. When she lost them, it was as if she lost her joy and it seemed to never return. Sam, he is very slothful and constantly complains of pain while making excuses for his lack of motivation. And then there's Yes'sa Man."

"Yes'sa Man?"

She giggled. "Yes. He was given that name because he lacks the ability to think for himself. You have to tell him every little thing to do and when you do, he always answers, 'Yes'sa regardless if he understands the task. He's a simpleton. Yes'sa Man was the only child of two slaves who are now deceased. His mother birthed him when she and his father were advanced in age and died before he reached the age of ten. Because of his lack of comprehension, he was passed from slave family to slave family and no one ever put any interest in him or showed him any love. His limited mental capacity excluded him from slave families' conversations. I'm told he entertained himself by sitting in corners playing with bugs."

"That's awfully sad."

"Yes, it is."

"We should reach my home shortly. I must explain that my home may not be what you were used to. Father had the house reconstructed. It's larger than the small shack that my in-laws had, but it is by no means a mansion. It has three adjoining bedrooms. I also have a slave quarters on the property."

She didn't bother to explain that the slave quarter was so small, that the helpers had to use blankets to separate their personal spaces in the small one-room shack.

"The farm sits on fifty acres of land and now it all belongs to me. Father lent me a few livestock, bags of seeding, and some fertilizer from his inventory. 'I gave you a little extra,' he said, although it was not free. Now that I have the inventory to get things moving, the helpers he lent me haven't been much help in turning the prospect into profit. Well, here we are." Suzanna stopped on her porch. She opened the front door and invited Cooper in.

Just like she'd said, her home was modest and simple. Cooper looked around the parlor and then back to her.

"I feel embarrassed that I've disclosed so much about myself to a stranger. Why did you allow me to talk your brain to pieces during our walk here?"

"I rather enjoyed learning about you."

She smiled. "I'm sure you're very exhausted. Let me show you to your sleeping quarters." She shook her head. "I mean...bedroom. By no means do I wish to pretend otherwise."

Remy walked into the parlor carrying a folded tablecloth.

"Remy, perfect timing. This is Mister Cooper Edwards. He will be spending the night. Please prepare bath water and dinner for him."

Remy had just completed dinner and was about to go to the shack she shared with the others. She visually examined Cooper up and down with tensed eyes. *This woman done brought home a stray dog.*

Her stares made Cooper nervous. *Perhaps a slave can recognize another slave or smell their own.*

"Remy, staring is impolite. Now, please make sure Mister Edwards has everything he needs and a hot meal."

Not moving her head, Remy's eyes move from Suzanna to Cooper. "Yes, ma'am." She looked at Cooper once more before walking away.

"Let me show you to your room." Afterward, she left him alone, closing the door behind him.

Sweaty and grimy, and in well need of a bath, Cooper had no changing clothes. But there he stood, next to a bed that was dressed in light pastel colored linen. He looked down at his dirty body and clothes and stuck his hands in his pockets. He paced the floors. It had been a very long time since he'd been in a home, much less, standing in a bedroom where he had been made welcome to use for the night. He was a slave, but she'd treated him like a human being.

About thirty minutes later, Remy softly knocked on the door.

Cooper turned around. He'd been standing all that time. "Come in."

Remy entered the room and quietly went about her business. Dragging a foot tub in the center of the room, she filled it with hot water and left all that he needed to clean himself. She returned with a warm plate of food and a glass of tea that she set on the table. She handed him a sheet. "You can use this to wrap in after you clean up. Leave your clothes outside the door." She closed the door behind her.

Cooper looked at the nice warm water with seeping steam, it looked so inviting. He turned to the hot plate of food where steam also rose. He contemplated, knowing that doing one would cause the other to grow cold. His body starved equally for both, but only one could have his attention first.

A few minutes later, he was sitting in the tub devouring the hot plate of food.

Having slept on hay, a hard cot, hardwood floors, grass, rocks, against trees and even in them after hearing voices in the woods one late night, Cooper was laying on a real bed for the first time in his life. He'd always imagined it being soft, *but this feels amazingly soft.* It was extremely comfortable. So comfortable that he didn't awaken until after noon the following day.

Awakened by heat, sweat, and from the daylight that shined through the window, Cooper pulled back the covers and got out of the bed buck-naked. Remembering his clothes, he cracked open the door and found them on the floor, cleaned and folded. After putting them on, he walked out of the room in search of Suzanna. He found the dining room where a covered plate of food and a note awaited him.

> *"Cooper, take all the time you need and do so on a full stomach. Enjoy! Suzanna."*

Cooper laid the note on the table and removed the lid to reveal cold burnt bacon, lumpy grits, runny eggs, and hard biscuits. Suzanna was a great hostess, but a horrible cook. Her efforts did not go unrewarded. He forced the lousy meal down and went outside where he spotted Suzanna and her three "helpers" in the field. He saw several farming tools laying on the ground. Picking up one, he entered the field, rolled up his sleeves, and began working.

Suzanna was busy working with her back to him, unaware that he had joined them. An unexpected gust of wind caught her hat, lifting it off her head. She turned to grab it and saw Cooper working. After retrieving her hat, she walked over to him. "What are you doing?"

"I believe it's called tilling the ground, my dear lady."

"It is, but why are you doing it?"

"Repaying my debt for your hospitality. You have been a very gracious hostess. And the breakfast was superb, by the way."

Pleased he liked her food, she smiled. Her mother-in-law had said that she would be a great housekeeper but not much of a cook. *He liked my food. I guess she was wrong.* "Sir, you need not repay me for the hospitality. Your kind words have helped plenty. Now, please...I can't have my house guest—"

"Madam, if I may. You said to take my time deciding my next move. Working helps me think. You have a lot of work and not many hands. Today, I offer you an additional two. Please allow me to continue."

She smiled and shook her head. "Of course. I could use all the help I can get. Thank you."

Though Cooper had started late, they accomplished more work that day than they ever had. The daylight was slowly being challenged by darkness, but Cooper continued working.

The helpers looked at each other and wondered when he was going to concede to the darkness. There was no need to ask Suzanna who was busy working, she was obviously following Cooper's lead, so they continued as well.

Soon, the night skies demanded a concession, but laboring continued. And when Cooper finally stopped, Suzanna and the helpers were exhausted.

"Whew. I ain't never work so long and hard in all my days of livin'." Sam opened the door of their shack and fell over in his bed.

Remy turned to Sam and Yes'sa Man as they entered their shack. "I wondered when y'all was coming in."

The next morning, Suzanna proudly cooked breakfast, covered it and labeled the note: Cooper. I hope you enjoy it. She included a smiley face drawing.

She met the helpers in the field and was surprised to see that Cooper had started the day without them. They each grabbed a tool and dragged it to the field, expecting another long day of hard labor.

As the day proceeded, Suzanna stood shaking her head while looking at Yes'sa Man who was like a child. He could never stay focused on any given task, and it was working on her last nerves.

"No! Do it like this." She grabbed the hoe and once again, showed him the proper way to use it. "You see. You understand?"

"Yes'sa."

"Yes'sa Man, I am a lady, not a man. It's yes ma'am."

"Yes'sa."

"Oh, forget it! But you have to learn how to do this. Come on, let me show you again for the fourth time."

"Like this?"

Suzanna took the hoe from him. "Noo! Do it like this," she said while digging into the soil, her foot on the hoe's shoulder. "Come here." She placed his hands on specific areas of the hoe. Bending over, she lifted his foot and guided it. It was an exhausting task to teach him what she had taught him the day before and the days before that.

Standing up, Suzanna dropped her head back. "Ughhh!" Her face aimed at the glaring sun in frustration, but the large bright beam forced her head down to ward off its bright light. She walked away shaking her head and resumed her work while ignoring his struggle to get the hang of it.

Remy knew exactly what to do, and without instructions, went about her business of work. But the time it took her to finish the few things that she was tasked to do, there was little time left to help out in the field. After only an hour, she was ready to leave the field. "Um' fin'na go do my housework."

"Alright, Remy." Suzanna stood straight up for back relief. The upward position brought Sam into view. *Again!* For the second time that morning, he was sitting on a crate. "Sam! We have a lot of work to do. I need you up and helping!"

"My back hurtin' sum'thin real bad, ma'am." He grabbed his lower back. "Gotta give it a rest." If it wasn't his back he was "giving a rest," it was his arms, legs, knees, pains that seemed to be in every part of his body and gave him *a convenient excuse.*

Suzanna shook her head and went back to work. It slowed production trying to get them to work. She got more work done when ignoring their slothfulness.

Cooper saw early on that Suzanna was not like any other white person he knew. The red-haired, freckled-face, short woman was not only unique in looks, but also in her approach to slavery. A method he thought was clearly being taken advantage of after witnessing how slack she was with them.

One evening before going to their rooms, Cooper approached her. "Madam, do you mind if I offer advice to encourage the helpers to work more effectively?"

"Sure. Please. If you have any solutions that would encourage their work behaviors, I welcome it."

As a former slave, Cooper didn't have the heart to force a slave to labor, so he improvised. He watched Remy leave the fields after they'd only just gotten started. His attention turned to Suzanna.

"No, that's not it. I've taught you this many times. When will you ever learn?"

"Yes'sa."

"It's yes, ma'am. Yes, ma'am. I am not a man, I am not a sir, I am a woman. It's ma'am!"

"Yes'sa."

"Ugh! Am I wasting my time?"

"Yes'sa."

"That's not the correct answer. Yes'sa is not the answer for every question."

"Yes'sa."

Looking past them, he saw Sam rubbing his knees while sitting on a crate. Thinking of them all, he smiled with bright ideas for each separate issue.

The next day before they started, Suzanna gathered everyone together. "Since we have no overseer, Cooper is going to be our acting overseer. I'm sure he's going to be a great asset to us all and the farm. Please do as he says." She looked at Cooper. "Good luck with your new crew." She went about her work, leaving him to tend to the slaves.

After an hour, Remy walked off, headed to the main house to do her chores. Sam went to the crate, placing it next to his work location, while Yes'sa Man chased a butterfly.

Cooper jogged to catch up with Remy. "Remy, may I speak to you for a moment?"

She stopped.

"You have done so much since I've been here. By the time Suzanna and I return from the field, you have everything in order for our conveniences, including a hot delicious meal. I just wanted to thank you for that."

She looked at him strangely. No white person had ever thanked her. "You welcome, Mister Cooper."

"Can I burden you further?"

"You the overseer, 'um to do what you say."

"No, Remy, I will only ask things of you. I will never demand anything. That's not how you treat a friend."

A friend. This white man up to something. He thinks he smarter than me. "Go 'head, ask."

"I know you have chores in the house, but do you think you can work a little longer in the field before going in? Just to help us out. Sam tries to do as much as his pain will allow. Suzanna works to the best of her ability, and Yes'sa Man, well, he needs a little help to point the way. Any additional help you can offer us will be more than we have."

Surprising to her, he didn't try to use *his head* on her. Everything he said was the truth. Never had she seen white folks in the field working harder than slaves. And he actually seemed to care for Sam's pain and understood Yes'sa Man's needs. "It's the least I can do. I think the house is clean enough this morning. I can stay out here a little longer." She lifted her tool and headed back to the field with a slight smile on her face while thinking about how refreshing his approach was.

Cooper walked up to Sam. "Sam, how's it going?"

"Fine, Massa."

"No need for formalities, my good man. Cooper will do just fine."

"Okay, Massa. I mean, Cooper—Mister Cooper."

Cooper smiled and knelt beside Sam who was sitting. "Tell me more about your pain."

"Oh, it hurts something bad, sar'."

"Is it hurting now?"

"Sittin' for a spell takes it away some."

"So, working for a while, then sitting helps to alleviate the pain?"

"If 'dat means sitting takes away the pain some, 'den, yeah."

"Gotcha. Let's try this. Try clearing this row, then rest your body, let's say, for the duration of a song. When the song ends, clear another row. You see these four rows, let's see if you can have them cleared before noon, then take a longer break before starting back. Then practice the same. Hopefully—"

"I see, I see. Catch 'dah pain fo' it catch me."

"Exactly. Try that for a while and tell me if it doesn't work. That will let us know whether we should try other methods. Meanwhile, we'll see what we can do to get you something for the pain."

"I sho' will, sar'. I sho' will." Sam got to work.

Cooper turned his attention to Yes'sa Man. He gave him a hoe, the same tool he was using. "Here, take this. We're going to play a game. Do you like to play games?"

"A game. Yes'sa."

"I thought you would. This game is called *follow the leader*. And the winner will get a big piece of cake. Do you like cake?"

"Yes'sa!"

"Great! Can you do this?" Cooper lifted the hoe.

"Like 'dis?"

"A little higher... Yeah, that's it. Now bring it down into the ground like this." He stabbed the ground.

Yes'sa Man did the same.

"Wonderful, you got it! Now, every time I raise mine, you raise yours. And when I bring mine down into the dirt, you do the same. That's called *follow-the-leader*. Are you ready?"

"Yes'sa."

"Let's practice once more to assure that you have it. Go ahead, show me how it should be done. And remember, the winner gets a big piece of cake if you can dig up that area before I dig up all of my area. But you must do it as I taught you. Show me how it's to be done." Cooper waited. "Raise it higher."

Yes'sa Man dug the hoe deep into the ground and threw soil to the side. "Like 'dat?"

"Exactly like that. You did great. Are you ready?"

"Yes'sa."

"You have to do it the same way each time, you understand?"

"Yes'sa."

"Let's go. ~Deep I go, with the hoe, up with the soil, throw it hard~" Cooper's made up song helped Yes'sa Man remember the instructions. "~Fast as I can, so I can win~"

Yes'sa Man enjoyed the song and sang along. Not able to quite remember all the words, he added some of his own. "Deep it go, in the ole hoe, push it hard, in the dirt and throw up, it go."

"He really messing up 'dat song, ain't he?" Sam laughed.

"Did he say 'ole hoe'?" Remy asked.

"Yep," Sam answered.

"No, that's not how it goes. It's..." Cooper corrected the song while Yes'sa Man sang along with him.

"~Deep I go, with the hoe, up with the soil, throw it hard. Fast as I can, so I can win~"

"~Deep it go, in the ole hoe, push it hard, in the dirt, I throw up, it go~"

"I sang it right, Mister Cooper?"

"Umm... Let's try it this way—"

"Dat's probably the best he gone do," Sam said.

"You're probably right, Sam," Cooper responded.

"At least he's doing it right," Remy acknowledged.

"That he is. And I won't do anything to confuse him," Cooper said.

Not only did Yes'sa Man remain on task, he sped up the lyrics and by doing so, he went faster.

"Oh, my. You are doing great. I can hardly keep up," Cooper lied, purposefully slowing down to allow Yes'sa Man to win.

"Okay, Mister Cooper, 'um goin' to the house to do my chores. But I'll be back to help y'all out later and will bring some lunch for everyone," Remy said. And thus, their lunch break was created.

"Thank you for your help. We really appreciate it. Oh, and Remy, do you think you can bake—"

She smiled. "I'm already 'head of you. He likes chocolate cake. I think I gots the ingredients for it. You just see to it that he wins."

"Of course."

The next day, Yes'sa Man was ready to go. Standing with a large grin, hoe in hand, exactly where they had left off. "I get another piece of cake today if I win?"

"Too much cake and you gone get fat," Remy answered for Cooper. "I tell you what, you win today and I'll let you help me make bread this Sunday. How about that?"

"I like bread."

"Yes, you can help me make it and get a big piece for yourself."

"I gone win. Come on, Mister Cooper. I ready to win."

And each day that followed; each new task, he caught on and was often challenging Cooper, Sam, Suzanna, even Remy to beat him. Soon, they all were his challengers. Clearing, planting, digging.

There was much to do and challenging each other was not only fun, it was very productive. Not long after, Cooper wrote out personal goals for them all. He made up a chart and tracked their performance. "An eye-pleasing achievement helps them to challenge themselves," he told Suzanna. "And it helps everyone to stay focused while I'm away conducting business."

After a while, the helpers' tallies were rewarded with payments, money he and Suzanna put aside for their freedom. He even taught Remy and Sam how to calculate it.

The monthly profits kept rising. Suzanna gladly shared the market's profits with Cooper, who used his earnings, combined with a bank loan to purchase a multiple-effect evaporator. The equipment made the sugar refining process easier and faster, and with it, their money grew just as fast as their product.

Over time, Suzanna was able to start paying her father back. But the settlement was not quick to decrease as he continued attaching higher interest every month. "The longer my slaves are in your possession, the more my plantation suffers the loss," her father argued, leaving nowhere in sight to pay off the loan.

A year later, they'd all conformed to the work schedule and ethics of Cooper Edwards. Starting before sunlight and ending when the skies no longer provided light for them. And they did so through self-motivation and strict dedication.

On many work nights, they all sat around the dinner table like family members, eating together, just like Suzanna's in-laws had done. They'd become her family, and it was important for her to keep up the tradition that made her fall in love with the farm.

Dinner times were full of laughter, conversations, and on occasions, wine was served. But none for Cooper, who after having one glass too many one evening, taught himself his limit.

"Who is Ben?" Suzanna asked Cooper while the two walked to the field early one morning.

"Who?"

"Ben. Last night, you mentioned someone by the name of Ben. A slave you met while on your journey. You said if he hadn't given you a ride, you might have been caught."

"I did?" Cooper was stunned.

"Yes, last night after dinner. You got quite intoxicated. Sam and Yes'sa Man had to carry you off to bed."

There it was...his weakness. One drink too many, and he became a whisperer of secrets. He'd learned his lesson. "Oh, Ben. Of course, my savior. Some stranger I stumbled upon while being chased out of the woods by a pack of wild dogs. I ran directly into Ben's wagon. He shot at the wild beasts, scaring them off."

"Indeed, he saved your life."

"He was my angel that day." *No more drinking for me.*

Thirty-two

Cooper had been sound asleep when the clip-clopping of horses and a wagon woke him. He wasn't expecting anyone and wondered who it could be at that late hour. He would not be honest with himself if he pretended that the unexpected visitor hadn't concerned him.

In the dark, he went to the window, leaned against the wall, and peeked from the side of the curtains. *What if it's more than one person? What if it's the hunters Ben had spoken about?* It was too dark to see.

He hurried to the parlor in hopes that the window in there would give him a better view. Against the wall, he stood as still as possible listening to the footsteps, one at a time, stepping onto the porch. He considered a hiding place while the footsteps got closer to the door and stopped. He looked in the direction of the doorknob that he could barely see as it was being twisted.

Pushing away from the wall, he started to run. Too late, the door was being opened. He aligned his body as far back to the wall as he could. With a heart that pumped profusely, a mind that raced rapidly, and feet that had frozen, he prepared to defend himself as the door opened, hitting and bouncing off him just as the unexpected intruder entered the house.

Thirty-three

Aside from the business relationship with her father, Suzanna hadn't spent any significant or special time with her family in over two years. She stood on the porch reading the invitation to spend Christmas with her family.

It was a little past noon with the sun high in the sky, giving off a blistering heat. She'd stepped away from the field for the noon break. The message had come the evening before, but she was just now getting around to reading it. She looked out into the field. Cooper and the helpers were going back out after their lunch break. Suzanna took the letter in the house and came back outside. She would have to give the invitation some serious thought.

Returning to the field, she walked up on the laughter and loud shouts that traveled across the field. After listening for a few seconds, she joined in, laughing at the funny conversations that accompanied work and enjoying the fun engagements that challenged the others to work harder and faster.

Working usually freed her mind, releasing it from thoughts she didn't welcome in its comfort zone. But it was hard to get the letter's message out of her frontal lobe. The conversation that had brought on laughter had become her life's norm. It was authentic love and it became the reason her decision to the invitation was not easily decided.

She was looking forward to spending Christmas with Cooper and the helpers that year. Their land was producing well. They could afford to share gifts, drink wine and be merry. On the other hand, to decline the invitation she'd received from her father would seem ungrateful. After all, it was his help that had afforded them hope and prosperity.

After work that evening, they all sat at the dinner table eating. She thought to share the message with them. "I received an invitation from Father. He wants me to spend the holidays with the family. Arrive before Christmas and leave after New Year's."

"Have you decided what you're going to do?" Cooper asked.

"No...I want to be with you all for the holidays."

"You gotta go...it would seem ungrateful if you didn't... We'll miss you, but we understand... Go, Miss Suzanna. It's alright," they each encouraged.

Their blessings had left her no excuses. "I guess I have to."

÷÷÷÷÷÷

The night of the Christmas party, Suzanna stared at a vanity mirror in her old room without a smile. Closing her eyes, she could hear chatter and laughter coming from the reception room downstairs. She dreaded socializing with her father's guests, but he wouldn't have it any other way. Her eyes swung open to her image in the mirror staring back. *Maybe I won't attend, and he can't make me.* She thought about her father's pressure and gave her best impression of his words. "It would be rude to our guests and insulting to the young man I've invited to meet you."

"Meet me?! The invitation clearly stated that this was supposed to be a gathering of family members."

"And it is," her father explained. "With me, your sisters, their husbands, and children. And a few of my associates who I consider family."

Looking in the mirror, she felt tricked. There had to be at least fifty people in attendance and only a small percentage of them were family members.

Suzanna looked herself over in the mirror. Turning from left to right, she confirmed the neatness of her gown, her hair, accessories, and make-up. She'd finally lost the stubborn plumpness that had stuck to her adult body long after her youth.

One last glance and it was time. She headed down the stairway, slowly descending each step of the spiral staircase. Perfectly aligned posture, holding up the front of her gown, carefully placing a foot on each step. Making it to the bottom, she walked toward the sounds of human voices and noticed a teenage slave boy playing a beautiful selection on the grand piano.

She lightly smiled while on her way to the davenport where she sat and was served a glass of wine by another slave.

The gentleman invited by her father came over to greet her. The last time he'd laid eyes on Suzanna, she had been thicker. While making his way over, he noticed the wine glass that sat on the table next to her was empty. *Great for starting a conversation.* He snatched up two glasses of wine from the servant's tray as he passed by and headed over to reintroduce himself. The closer he got, the wider his smile spread with admiration for her natural beauty that was very refreshing to him. Her now well fit frame complemented the lovely dress she wore as she sat with legs crossed, looking bored to death.

"I do love how pretty your face is with your hair pulled back. It shows your natural beauty," the suitor complimented while handing her a glass of wine.

She looked up and saw the young man in his mid-twenties that she'd seen maybe once or twice before. It really didn't matter. *He'd paid me no mind before, why do so now? Because of my father? No, thank you.* "Thank you, but I don't care for red wine, I prefer white."

"Of course. And that you shall have." He left to satisfy her needs.

Suzanna looked around the room from one end to the next. Everyone seemed to be enjoying themselves, except for her. It was not that she couldn't, it was that she didn't want to. She would much rather be at home, enjoying her real friends whom she didn't realize she would miss so much. Especially during the holiday occasion.

Cooper and the helpers had insisted that she go and enjoy herself, but there she was at the fancy party, wearing a fancy dress, with fancy people and only thinking about those who didn't need to dress fancy to impress her, especially Cooper.

Suzanna loved her husband, and his loss had been devastating to her. She never thought she would experience such love again until she met Cooper. He was such a kind and gentle man, one who made her feel safe and cared for. He treated her special, as if she was one of a kind.

When she met him, she was thicker and had put forth no efforts in caring for her looks. But since he'd been in her life, she felt pretty and wanted to make sure that he saw her beauty inside and out, so she had begun fixing herself up. The more she worked, the more weight she lost, the more attractive she felt, and the more attention she put into caring for her hair, face, and body.

"A crystal-clear glass of white wine." The suitor was back in her face, holding two glasses of wine. She took one as he sat next to her, crossed his leg, and yanked down the front of his waistcoat for comfort. "So, your father tells me that you are nurturing your own farm?"

"Yes." She sipped.

"I've never heard of such a thing. A woman of your wealth, pretty and graceful, out in the field working like a common field hand. There is no cause for that. What possessed you to take on such a responsibility? Your father is one of the wealthiest men in the state. It's quite deplorable really." He took a sip from his glass.

Suzanna sat quietly, holding the glass of wine that she wanted to toss in his face. Fortunately, for him, it wasn't in her upbringing to disrespect a male because "It is he who has authority over the woman," as her father had often imparted to his daughters. She stood and turned to the suitor. "Excuse me."

He hurried to stand. "Would you like to dance?"

"No, thank you. Suddenly, I'm not feeling well. I regret that I must return to my room. Do enjoy your evening." Giving the unfinished glass of wine to him, Suzanna walked away. Holding up the front of her dress, she rushed up the stairs to her former bedroom, closing and locking the door behind her.

She was furious as she paced back and forth in her room. "Working as a *common field hand* has given my life more meaning than any of you could ever imagine. Wealth doesn't define me. My money came from hard labor. I'm a self-driven, strong, independent woman!"

Being in that house and around those people, whom she had nothing in common with, gave her the blues. She didn't want to share in their conversations or be invited to any of their social functions. The more she dwelt on it, the more she wanted to leave, to go back home to be with her friends, to be with Cooper Edwards.

Her thoughts had made its way back to him again. She knew she felt some kind of way for him, more than she'd realized, but she didn't understand those feelings until that night. "I wonder if he feels the same."

She walked to the window and pulled back the curtains. "It's so dark out. Christmas is just hours away, and I plan to enjoy it!"

Thirty-four

Suzanna walked up to her father having thought of the perfect time to confront him. "Pardon me," she said to the man who her father was speaking to. "Father, may I speak with you a moment?"

"Suzanna, I'm having a conversation with—"

"I do apologize, but it's urgent."

Her father looked at her, then at the man. "Excuse my daughter's impoliteness. I did raise her better."

"And that you did, Father, but this can't wait."

He looked at the man. "Excuse me." With a hand on her back, he tried to guide her to his office that was feet away, but she braced against his efforts.

"Father, I'm going home."

"What? After New Year's, of course. I've planned an amazing celebration."

"No, I'm leaving tonight."

"I forbid it. I will not have my daughter, a female, taking a wagon in the middle of the night."

"I am very capable of taking care of myself. And yes, I will need to use one of your horses and a wagon. Thanks for the offer."

"No, Suzanna and that's final!" He turned to attend to his guest.

"Then, I shall walk!"

Getting the attention of the guest, he turned back to her. "You lower your voice and mind your manners, young lady!"

"Good evening, Father. I'm leaving!" Lifting her dress, she turned and went upstairs.

"Suzanna! Suzanna, I demand that you get back here at once!"

"I'm a self-made woman and I am beyond demanding."

Rushing to her, he grabbed her arm but noticed the guests' attentions were on them. He released her. "Everything is fine, everyone. Please return to enjoying yourselves." He whispered in her ear. "Young lady, I am your father and you will do as I say."

Still holding her dress, she briskly walked away.

"Suzanna! Suzanna! You get back here this instant!"

Never looking back, she continued walking. "Father, your friends are more important to you, I'm sure, and mine are more important to me. I'm taking a wagon and horse. I will return it after the holidays."

÷÷÷÷÷÷

The night skies were dark, but she made it home safely. After pulling the wagon to the far front end of her house, she made her way to the porch and struggled to unlock the door. A final twist and turn and the door opened into a pitch-dark room.

Hitting Cooper, the door stopped and bounced off him as he waited with inflaming nerves, anticipating a fight to defend himself at all cost against whoever had just entered.

Suzanna placed her luggage on the floor and closed the door behind her. A gust of air from outside swept the sweet smell of her perfume to Cooper's nostrils. He smiled at the familiar fragrance. "Suzanna?"

A heart clutching scream and a few quick steps backward landed her back against the door.

"I'm sorry, I'm so sorry." He reached out to her. "Are you alright?"

"You frightened me."

"I know. I apologize."

He lit the room. The lantern's glow shone on her face in such a way that it mesmerized him. He had never seen her look so elegant. She wore a beautiful eggshell color full length ruffled gown that was adorned with strands of pearls. Her long red hair was pulled back with a few natural locks curling gracefully around her face.

"Why were you behind the door? Is everything okay?" She noticed his stare.

"I thought I heard..." His eyes admired her lovely pink lipstick. Suddenly, his hormones were doing things they had not done in years, persuading him to take a woman into his room and make untamed love to her. But at what cost to their friendship. *If I touched her in a way that she finds inappropriate, she could banish me from the farm.*

"Cooper? Why were you standing behind the door?"

Failing to answer, he couldn't help himself. He was daring to cross the line and engage in the unthinkable; a slave making love to a white woman. Surrendering to the fight, he picked her up and with his eyes never leaving hers, he carried her into his bedroom, and there, their friendship reached a level that could not be undone.

Suzanna never battled against his touch. Her body wanted the man that had caused private tingles in places that she dared not speak of. That night, those thoughts caused her to become helpless to his seduction. While underneath him, him on top of her, their bodies in complete agreement with burning passion. Her yearning surrendered to his lust.

Thirty-five

*I*t was extremely cold that particular Christmas morning. Droplets of rain forced the helpers to rush into the house to escape its coldness. Entering through the back door of Suzanna's home, the guys shook off their coats, Remy shook the blanket that covered her. They immediately started the celebration, honoring Suzanna's promise to not work on Christmas day.

Sam loaded logs in the fireplace and Remy started breakfast with Yes'sa Man's help.

While they began their morning, Suzanna and Cooper slept soundly in his bedroom, still wrapped in the moment of the night before.

With breakfast just about finished, Remy went into the parlor. "Sam, Mister Cooper still sleep?"

"I think so."

"Can you wake him up for breakfast?"

"Okay."

She went back into the kitchen.

"Mister Cooper?" Sam knocked. "Mister Cooper?" He knocked again. "He must be sleeping hard. Mister Cooper?" Sam entered the room. "Merry Chris—"

"Sam, close the door!" Cooper shouted, waking up Suzanna who rushed to cover her pale exposed breasts.

Sam couldn't break free of his shock.

Cooper draped Suzanna with the blanket. "Sam! Close the door!"

The words snapped him into reality. He immediately backed out of the room, slamming the door that got Remy and Yes'sa Man's attention. They rushed to the parlor.

"What was that?" Remy asked.

"I almost fell. Had to catch muh' fall that's all." He walked over to the fireplace and continued tending to it.

"Did you wake up Mr. Cooper?"

"Yeah, he coming."

Remy and Yes'sa Man went back to the kitchen.

As soon as Sam fled, Suzanna rushed to put on her clothes and hurried out of the room. Passing by Cooper, she stopped. Voices were coming from the kitchen, that was around the corner from the dining. The wide doorway was in direct view of her bedroom. They would surely see her go on in.

Suzanna stood still, clothes hanging off her, shoes in one hand, accessories in the other, her hair a mess, with Remy and Yes'sa Man in front of her and Sam behind.

Cooper rushed out of his room wearing only pants and shoes. He went out the front door, ran to the back of the house and opened the kitchen door. "Remy, Yes'sa Man, can I see you two outside?"

Shaking her head, Remy refused, not bothering to look back. "Gotta finished this breakfast, Mister Cooper. It'll be ready shortly."

"Come on, I wanna show you something."

She looked back at him. "You ain't even dressed. You better go put on sum' clothes buh'fo you catch your death."

"Now, why would I be out here catching my death if I didn't have something to show you?"

Taking off her apron, she stubbornly walked to the door. "What?"

Grabbing her arm, he pulled her outside.

"No, no, no. Ain't got time for this now, Mister Cooper."

"Yes, you do. There's always time for fun." He picked up a hand full of wet, cold leaves and tossed them on her.

"A game!" Yes'sa Man hurried out and joined in.

Hearing the laughter, Suzanna moved a foot, then another closer to her bedroom door.

Retreating from the hands full of leaves coming his way, Yes'sa Man fell against the screen door, scaring Suzanna who stood in his view. But he did not see her. With laughter, he continued enjoying the fun, giving her time to escape to her room.

Feeling the disdain of a shirtless man, Jack Frost blew its unbearable breath and Cooper dashed into the house just as Suzanna's bedroom door closed. The others followed his lead.

Remy and Yes'sa Man resumed preparing breakfast.

Cooper rushed in front of the fireplace.

"Here you go." Sam covered him with a blanket.

"MERRY CHRISTMAS!"

Remy and Yes'sa Man turned to the sound of Suzanna's voice. Surprised, they too shouted "Merry Christmas" and rushed into her open arms.

It felt so good. That thing called love that is shared in a family dynamic. Suzanna closed her eyes and embraced it. She'd never felt that type of love from her biological family. With teary eyes, her head rested on Remy's shoulder.

"'Um just about through with breakfast," Remy said.

"Let me help you. Yes'sa Man, you can take your leave. I'm sure Sam could use your help," Suzanna said.

"Yes'sa." He left.

"Does Mister Cooper know you're here?"

"He sure does."

Remy looked back at Suzanna who was gathering utensils. *He sure does.* "Hmm."

Christmas morning breakfast was perfect. A feast fit for royalty. They gave grace and dug into the piles of bacon, sausage, grits, flapjacks, eggs, biscuits and gravy. The conversation around the table came naturally. No talk about work, only fun stories, laughter and a little private flirting between Suzanna and Cooper that they tried to conceal from the others.

Although engaged in laughter, Sam didn't say too much. He was still feeling a bit awkward about what he'd witnessed earlier.

Noticing his behavior, Cooper attempted to set his mind at ease. "So, Sam, you've never shared your life story with me. I've told you about mine, please share a little about yourself."

While looking at his food, Sam tightly gripped the fork and stabbed it into the sausage that was on his plate. After getting everyone's attention, he picked up a knife, cut the meat in half and pulled the fork out. He sliced it again and continued to do so, grinding the fork and knife on the plate. Scraping and squealing, making the ladies cringed with every stroke. Finally, the meat could be minimized no more. Placing the knife on the table, he stuck the fork into a miniature piece and held it up. Looking at it, he turned the itty-bitty piece from side to side, staring at it with wide eyes, locked into the past that he brought into the present.

"See 'dis here meat? 'Dat be what my life be like buh'fo' Massa lend me out to Miss Suzanna and you come along."

The room was silent. No one lifted a utensil or said a word. They just sat there staring at him, offering their undivided attention.

"See, Mister Cooper, you don't know what it feels like to be a slave."

Cooper leaned back. His thoughts left the room momentarily but quickly returned when Sam spoke again.

"You don't know what it be like to be a man but treated like a boy no matter how ole you get. To know you somethang, but treated like you nothang till you start believin' it."

Sam turned and twisted the fork, examining the small piece of sausage as if he was searching its soul. He grew sad, put the sausage and fork on the plate and continued. "One day when I be 'bout fit'teen, my mama, she sends me to chop woods for a fire. Overseer wasn't too far oft from me, so I heards' him make a wager wit' his boys 'dat he, 'dey old man, was stronger 'dan 'dey. 'Dey took him up on the offer and each broke a limb off a tree. 'Den 'dey unrooted plants from the groun'. I stand 'dare lookin' until the overseer noticed me. He said somethang to his boys and 'dey all come over to me. I be 'dey new wager. 'Who can break a limb first' 'dey old man said. 'Dey pushed me down and each one grabbed a leg or an arm and pulled hardest 'dey can. But 'dey couldn't get 'dem to break, so 'dey put a foot to me and started twisting and pulling, turning' til each one heard a pop on the arm or leg 'dey be workin' on."

"Oh my God." Suzanna covered her mouth.

Cooper closed his eyes and shook his head in disbelief.

Remy folded her lips in, trying to hold back tears.

Yes'sa Man just sat there staring at Sam, who continued telling his story.

" 'Den 'dey kicked and stomped me. Tryin'na get me to stop crying. But I was hurtin' sum'thin bad. Sum'thin real bad. I yelled at the top of my lungs, but nobody heards me. But I kept on screaming 'cause the pain be like nothang I ever felt buh'fo'. I scream till no mo' sound could come out me. 'Muh mama figured I was gone too long, so she come to see 'bout me and saw 'dem beatin' me. She ran and got Massa, and he stops 'em and gots the doctor to fix me back up...but he sold me off 'cause I was no good to 'em after 'dat. Said the only value I had was to be sold. When you sees me stop working, I not stop 'cause I lazy, I stop 'cause 'dose pains never left me 'lone. More on cold days. But since Mister Cooper come and gets me new warmer clothes, I can stand 'dah cold better. And Remy, she rubs me down every night wit' 'dat cream she makes. The pain don't hurt so much no mo', but it ain't never left."

Tears welled in Remy's eyes. Too full, they released. She unfolded her lips and sniffed. Opening her mouth, she exhaled. The reverberation of her trembling breath prepared them for her story.

"I had me a family... Two baby girls and my man. He be a strong dark, handsome man and I loved him—oh, how I loved that man. He comes to me one night and say, 'Baby I gotta leave. I can't take you and the girls, but I promise I'll be back fo' ya' as soon as I figure out how. But I loved that man. Didn't thank I could live wit' out 'em. So, I begged 'em to let us go, and he gave in. When we gotta chance, we ran off. We ran the whole night and thought we gone make it. We knew we had a long ways to go, but we didn't hear no dogs or no folks. So, we be sure we gone make it."

Remy sat up straight, spoke slowly, measuring every word as if she was reliving the traumatic experience. "The woods was dark—so dark till sometimes I couldn't see my man 'cause he so dark just like the night. The girls got tired, so we stop fo' a rest and fell asleep. When we woke up, the daylight be up too. I see my man standing and looking confused wit' his hands on his hip. I know to not bother him when he's thankin', so I gave the girls the bread I packed. Then he comes and eats wit' us, and we started movin' again."

She frowned. "Then we hear hounds...but...they not be behind us, they be in front of us. Coming right at us. So, we turned and run the other way. But the overseer and his men caught up wit' us and dragged us back. It only took us a little ways to get out of the woods. We had run a whole night and it only took a short time to get back on the plantation. Turns out my man got confused and headed us back to the plantation."

"Mmp, mmp, mmp." Sam shook his head.

"They took us in the barn and mocked us for a while befo' they beat us. Even the babies. They beat my sweet little girls. Then they left us in the barn strapped up for days. Gave us no food, no water. I remember it was so hot in that barn, I thought they gone leave us in there to die. Then the overseer and his men comes in and tell my man how dumb he is. Said he didn't know comin' from going. They killed my man down in his heart when they told 'em that it be because of how dumb he is that his whole family got caught and that his girls would be sold to a owner who likes young black nigga girls. They sold my two girls. They wasn't but five, and seven, and they sold 'em to a man who likes 'em young. Then they laughed at us...tell us how much pleasing they gone be for they new owner."

Remy's face became more intense. Shaking her head, her eyes nearly disappeared while squinting. "Then they sold Roy." Unable to keep her composure, a high-pitched cry burst free. She dropped her head. "Oh, God, they sold my family from me."

Suzanna passed her a cloth napkin.

Taking it, Remy wiped her tears and continued. "Massa kept me for his self." Her breathing elevated, became heavier, louder as she cried, "...and raped me the first night they sold my man off and gave me one girl baby from him. Then when she was old enough to sell, he sold her off to another owner who he said likes 'em young. Massa kept at me and gave me two mo' babies till finally, no mo' babies could come out me. Then he stopped coming at me when I had nothang left in me. Nothang left to live fo'."

Tears rolled down faster. "I just wanted to die. Ain't no life to live if the life in you dead." She stopped for a while, and after clearing her throat, she dried her face with the napkin. "Then when Massa died, his wife sold the plantation and the possessions to Misses Suzanna's daddy, and now this where I be." Taking a deep breath, Remy got up from the table and started clearing it. With a stack of plates in her hand, standing in front of the table, she broke down and cried.

Suzanna gave her a hug.

Not wanting anyone to see her weakness, Remy tried to free herself from Suzanna who wouldn't let her go. For years, she had buried her pain in the depths of her soul and now it had been exhumed, leaving her emotionally exposed. She fought harder to be freed, but Suzanna refused until she finally gave in. Releasing a flood of tears, her body lost its strength. She fell from Suzanna's arms and collapsed to the floor.

Suzanna beside her and comforted her.

Sam got up and stood over them.

Cooper knelt beside them and rubbed her back. He motioned for Suzanna to move, then picked up Remy, carried her to the parlor and laid her on the settee.

Everyone followed them, except Yes'sa Man, who was left behind staring at the leftover food. "I thought we 'posed to be happy on Christmas Day."

Thirty-six

$\underline{S}$uzanna batted her eyes, making Cooper smile. They didn't need words to set up the unspoken appointment, their heated desires administered the date. As soon as the helpers left after dinner, Cooper was all over Suzanna, and she loved every minute of it.

Their hidden love had pierced their shielded secret like a bright sun appearing from behind tall mountain. They could hardly keep their hands, eyes, and bodies off each other, yet they never allowed it to complicate their commitment to the farm. No late sleep-ins or flirting while working, Cooper and Suzanna were all about business. If he'd learned nothing from the Hartford's, he'd taken that in.

Another year was approaching, and Suzanna was making her latest payment to her father.

"Hmp...that's three payments at once," her father acknowledged.

"That's correct, Father. Soon, you'll have the final payment."

"How do you mean?"

"Father, I'm tripling payments. By our calculations, the last should be in a matter of months."

"How did you come to that conclusion?"

"That conclusion? Father, I—"

Cooper jumped in. "Sir, based on our calculation, we have three more payments left. Am I correct?"

"Who are you?" Peter asked Cooper.

"I'm..."

"That doesn't matter. What matters is the fact that my father is trying to take advantage of me."

"This is business, Suzanna. And the very reason why women should stay in their places."

"Stay in their places! I am very capable—"

Cooper intervened, "Suzanna, allow me. Sir, do you have a contract, a written agreement, or some form of documentation bidding Suzanna to the elevated interests and seemingly unending fees that continue to rise?"

"Who do you think you are? You do not question me! This is a family matter."

"I do believe it was you who just stated that this is business. If you do not have any signed documents, we will supply them for you to end this business matter once and for all. I'm sure you'll find our fees based on the supplies you sold to your daughter years prior to be quite reasonable and fair. We will also include documents for the purchasing rights of the slaves, Sam, Remy, and—"

"You will not! They are a separate matter altogether."

"Fine. We shall discuss purchasing them at a later time. You're right, one thing at a time." Cooper turned to Suzanna. "Come along, my dear. You have a great day, sir." They left without looking back, leaving Peter steaming.

Suzanna was glad to have Cooper by her side when dealing with her father. He was a natural when it came to managing the farm's business. He purchased only the inventory needed based on the seasonal growth of the products to be sold that year and had established great business relationships. He knew who to market the products to, the exact times to market them, and how and when to negotiate.

With books he'd read from Massa Hartford's library and those he'd recently purchased, he'd learned everything there was to know about harvesting, business management, and investments, and his efforts were very successful.

They produced quality sugar cane products that rose in demand. And Copper's commerce deals and professional contacts were constantly increasing. His keen business sense had caused the farm's profits to double in less than a year. The only issue was that the demand for their products had become too much for the five of them to work alone.

"I'm sure Father will rent us more field hands."

"Yes, but at what rate? I'll create a contract that I'm sure will be pleasing to him." Cooper conditioned the lease to return the slaves each evening to help lower the cost and eliminate additional food and housing for the slaves.

"I think it will be wise to conceal our relationship with Remy, Sam, and Yes'sa Man from the slaves. I wouldn't want it to get back to Father. His traditional ways are unchangeable."

"I agree."

The helpers understood the need to be discrete and knew that Cooper and Suzanna were working towards their freedom. To prepare them to live as free men, Cooper began teaching them to read, write, and do math, tools they would need to survive outside of slavery.

Everything was going well. No problems, no complications, no sticky issues that lasted beyond control.

One evening when they sat around the dinner table in prayer, a word away from saying amen, they heard, "When y'all gone get married, since y'all act like married folks in the bedroom?"

Eyes sprung open, heads popped up, hands released, all attention went to Yes'sa Man, who waited for an answer to his invasive question. In a moment's time, the question turned on Cooper, and so did their eyes and ears, waiting to hear an answer.

Trapped by their stares, Cooper released Sam's and Remy's hands and looked at Yes'sa Man, who was staring back. He smiled to ease the discomfort. "This food looks delicious, Remy," he finally thought to say.

"Thank you, Mister Cooper," she said with her proper words that she was learning to use. "But I sure would like to hear the answer to that question."

Of course, you would. Cooper looked at Sam, his eyes and facial expression pleading for help.

Sam shrugged his shoulder. *I'on know what to tell ya'.*

Releasing Yes'sa Man's and Sam's hands, Suzanna sat up straight and cleared her throat.

Cooper briefly looked at her, then Yes'sa Man who was still staring. Huffing, he smiled. "If you all don't mind, I would like to have that discussion with Suzanna alone at an appropriate time." Never minding their stares, he picked up his fork and knife and began eating.

Remy looked at Suzanna. "Actually, I do mind."

Taking a hard-lumping swallow of his half-chewed food, Cooper looked up at Remy. "Of course, but I think such a question should be discussed amongst the two involved. We shall speak on the matter and share our thoughts with you all at a later time. Now, if you don't mind, I would like to enjoy this delicious meal you've prepared before it gets cold."

That was it. Nothing else was said about it. Food was eaten, the table cleared, and the helpers returned to their cabins that had been enlarged and now included three small bedrooms that were divided by walls instead of blankets.

÷÷÷÷÷÷

The temperature in the room was perfect for cuddling. After changing into his bed garment, Cooper joined Suzanna, who had also put on her nightdress and was sitting on the settee in front of the fireplace.

"This is nice." Suzanna laid her head on his chest as they both listened to the crackling sounds of the fire.

He'd said they would discuss it later that night, but there he sat, her head on his chest, his arm wrapping her in his love, the two giving reverence to the serene atmosphere. And her wanting to yell, beg for an answer to the out-of-place question that still lingered.

Cooper took a deep breath.

"What's wrong, my love?" she asked.

"Nothing... Well..."

"Well, what?"

"Suzanna, I love you, you do know that?"

"I do."

"And I want to marry you, it just that...I'm already...I'm already overloaded with the farm's business and to add something as important as marriage, it would be a bit bearing for me. Can you give me—"

"Take all the time you need. I'm not worried. When you decide to make me an honest woman, I will be here waiting. Cooper, I love you and I will wait for all eternity if you need me too."

Looking down at her, he stared into her eyes. He lifted her chin, gently placed his lips on hers. His tongue found its way into her mouth, his hand to her breast and the heated action became too hot to carry out in front of a burning fire. They moved their passion into the bedroom and set his bed ablaze.

The next morning, Cooper left Suzanna in his bed and walked right into Remy, who was in the kitchen preparing breakfast.

"Good morning," she said cheerfully.

That depends. "Good morning, Remy."

"How did you sleep last night, or did you sleep at all?" she teased.

He grinned. "I slept fine, Remy."

"So, you gone tell me if you proposed to Misses Suzanna or not?"

So much for a good morning. "Misses Suzanna and I settled. We decided that it would be best if we waited."

"What y'all waiting for...you love her, don't you?"

"Of course, I do."

She stopped preparing breakfast and turned to face him.

He felt a lecture coming on. Putting his hands in his pocket, he dropped his head as if his mother was about to chastise him.

"Mister Cooper, you have a choice that we slaves don't have. You can choose to marry who you love. Ain't nothang worse than being forced to love somebody, then when you love them, that love be taken away from you. So, when you can love freely, never take it lightly." She turned to the stove. "Now breakfast'll be ready soon."

He shouldn't have said anything, but he felt compelled. "I didn't always have a choice, you know."

She stopped and turned to him as if to teach him something that he would never understand. "You're not a slave, Mister Cooper. With all due respect, you'll never understand what we go through." Turning to the stove again, she continued cooking.

Thirty-seven

A year passed with no mention of the word marriage. Life on the farm and for the five was moving ahead with only minor setbacks, which forced Suzanna and Cooper to lease more slaves from her father. But they got through those struggles and soon things were back on track. The cane season ended and transitioned to the corn season.

On one particular occasion, Cooper and Sam went into town to conduct business. Cooper completed his business and went to the jewelry store to pick up an order.

Later that evening, they all sat at the dinner table laughing and eating. Remy had baked one of her special cakes to commemorate the success of their harvest for that season. When she came out of the kitchen with it, they were all standing, looking at her. Cooper had one hand behind his back.

"What's going on here? Y'all look like 'um the dessert?" She placed the cake on the table and turned around to see Cooper holding a small wrapped rectangular box.

"What's this?" she asked.

"From all of us," Cooper answered.

Tears formed when thinking that no one had ever given her a gift. She wanted to take it but didn't know how to. The whole experience felt strange.

"Remy, my arm is growing quite weary," Cooper said.

"Remy, are you alright?" Suzanna asked.

"Yes."

"Well, if you be alright, take the present," Sam urged.

Remy turned up her palm and waited for Cooper to place the gift in it. Once holding it, trembles forced her to sit. She carefully placed the elegantly wrapped box on the table as if it was fragile. Sitting back, she stared at it for a moment, wanting to remember how nice the box looked before unwrapping it.

"Open it!" Yes'sa Man yelled, breaking her sentimental moment.

Remy picked up the box and looked it over. It was so pretty. She turned it side to side, dreading peeling away the beautiful paper.

"You'll have to open it if you want to know what's inside," Suzanna said.

Remy methodically untied the bow and strings until she was finally able to undress the box and lift its lid. Her hand went to her mouth, then to the box as she lifted a silver necklace with six small and one large heart-shaped charms dangling from it.

Pointing to each, Cooper explained, "The five small hearts are symbols for each of your children. The large heart represents your husband's heart."

Covering her mouth, she broke down and cried in the midst of his explanation.

Suzanna sat next to her. The men gathered in close and they all comforted her.

Smiling through tears, she humbly thanked them for the thoughtful gift.

After giving hugs to Remy, Cooper walked over to Suzanna. He took a box from his waistcoat, got on one knee and pointed it to her. "Having you as my wife would make me a very happy man."

With a huge grin, Yes'sa Man loudly clapped repeatedly, drowning out Suzanna who answered, "Yes! Yes, I would be honored to be your wife!"

‡‡‡‡‡‡

"I don't know if I shall invite my family," Suzanna said while tilling the ground.

"Of course, you gotta invite your family. They your family...wouldn't be right not to invite 'em."

Working beside Suzanna, Remy rapidly moved, trying to do her share of the field work before going to the house to prepare lunch and do house chores. She no longer stayed in the house the remainder of the day as she had done in the old days but always returned to the field as soon as the house chores were completed.

Three weeks had passed since the wedding proposal and Suzanna was wrestling with the decision of whether she should invite her family to her wedding.

Cooper had complicated things by neglecting to speak with her father, who religiously subscribed to the older tradition. His failure to ask for his daughter's hand in marriage would be seen as an insult.

"Oh, I don't care. I mustn't worry myself numb. Cooper will be my husband, and I shall be his wife. It is our decision that prevails over all others' opinions. We don't require Father's permission to be happy." Yet, she still had a decision to make and regardless of her verbal words, inwardly, she would prefer having her father's blessing. She'd disappointed him once when she had married her first husband. For her second marriage, she wanted her family's presence.

"I don't know, Remy. Should I have a big wedding or a small intimate celebration?" She constantly worked while considering her options. "If I have a big wedding, I will need a glamorous wedding dress. And of course, I would have to invite my family. On the other hand, if it's small and intimate, I could wear something soft and simple, but pretty. It must be gorgeous regardless of the wedding size." She went on and on, every thought she had, she made known except wanting her father's blessing.

No wedding date had been set because she couldn't make up her mind. Suzanna had failed to formally introduce Cooper to her father, who'd wondered about the new man in his daughter's life. All he knew of him was that Cooper was interfering in their business and did so on their first meeting.

When Suzanna moved to the farm, her visits to her father's home didn't always feel welcoming until after her husband's death. Her father often hosted many parties and gatherings but had only invited her to a couple. And when she did visit her family, their social interest made her feel awkward, like an outsider. Suzanna's father was clearly embarrassed by the humbled life she'd chosen and never failed to make his position known.

Suzanna, what are you wearing?
What in God's name have you done to your hair?
When you get here, hide your wagon in the barn. I would die of shame if any of my guests were to see it?
It perplexes me why you don't fix yourself up to look like your sisters and other ladies your age.
Your sisters and friends have all married well, but you chose to marry a commoner.

"Introduce them."

While shoveling, Suzanna was lost in her thoughts and didn't hear Remy.

"Misses Suzanna?"

"I'm sorry. Yes. What did you say?"

"I said, you have to introduce your father to Mister Cooper. Yo' pa up in age now, maybe he's changed. The last few parties he had, he invited you. Maybe that be because he misses you and wants you around him more. Besides, it's the right thing to do."

"What if he rejects Cooper?"

"I don't think it'll bother Mister Cooper more than it'll bother you. That's why you scared. Not fo' Mister Cooper, but fo' yourself. You know what you should do? You should invite your pa over for dinner, talk about how things going on the farm since you done paid him out for the inventory. Then tell him how Mister Cooper be the reason why the farm is prospering. Then he can get to know Mister Cooper fo' his'self and see that he be good for you."

Suzanna stopped working. "That's not a bad idea."

"Then if he gives his blessing or not, it'll help you decide what kind of wedding you want."

"That's a great idea, Remy... But of course, if I invite Father to dinner, that will mean you all—"

"We know, Misses Suzanna. We know our rightful place in front of company."

"I really hate to ask you all to do such a thing. It's so unfair."

"I know. You know you and me didn't make this world, but we do gotta live in it."

"Have to," Suzanna corrected.

"Huh?"

"You said, 'we do gotta live in it'. It's, we do have to live in it."

"Have to. We do have to live in it." Smiling while working, Remy enjoyed learning how to talk proper.

That very day, Suzanna sent her father the invitation by messenger.

Reading the invitation at his desk, Peter immediately wrote a rejection letter.

"I would love to be a guest at your dinner table, Suzanna. Unfortunately, I will be away on business on the proposed date."

Signing his response, he stopped. *Who is this Cooper fellow?* A stranger he'd only met once and had inquired about in town, but no one could offer any background on the man who seemed to have dropped out of the sky. He tore up the rejection and wrote an RSVP.

‡‡‡‡‡‡

Suzanna and Remy worked hard to prepare for her father's visit. "Everything has to be perfect." Suzanna looked over the table one final time. Her father's arrival would be soon, and it was making her a nervous wreck. She sped off to her room.

Minutes later, Suzanna returned, tugging on her dress and teasing her hair. "He will be here in a moment's time." She turned to Cooper. "How do I look?"

"You look amazing. You mustn't get so worked up. It's going to be wonderful." Gripping her shoulders, he stopped her. "Hey, look at me. It's going to be fine." He pulled her in for a warm embrace but slacked off when they heard a wagon and horse.

"He here!" Yes'sa Man shouted while looking out the front window.

"Come over here." Remy waved with her hand.

Suzanna nervously checked everything while everyone rushed to take their places. The helpers were uniformed in black and white attire, clothing Suzanna had gone into town to purchase for the special occasion.

Thoroughly trained for the task, Yes'sa Man stood by the door, opening it before Peter knocked. He took Peter's coat, hat and cane the moment he walked in.

"Father." Suzanna rushed to greet him with a hug and kiss. She turned to Cooper. "Father, this is Cooper Edwards from Virginia. The son of the late Corpel De Luca, who originated from Italy and Lady Elizabeth Edwards from Virginia. Mister De Luca was a wine connoisseur." She hoped that the bit of information would reduce probing questions and impress her father.

Peter gave Cooper a firm handshake.

Cooper knew that the long hand grip came with questions.

"Edwards, from Virginia?"

"As Suzanna explained, Father migrated from Italy."

Still gripping his hand, Peter shook his head. "I see. I see."

"Father, we've prepared hors d' oeuvres."

"We've prepared?" Peter frowned.

"Yes, I helped Remy to make them."

"You're turning into a full domesticated servant and field hand, aren't you? That's a step away from slavery. My word, Suzanna, where did I go wrong?"

"I happen to enjoy learning of any sort, Father. And yes, that includes cooking." Suzanna felt the presence of agitation growing while guiding her father to the dinner table. "Please, take a seat."

Grimacing with a raised eyebrow, Peter looked around the large open eating room. It was his first time in the house since it had been built. The frown on his face expressed his thoughts about Suzanna's decoration taste.

Sam went over and pulled out his chair, prompting him to sit.

As Remy served the appetizers, Peter wasted no time getting to know Cooper. "So, Cooper Edwards, is it?"

"Yes, sir."

"Are you going to marry my daughter or continue laying up with her like you're bedding a whore?"

"Father!"

Smiling as he often did to keep calm, Cooper reached over and squeezed Suzanna's hand, staring into her eyes. "You are a beautiful, vibrant woman. I love your smile, your thoughts, your walk, your laughter, every freckle on your face, even the smell of your flatulence."

She giggled.

"You make me the man that I am. You push me to be my best. You are an honorable woman and any man would be lucky to have you as the love of their life. I love how strong you are and I'm not intimidated by your brilliance or your desire to build your legacy. You are a gracious woman, yet you are strong-willed and I loved that about you. I love you, Suzanna. From my heart to my soul, I love every part of you." Cooper turned to Peter. "Sir, I wish to make your daughter my wife because she has taught me how to be a husband."

Peter's stare remained on Cooper, who didn't know what to make of it. Finally, he stood and threw his napkin on the table. "Do you think that I would just hand my daughter off to you? A stranger from Virginia. I've traveled all over and I've never heard of a Corpal De Luca, some wine connoisseur from Virginia. You could have come from underneath a rock for all I know!"

"Father, you are out of line!"

"No, he's out of line!" Peter argued.

"I understand, sir, and you have every right to protest for your daughter's welfare. If you would give me the time, I would be happy to make your acquaintance."

Peter eased into his seat. "Hmp...Tell me more about your father."

"Of course."

By dessert time, Peter was happy to learn that he came from a family of prestige and not only was he ambitious, he was also well-educated, an opinion he'd gathered from Cooper's expansive vocabulary. Being the proud man that he was, he would never use the word "impressed" to describe his feelings for Cooper, but he was. Cooper's level of business knowledge was obvious in the farm's prosperity.

"And Cooper spear-headed it all," Suzanna proudly stated. "We recently acquired thirty additional acres of adjacent land and our revenue is increasing quite handsomely, Father."

Consuming the last of his second piece of pie, Peter dropped his napkin on the table. Disregarding the word "we," he thought about *his* daughter's prosperity. Standing, he picked up his glass and raised it.

They did the same.

Peter looked at Suzanna. "I'm proud of you. You have put all my doubts to rest." Then to Cooper, he continued, "I trust that you will make my daughter an honest, happy woman. And with your knowledge and skills, I'm sure that you will help *her* land continue to prosper. To your engagement." He nodded, and not waiting for them, drank down his wine as if he was in a hurry. He left the table and took his things from Yes'sa Man and after putting on his hat, he wished them a good night.

Suzanna jumped into Cooper's arms. "Thank you. I'm so happy. I love you so much." She rushed over to Remy and pulled her toward her bedroom. "Come on."

Remy stopped. "But I have to clean up."

"Oh, I'll help you later. We have a formal wedding to plan."

Watching the two walk away, Cooper laughed. "Sam, Yes'sa Man, why don't we help the ladies out by cleaning up while they plan *their* wedding?"

Thirty-eight

Waving good-bye, Cooper and Suzanna headed for the train. Their wedding had been perfect, leaving Suzanna gleaming with joy. The newlyweds left for their honeymoon a few days after their wedding and the help worked the farm in their absence.

In their honeymoon suite, Cooper was getting dressed. "Darling, are you going to join me?"

Suzanna lay across the bed. She rolled over to face him.

"What's wrong? Are you not feeling well?"

"Just tired. All the planning, the wedding, reception, traveling and moving non-stop since our arrival have taken its toll. Do you mind if I stay in for the night?"

"Of course not. I'll go out and grab you a bite to eat."

"Take your time. I'm going to undress and rest for a spell." She turned on her side.

"Alright, darling." Cooper kissed his new bride and left.

Walking on the sidewalks of the large beautiful city of San Antonio, Texas, Cooper noticed a local tavern. "Surely one drink can't hurt." He walked in, took a seat at the bar and ordered his "one drink." He leisurely consumed the glass of brandy and minded his own business.

A man sat next to him and after ordering his drink, he turned to Cooper and stuck out his hand. "Darwell Lingston."

Cooper slowly reached out and shook his hand. "Cooper Edwards."

"Nice to be in your company. I do hate drinking alone." He looked down at Cooper's nearly empty glass. "What are you having?"

Cooper hesitated. His fear of bounty hunters had never left. He was always easily spooked. "Brandy."

Darwell turned to the bar. "Barman, a finger of brandy served neat for the fellow sitting next to me." He looked at Cooper and smiled.

The barman was pouring a finger length amount of brandy with no ice as requested by Darwell before Cooper could raise a hand to oppose.

"Cheers to meeting new people." Darwell raised his glass and waited for Cooper to join him.

Cooper stared at his glass like an alcoholic facing a losing battle.

"Take the glass, my friend, and let's find a reason to toast."

Cooper smirked. "I'm a new husband. Just got married a week ago."

"A perfect reason to celebrate."

Yeah, it is a perfect reason. Cooper raised his glass and gulp down the wine. "Barman, another round on me."

A small conversation and Darwell was ready for thirds. "Keep 'em coming until I say when."

"But I shouldn't. I need to get back to my new bride."

"You'll have a lifetime together."

The barman refilled their glasses.

Cooper figured he'd let the filled glass sit. It was still early. After looking at the glass for a few seconds, he quickly changed his mind. "You know what? My wife is probably asleep. I shouldn't disturb her. Might as well enjoy the company."

"Here's to a sleeping wife." Darwell raised his glass.

Two hours later, they were quite intoxicated and indulging in an interesting conversation. Cooper's inebriated loose lips were giving Darwell a very intriguing story. His drunken words crossed between Cooper's and Jesse's dialect. "Dis' not be muh' first marriage... I was, I mean, 'um still married' tah 'dah most beau-ful woman in 'dah world."

Not able to keep up with them, the barman left the bottle that Cooper grabbed and poured. "But I love my Suzanna...I 'den know you could love two women at once, but I do. I love 'dem both." He stared.

The evening drew to an end. The two men left the tavern barely able to stand. Before departing, Darwell pulled out his business card and through slurred words offered his specialty services to Cooper. "Take muh card." He tucked it into Cooper's front pocket. "I can help you."

They shook hands and staggered in different directions.

The next day had stripped Cooper's memory of the night before. After falling into bed, the last thing he remembered was staring at a glass of brandy.

At noon, Cooper and Suzanna strolled arm and arm on the city's sidewalks. The city was everything Cooper had heard about. Tall buildings, banks, restaurants and— "...a clothing store." Suzanna pointed. "We must go in."

"Good afternoon." Darwell stepped in front of them.

The couple stopped. Immediately, an additional thought of the night before returned to Cooper. "Suzanna, this is—"

"Darwell Lingston." He gripped the rim of his hat and nodded.

Suzanna smiled and slightly curtsied.

Cooper turned to Suzanna. "Darling, go on without me. I'll be in shortly."

She kissed Cooper on the cheek and nodded to the man before leaving.

Darwell waited before speaking. "Are you still interested in the business we discussed last night?"

Cooper was baffled. "I beg your pardon. You will have to refresh my memory as I seemed to have forgotten our conversation past my third drink."

"Of course. I'm having withdrawal as well from our indulging evening. You said you were interested in retaining my services."

"And what services might that be?" Cooper looked quizzical.

"You explained...a lot. It was quite a night. We talked about much." Darwell was careful. Who knew if Cooper was the same man sober that he was when he was intoxicated? His type of business was too important to jeopardize. "...Yes, 'um...I see you have forgotten our conversation. Perhaps you might be reminded if you look in the pocket of the waistcoat you wore last evening. If you are still in need of my services, my card that you will find there will help you locate me. And do so discretely. Without the presence of your new bride. Farewell, my good fellow and do enjoy your honeymoon." Darwell hurriedly excused himself, walking away without looking back. Sixteen broad steps forward, a right turn at a street corner, and he was gone.

Although he had on a different waistcoat from the night before, he immediately checked his pockets, rapidly patting himself down.

"Whatever are you so frantically searching for?" Suzanna asked.

Thirty-nine

The honeymoon was over.

After telling Suzanna that he was searching for the key to the room, the two went back to the hotel and were stopped in the lobby by the attendant. "Madam, this is addressed to you."

"Why would I be getting a message on our honeymoon?" She rushed to read it, then looked up at Cooper.

"What?"

"Father has taken ill."

"Is it serious?"

"Gravely, it says."

The timing could not have been worse. They'd missed work for the wedding and honeymoon, putting them behind in productivity. Not only would they be cutting their honeymoon short, they would also have to rush home to be by Peter's side.

"You return home, I'll go to be with Father."

"And I shall be by your side. I'm your husband, I will not allow you to face your father's illness alone."

After a week and a half at her father's, Peter survived the terrible bout of pneumonia and returned to his grouchy self.

Suzanna and Cooper seized on the visit and his vulnerable state.

"Why won't you sell them to us?" Suzanna asked.

"I am willing, but you have failed to accept my offer." Peter sat back in his office chair, still weakened from the illness he was recovering from, but as greedy as ever.

The evening he visited Suzanna for dinner, he'd taken notice of the once shallow, lazy, and dead-spirited slaves whom he had leased to Suzanna. They'd transformed into well-mannered, attentive servants, who had helped her farm prosper despite only being the three of them. Surely, he could not let them go at a worthless slave's value. "I'm not refusing to sell them. That would make me a foolish businessman. But I'm afraid you've had them for so long that I cannot possibly recuperate all that I've lost in their absence. Therefore, I must be compensated for my loss and their value."

Cooper became livid. "How much are you increasing their value to now, Peter?"

Peter wrote the amounts on a slip of paper and slid it to Cooper.

He picked it up, read it and looked at Peter. "Are you mad? These prices triple the cost of strong, healthy slaves in their twenties."

"It's my final and only offer and it's non-negotiable. Until you are able to buy them outright, their rental cost has doubled. I'm constantly losing money as long as you have them in your possession. Now, leave me, so I can get some rest. This discussion has drained me."

"But, Father."

"Come along, dear." Cooper pulled Suzanna's arm.

They stormed out of his office. His greediness did not deter them from securing the helper's freedom. They would just need more money and time.

The farm continued to grow and was doing well financially, but there was only so much the small farm could produce.

"We can purchase more of the adjoining land, but in doing so, the huge sacrifice would leave us just enough money to procure the inventory.

We won't have enough money left to include the purchase of slaves needed to work the fields," Cooper said to Suzanna.

"What do you suppose we should do?"

"I've already spoken to the land's owner and asked if he would divide the land. He agreed but increased the acre's amount to a price that would still leave us short."

"We can always borrow from my father."

"Never. We'll just have to figure this out."

"There's no other way we can do this without going into debt. Except for one thing," Suzanna said.

Cooper and Suzanna held a meeting with the helpers. Cooper explained, "We have what's needed to close the deal on the land, but with its increased value per acre, we won't be able to stock up on inventory without going into debt. A consideration that may not be a good option for us at this time because of the unpredictable possibilities of seasonal harvesting. But there is another option."

"And what's 'dat?" Sam asked.

"We have money put aside for your freedom. It's not quite enough to purchase your freedom at this time, but it can afford us enough inventory to get us started," Suzanna answered.

Cooper continued, "And in doing so, we can make more money, which helps us pay for your freedom."

Remy looked at Sam, he looked at Yes'sa Man, and they all looked at each other. Cooper and Suzanna had been good to them and now it was their turn to show their appreciation. Remy smiled at Sam, who nodded. Yes'sa Man smiled, staring at Cooper.

"We…give…you…our…blessing," Sam said. Pronouncing every word the way Remy had been teaching him in the evenings. It was great to be in a place of power, and he wanted to make sure that he managed it well. Cooper had begun teaching him how to manage the farm, giving him the position of the overseer. Preparing him for what was to come.

☩☩☩☩☩☩

Cooper took a ride to the river where he loved to sit and think. There, his mind streamed like the flowing waters, constantly filtering thoughts of what could be and putting it up against what should never be. His mind stopped for a moment. The moment he'd been waiting for since he'd run had arrived. But a lot had changed. So much so that it had given him second thoughts of his former plans.

He was no longer Jesse, who took trips to the woods, laid out in the grass with limited time. He was now Cooper, who could sit on the banks of the river for as long as he wanted, on the property he owned. Instead of his dream of leaving the Hartford Plantation, he now dreamt of returning to it. Now that life had presented him with the opportunity to make his dream come true, his life had also made that decision a nightmare of complicated issues. Before marriage, he had wondered if he could. After marriage, he questioned if he should.

Why continue to wonder?

The opportunity was present. They needed more money for Sam, Remy, and Yes'sa Man's freedom, which required more land and inventory, which called for more slaves to work the fields.

Cooper's mind shifted. It was made up. No more doubting, wondering or deliberating. He went in hard on his goals. Working and planning, taking no days off. In the rain, on cold days and hot. He wasted no awakened hour. In the field, he worked his body. In the house, he worked his mind, writing, calculating, strategically planning. Laboring under stress, getting bright new ideas, canceling foreseeable problems. His mind never rested. "Maybe fewer acres, more seeds...a few more pieces of equipment would leave enough money to purchase the slaves needed." He stopped and sat back. "That's it. I can do it. I finally have enough to purchase her."

"Who?" Suzanna asked.

Forty

"Another mule." Cooper answered Suzanna, who'd walked in their bedroom and overheard his spoken thoughts.

Of late, he couldn't keep his mind off of her. Her face had faded in his memories over the years, but not her lips and the smile they formed. His mind had captured it so perfectly, her eyes, her beautiful dark shiny skin, never to be erased. He worked hard to bring his vision of her into reality.

The days were long and the nights were short. From sunup to sunset, everyone worked relentlessly. Days, weeks, months, a year passed, and their hard work had paid off. The farm had its most successful year ever and the wheels were in motion to purchase a hundred acres of the adjoining property and the inventory and slaves to work it.

"We here, Mister Cooper," Sam said after stopping the horses and wagon.

Cooper got off the wagon and walked into the bank to make the withdrawal. He could now move forward with his plans to purchase the land, inventory, his family and Nina.

To commemorate their success, Cooper and Suzanna hosted a black and white evening for the five of them. They all dressed up on a Sunday evening wearing black and white formal wear, preparing to eat a fancy dinner prepared by Remy and her help, Suzanna.

Cooper owned two black waistcoats and Suzanna had laid out the best fitting of the two, the one he'd worn on their honeymoon. He put on the waistcoat and noticed that something was missing. "A white handkerchief." He tried to stuff one into his front pocket but was restricted. "What's this?" He reached inside and pulled out a business card. Images flashed across his mind. That of a tavern, a man, several shots of brandy, laughter, a secret conversation. *What have I done? What secrets did I disclose? What harmed did I cause?*

Cooper looked at the man's card and recalled his words.

"Yes, 'um...I see you have forgotten our conversation. Perhaps you might be reminded if you look in the pocket of the waistcoat you wore last evening. If you are still in need of my services, my card that you will find there will help you to locate me..."

He remembered wanting to check the waistcoat when they returned to the hotel, but Suzanna's father's illness took precedent, removing all urgent matters. When they had returned home, catching up on the work that they were terribly behind on had become a top priority. But now, the thought had resurfaced. He read the card that had all capital words.

"WHEN YOU CAN'T, I CAN.
CONTACT ME, THE PURCHASE MAN!"
Flipping it over, he found how to contact the "Purchase Man."

"'When you can't, I can, contact me, the Purchase Man.' What does that mean?" Cooper whispered. He couldn't remember why the man would have given him that card but knew it had something to do with his loose drunken lips. "Land? Perhaps we discussed purchasing land."

Yes'sa Man knocked on the door. "Mister Cooper! Dinner's ready!"

Turning to the door, Cooper tucked the card back into his pocket and left the room.

Suzanna smiled. The waistcoat she'd picked out for their honeymoon complimented his muscular tone. She felt so lucky to be married to such a *handsome, gorgeous man, who's also so good in...*

"This is the last of it. I sure hope everything tastes good. Miss Suzanna and I worked so hard on it," Remy said, breaking Suzanna's thoughts as she set a large bowl of mashed potatoes on the table.

"It looks wonderful, ladies. I'm sure it's going to taste divine," Cooper said while sitting.

The helpers sat at the table feeling proud of their fancy clothes. For the special occasion, Suzanna and Cooper had taken them into town and helped them pick out black and white attire especially for the evening. To a white person, their clothing would not mean much. But for them, they felt that they were as sophisticated as any of those who held themselves superior to them. Their wardrobes made the evening all the more special.

After dinner, they sat around the fireplace sharing stories, enjoying each other's company, and drinking wine. Because of the recent recollection of lost memory, Cooper stopped his glass at half full.

Sam shared his best funny stories and Remy, while caressing her necklace, talked about her dreams of seeing her family again. "If I ever get my freedom, I'll find 'em and find some way to purchase them."

Cooper's eyes widened. That was it...that's what he'd told the man. He couldn't believe that he'd revealed his life story, but he had. That night, after drinking one too many drinks, he had shared his deepest secrets with a stranger. *It must have been fate; The Purchase Man. That's what that means. He purchases slaves for former slaves who are unable to make the transactions themselves because of their runaway status.*

"Cooper... Cooper... Mister Edwards?!" Suzanna got louder to get his attention.

When Cooper was mentally fixated on a thought, he became deaf to even the call of his name. His gaze never left the burning fire.

"Cooper!" She grabbed his arm that was propping up his face, making it fall, his head tilted over.

"What in the world could possess your thoughts so that you were not able to hear my calls?"

"I'm just tired, my love. I guess I fell asleep with my eyes open."

"Yes'sa Man asked you a question."

"I'm sorry, I didn't hear it." He looked at Yes'sa Man. "I'm sorry, please repeat it."

"When we gone buy more slaves wit' our money?" Yes'sa Man asked again.

"Not at this time, Yes'sa Man," Cooper answered, "but I am thinking about it."

"So how're we gonna work the fields by ourselves?" Remy asked.

"Yeah, 'cause that's a lot of land. Too much fo' us five," Sam added.

"That's true," Cooper responded. "The transaction will take a great deal of consideration because of the cost of the land and inventory. We can't make mistakes that could cost us a great deal of money that we can't afford to spare. Slaves too young may not be ready for the workload that will be required of them. Those too old may only have a few years of work left in them but could help with other chores, yet they would be cheaper for us to purchase. Now, while slaves in their twenties and thirties are strong, they will be too expensive. My decision has to include a balance between money and labor."

"Well said, my dear husband."

It was well said alright. Cooper had given the justification for the precise types and ages of Nina and his family and the reason to purchase them while effortlessly persuading Suzanna. *Now, all I have to do is contact Darwell Lingston and get things moving.*

The very next day, Cooper went into town and sent a telegram. In a matter of days, The Purchaser responded and was given all the names and the location of Cooper's family. To Cooper's surprise, the estimated cost for each slave was considerably less than he'd expected, but he had to pay double the value of each to afford negotiating.

"Any remaining funds, excluding expenses will be returned to you." Darwell considered himself to be a fair man.

"Why are you doing this?" Cooper needed to know, hoping to hear an answer that would convince him that *The Purchaser* wasn't swindling him.

"I see. You're wondering if you can trust me. I understand. When I was seven years old, I watched helplessly as my best friend, a slave boy, was snatched out of his mother's arms. His screams and cries pained the ears of us all and became more devastating when his mother was slapped to the ground while trying to save her son. She went to my father and begged him to allow her to go into town to get a job in the evenings to pay for her son's return. 'You will be permitted to do so, but only if you buy his freedom from his new master, then return him to me as my slave,' my father said to her. So desperate for her only child, she agreed and was given permission by him to work.

She worked as a caregiver for a modest family in the evening hours, and for free as a servant to my family on days. When I turned eighteen, I witnessed the woman give my father every dime she'd earned to purchase her son. I saw when he took the money from her hands. Eleven years of no rest, working for two families to get her son back. My father smiled and said he would take care of it. That mother cried, tears falling non-stop as she walked away, happy, thinking she would be reunited with her son. A week later, she was sold to the very plantation that her son was sold to. But her story, my friend, does not bear a happy ending.

Allow me to digress. You see, I was helpless then, but I am not helpless now. And I still hear their cries. They haunt me as if it was just yesterday," he said sadly. "They are the reason I do this. And like you, I never use my real name, Jesse Hartford."

Cooper was bewildered. "How did you—"

"Because I passed you on the road some years back when my partner and I were headed to my uncle's funeral. Walter Hartford. I didn't know it was you until I made it to the Hartford Plantation. And then I remembered when they were talking about this white-looking runaway slave. I remembered you looked so familiar when we spoke. You looked a lot like your father, my uncle. Except for the hazel eyes. It was you, the slave they were speaking of. We are cousins, you and I. You were pretending to be the master of an old slave by the name of Ben. I found Ben and once I got him to trust me, he told me everything and guessed that you had headed out West. I make it my business to know all things and everyone, although no one really knows me, you now have the pleasure of knowing that I am your family. I learned that you'd made your home in Louisiana and were honeymooning in Texas where we met."

Cooper's heart jumped rapidly. Suddenly an old hunting fear took over. The roguish look in his eyes spoke volumes to Darwell.

"Calm down, my friend. There's no need to attack or run. I can assure you that I am not here to capture and drag you back to the Hartford Plantation. Dear God, no. I'm here to help you...to do exactly as I stated. To retrieve your family on your behalf. Why? Because I died as my father's son years ago and became everything that he's not. And I'm proud of the lives I have helped in honor of my friend whose mother hung herself the night she was sold. When she arrived at the plantation, she learned that her son had run, was caught and hung years prior while she labored for his return.

I questioned my father during one of his drunken *spats* about the whole ordeal, and he acknowledged knowing all along that the mother's son was dead and that selling her to the same plantation would break her heart."

Cooper gave him the money. "Here. Thank you for helping me."

"I promise to do everything I can. My word is my contract. I provide no paper trail in this business."

"I understand."

"Within a year you will receive four messages. Each will have a number. One means I've landed on the plantation, two means I'm negotiating, three means I've made the purchases. I can't promise that I will be able to purchase everyone on your list, but I will do what I can. The last message will be the number four. It means that I'm on my way to a designated location that I know you are familiar with."

"How will you know that?"

"As I said, I make it my business to know all things. If I run into any problems, the message will have a zero. This means wait to be contacted. Please make no efforts to contact me. I will be in touch when it is safe to do so. If not me, you will hear from my partner,

Margaret. You've met her on our way to my uncle's funeral. Do you understand?"

"Yes. I understand—"

"A simple 'yes' will do. It is how you should communicate. Keep everything simple. It's best that way. Do you understand?"

"I do, I mean, yes." Cooper smiled, shook Darwell's hand, and they parted. Cooper went one way, Darwell another, walking as if his steps had been pre-calculated. Exactly sixteen steps, a right turn, and he was no longer in sight.

Forty-one

The sun had yet to come out. Cooper eased the door shut and headed for the field with limited light in the sky. Feeling his way around, he did what could be done in the dark without allowing the morning's dimness to limit his ability to work.

About thirty minutes later, Sam came out and began working. Not long after that, Yes'sa Man appeared, rubbing his eyes, trying to force complete alertness. He went near Cooper as usual and started copying him. "Um'ma win today, Mister Cooper." He yawned and took a long wide stretch to get started.

"We shall see, Yes'sa Man." Cooper no longer had to let him win. He'd become quite competitive.

"Here y'all go." Remy came out with a basket of biscuit sandwiches just as the sun was rising. She joined in the work.

They wiped sweat, did body stretches, drank water, and even slowed down at various times, but they never stopped. Cooper was on a mission, in pursuit of his greatest conquest, to be reunited with Nina and his family. He started each day the same. Working tenaciously before sunrise and long after it had dawned. Some days, Sam would work the long hours with him and other days it would be Remy and Yes'sa Man.

When Suzanna tried to work alongside him, he rejected her help. It didn't feel right to have her laboring in the fields so that he could reunite with Nina.

Oftentimes, he would regret his decision, never about his family, but about Nina. Suzanna was such a good wife to him, and he loved her.

He loved everything about her. He felt that what he had done to Nina then, was just as wrong as what he was doing to Suzanna now. Yet, he didn't know how to fix one without neglecting the other. But he was going to do everything in his will to make sure that it all worked out.

While taking a work break, Cooper stepped off the porch and walked to the center of the road. He looked all around the property at the house, the helpers' home, the field, the two large barns and smiled. They had the land and the inventory had been purchased. He turned to the new structure where one large cabin and two outhouses were being built to accommodate the new slaves. *Yes, it's all coming together.* There was no turning back, no changing his mind.

Cooper had given instructions to Darwell Lingston to acquire ten slaves. His mother and stepfather, his six siblings and his wife Nina. The tenth would be of his family's choosing. He forbade the purchase of any children. Although he hated the thought of parents leaving their children behind, he needed the adults to work the farm and to eliminate any suspicion that Suzanna might have because of his selections. If everything went well, the adults would have the opportunity to later purchase their spouses and children.

The early morning-late night routine continued for months, bringing forth the approaching time for Cooper's family to arrive. He had received the second number and was looking forward to the third that meant the purchases had been made.

The relentless work that went into the newly purchased property had put them ahead of schedule, and the need for the slaves was past due.

Suzanna privately worried that he'd made a bad decision by soliciting the help of someone whose only guarantee was his word that he could get the best slaves for less money, which was what he'd told her.

Everyone was getting anxious.

"How long?"
"How many?"
"Have you heard anything?"
"Maybe you were conned?"

"I'm sure I'll hear something soon." Was no longer satisfying their questions. They required further explanation because the long hours in the field, minus Suzanna's help was taking its toll.

Sitting at the dinner table one evening, long after the sun went down, and following a long day's work, Sam, Remy, and Yes'sa Man waited for Cooper's answer to Suzanna's question. He'd heard it many times before. "How much longer? We need help and we need it now."

"I know it appears that it is taking a long time, but I'd arranged for the slaves to arrive in a year's time. The time I knew we needed to prepare for their arrival. It is not the order that is in delay, on the contrary, we are ahead of schedule. And that's the reason the order seems to be tardy." Finally, he got them to understand, and the questions stopped coming.

A few months later, the day finally came when Cooper received the last message. The number four and a map. With a smile, he was quite familiar with the location. In the lower right corner of the letter were three numbers.

6-1-7-A. The month, date, and time of day.

After receiving the date and location, he prepared to leave. Suzanna assumed that she would be accompanying him. He walked into their bedroom and saw her filling a small suitcase. "Sweetheart, what are you doing?"

She continued packaging, failing to see the surprised look on his face. "We have to leave to meet our new helpers."

"Of course."

"I've already prepared your things. Get ready for dinner, Remy will be setting the table shortly."

"Yes, my love." He left the room trying to figure out what he would say to change her mind. He had not anticipated that she would want to accompany him.

During dinner, everyone was excited. Yes'sa Man was shouting questions so fast that no one had a chance to answer them all.

Suzanna, Remy, and Sam shared laughter while Cooper sat quietly, trying to figure out the best way to disappoint his wife.

"Is everything alright? Did you receive another telegram?" Suzanna asked.

"No, but I'm afraid I have some bad news. Well, not bad, disappointing, I should say. Darling, you can't accompany me. Up until this moment, the gentleman has kept his word. But to be honest, I'm not sure if I can put complete trust in him. I'm not sure if he's obtained the slaves by some illegal transaction and I do not want you involved if that is the case."

"I'm sure it isn't. I have to be there upon their arrival."

"No, you don't. There is no cause for your presence."

"If your concern is true, you might be riding right into a trap. You are not known around here. I am, and so is my father. No one will ever harm me."

"My love, it's not that simple."

"Well, I insist and that's final."

"No! And that's final!" He stood "There's no need to take luggage. I shouldn't be gone that long. It's best to leave this evening instead of waiting for morning. I'm hoping that I can get to the location prior to his arrival. That way I can check out the area to make sure it's safe and secure. Bye, Suzanna."

Upset, she turned her head, never bidding him goodbye.

"I will see you all soon. Good evening, everyone." He left.

"I'll get everything cleaned up." Remy started clearing the table.

"I'll help," Yes'sa Man offered.

Cooper took the large wagon and went on his way. Thoughts crowded his mind. He was scared, afraid of what he might see. What had happened to them after he'd run? He wondered if his family had been punished, sold, or worse, had died? Were they mad at him?

In his company was the clacking of the horses' shoes, the shaking of the wagon, and the scenery of the drive. They did nothing to take his mind off of what was awaiting him. Then he looked up and saw it, a wagon stopped at the foot of a hill near a tree. Slaves standing, sitting, some resting under the tree's shade, obviously trying to cool themselves from the heat while waiting for their new owner. *They are early.*

Cooper's brother, Micah, who was the second oldest, saw the wagon approaching them. The others looked out to see what had gotten his attention.

Cooper smiled with mixed emotions. Getting a little closer, he could make out some of their faces. "Nina."

As if she could hear his whisper, she stood, her hand rushed to shield her eyes from the sun. When the wagon got a little closer, she jumped up and down. Screaming, she ran to meet him.

Cooper stopped the wagon, hop off, and ran towards her as she rushed into his arms, nearly knocking him over.

"What she doing?" one of the females asked.

"Maybe it's a childhood friend from her last plantation." Another female stood, trying to see in the distance.

"Whoever it be, it's somebody she knows," Cecil, Cooper's brother said.

"It has to be Jesse," Micah told the others, and they all walked toward the wagon to see.

In shock, the females cover their mouths, the men laughed.

"Look how good he looks. How he dressed. That's my big brother," Cecil announced.

Cooper walked over, shook hands with the men and hugged the women. "It's wonderful to see you all."

"Boy, where you learn to talk like that?" Cecil had a huge smile on his face.

Darwell Lingston tilted his hat to Cooper and rode off without a spoken word. It was the way of his business.

Cooper looked around. "Ma and Pa, where are they?"

Micah explained, "The man said a new plantation was looking for slaves. Said he'd been watching us and thought we'd be perfect for the new owner."

"He said the new owners would treat us good. Now, we know why." Thomas, the baby brother, laughed.

Micah continued, "Ma and Pa still alive, but they ole. They told us to go. Wanted us to have a chance at life. May, our baby sistah, she stayed back wit' 'em. She takin' care of our babies for us since we couldn't bring 'em."

In a panic, he looked them over, grabbing their arms, turning them around, examining them.

"Massa Ordell, he treats us sum'thin bad when you run off. But afta' awhile, he settled down. Finally, figured that the mo' he beat us, the less work he gets out'ta us 'cause of the wounds," Micah explained.

"I'm so sorry," Cooper said.

His sister, Reah, grabbed his hand, swinging it. "It don't matter none. You be a brave man for all the slaves on the plantation. *Our brother* was loved by all the slaves 'cause he was brave a'nuff to run off and didn't get caught. Now, here you be. All dressed up, lookin' fine, and done come and got your fam'ly."

"We was beaten bad, true that be. But today, we learn why and it was worth it. I'll take a beatin' for my freedom any day," Cecil said. But they were not free.

On the way back to the farm, Cooper purchased them food along the way. While they ate, he pulled Nina aside. The two sat underneath a tree. After they'd eaten, he collected the courage to explain his new life to her.

"My new wife...she's white."

"Your *new* wife. But you married to me. Wait, did you say, white?"

"Yes, I did. And yes, we are still married, but I'm also married to her."

"I don't understand. How can you be married to her? You be my husband. What that mean for us?" What did it mean to her as a black woman for her husband to be married to a white woman?

Cooper reached for her hand; she pulled it back. "Nina...Nina, I love you and I promise that we will be together. It's just... We'll have to be together in secret. No one can ever know that you are my wife." He tried to assure her that the life he was living now was a sacrifice that made it where he could be with her.

Nina listened in silence. She didn't want to be the slave girl who the master sneaked away to bed.

He reached over and caressed her face, turning it to him. She looked into his eyes and saw the man she'd fallen in love with. *Jesse.* He was the only man she had ever loved. "Okay."

After sharing the news with the others, they all understood and agreed to do whatever he asked of them. "One final thing. None of you can ever call me Jesse. Ever."

"What do we call you?" Micah asked.

"Cooper. My new identity is the life of Cooper Edwards."

"So, we call you Massa Edwards?" his brother Cecil asked.

"The others call me Mister Cooper. That will do." He explained that the helpers had special privileges because of the conditions of their lease. They, on the other hand, had to play the role of slaves because Suzanna and the helpers could never know of his relationship to them or else it would jeopardize his and their freedom.

They all agreed to his conditions and were feeling joy thinking about their new lives that awaited them.

Forty-two

Cecil, the third brother of the family sat in the front of the wagon with Cooper as they traveled back to the farm. None of the siblings had ever left the Hartford Plantation, so there he sat, with a big ole smile, as proud as he could be. He looked over at Cooper and patted him on his back. The life they once knew would be no more thanks to his big brother.

Looking ahead, they'd made it just up the road from the farm.

"There's Mister Cooper. He comin', he comin'!" Yes'sa Man said.

Everyone looked up and saw the wagon coming up the road.

Suzanna had no idea when he would be returning, but she was sure she didn't want to greet her new slaves looking like a dirty field hand. She dropped her tool and ran to the house as fast as she could. Standing in front of the mirror, she washed the dirt from her body and rushed to change clothes. When she returned to the porch teasing her hair, Cooper was getting off the wagon. Suzanna jumped off the porch and rushed into his arms. "It so good to see you. Our last conversation left me filled with worry. We mustn't ever leave a disagreement unresolved again." With puckered lips, she got up on her tiptoes and waited for his lips to meet hers.

Feeling uncomfortable in Nina's presence, Cooper quickly obliged. He grabbed her arms from around him and led her by the hand to meet their new slaves.

Cooper and Suzanna had purchased a total of ten slaves. From the lineage of his mother, Willa, and after Cooper, the second born, Micah and his wife, Sarah; the third born, Cecil and his wife, Bertha; the fourth born and first sister, Reah and her son, John; the fifth and six siblings, who were twins, brother, Thomas and sister, Jalean and her husband Mark; and finally Nina, who was introduced as the cousin of the siblings.

Cooper didn't hide the fact that the lot of slaves was all family, he just didn't share the most important part of the truth, that they were his family and Nina was his wife.

The cabin rooms' assignment was left for the family to decide since Cooper didn't know which of his family members would be coming. He had not seen them in a very long time and wanted them to feel as comfortable as possible with the new situation.

When Sam led the family to their house, Nina followed but found it hard to take her eyes off of Cooper, who was walking in the opposite direction towards the house that he shared with the woman who was wrapped in his arms. *His arms should be around me. He should be making love to me tonight, not her.* The calmness she thought she would be able to retain began to unravel. Feeling her heart tearing apart, she stopped.

"Come on, honey." Bertha pulled her arm. "Let's go see our new house. Look at it. It's so big. Sam said it got seven bedrooms. That means you'll have your very own room."

Nina looked at Bertha who was leading her away. "Bertha, I don't want my own bedroom, I want my own husband," she whispered.

"I know, I know. But you'll have to make do. And I'll be here to help you get through it."

"Look at this house." Jalean looked with wide eyes.

"Cabin," Cecil corrected. "The man called it a cabin."

"It don't even matter. It's huge. Like a massa's house." Sarah was amazed.

"It sure is." Reah looked around in every direction.

They'd traveled in the back of a wagon for days, slept on top of each other and prior to that, several of them shared small two-room shacks. The moment they stepped into the oversized cabin, they ran around like children, calling out to one another to come and see the various furnished rooms.

"This be our room. Cecil, look baby. We got a bed, a bureau, and a chair and bed table." Bertha was overjoyed. "I sure wish my ma could see me now. She'd be so happy fo' me."

Not only did the cabin have seven bedrooms and was fully furnished, but it also had a connected kitchen house in the back, a large family room, soft comfortable beds, and two out-houses that had covered walkways extending to the cabin. Cooper personally designed every part of it to assure that they had all the necessities they needed.

When Remy saw the slaves, she went over to Yes'sa Man. "Come on and help me cook."

"But we gotta work," Yes'sa Man said.

"It's just for today. Now that we have plenty help, we got time to stop and cook them a nice big meal for their first night here." When dinner was ready, Remy, Yes'sa Man and Cooper took the food to the family's cabin.

They ate that evening as they never had before.

"That woman can cook!" Thomas, the twin, leaned back on the settee holding his full stomach.

It was late, time to retire for the evening and get ready for the big day that followed. A day they found themselves looking forward to.

"A slave glad to start a day of work. How crazy that be?" Micah was getting off the settee.

"It's for our brother. Ain't gone be nothin' like workin' on the Hartford Plantation." Cecil stood in the midst of the family.

"Yeah, but we gotta do our part. Can't mess it up for 'em," Micah added.

"We ain't. This be fam'ly. Our fam'ly. It be like havin' our own plantation," Cecil said.

Before daylight the next morning, Cooper, Yes'sa Man and Sam were already in the field when the slaves walked out. Each slave listened carefully as Cooper gave them instructions and assigned duties. After receiving their orders, some walked off and started work. While a few more were still receiving their duties, Suzanna walked up to work.

"Excuse me," Cooper said to the slaves and pulled her aside.

"Cooper, darling, you failed to awaken me this morning. Oh, never mind, do you want me to go about my normal duties or do you have something different in mind for me today?"

Reah, her son, John, and Sarah, who Cooper had been speaking to listened to their conversation.

"Did she say, normal duties? She tryin'na work the fields?" Sarah asked, Reah.

"Yeah, that's what she said."

"Sweetheart, I had no plans to awaken you." Grabbing both her shoulders, he pushed her from behind, leading her in the direction of their house. "We have slaves now. There is no longer a need to have you toiling in the fields."

"But—"

"No but, Suzanna. The field is no place for the first lady of the farm to be. Now, that we have help, your place is in the home, not in the field."

"But, darling—"

"Suzanna... No. Go on, I'll be in shortly."

Smiling, she squeezed his hand and headed back to the house.

While working, Nina watched their body language. *She looks like she loves him.* It filled her with remorse while coming to grips with the reality of her new life.

Cooper watched as Suzanna headed to the house. He returned to the field and after gathering his thoughts, he continued instructing the others. "Let me or Sam know if you have any questions."

They shook their heads and got started.

Turning to Nina, he looked towards the house before going to her. "Here, let me show you how to use that."

"I know how to use it. I been in the fields all my life."

"Nina, I need you to…" He looked around, making sure no one was looking. His words changed to a whisper. "I'm sorry about that. I…I will not have you feeling uncomfortable in her presence. I'll do whatever it takes to protect you." He privately squeezed her hand.

"I…never mind."

"Please, tell me. Anything."

"I been meaning to ask you. How you learned to talk like that?"

"Miss Delilah taught me from my childhood until she moved away. I'd always talk this way, but I kept it concealed."

"When we were married, I thought I knew everything about you. But there was so much I didn't know." She returned to work, leaving him feeling her disappointment.

"We'll talk later."

She never stopped working, never even looked his way.

÷÷÷÷÷÷

Working with his family was new to Cooper. He knew that the Hartford's had instilled strong work ethics in each of their slaves and that those qualities would carry over to their farm or so he thought.

Micah, the eldest of the group constantly stopped working to get water; then he had to go relieve himself of it several times throughout the day. His wife, Sarah, kept asking how long they would have to work before they could take a break.

The twins, Thomas and Jalean argued with each other throughout the day. Conflicts that interfered with work when they stopped to get into each other's face.

Reah's son, John, was mentally challenged and only remained focused for short periods of time.

He had no problems out of Cecil's wife, Bertha, but Cecil moved like an old man. Thankfully, Nina, Reah, and Jalean's husband Mark, worked harder than them all.

After a few days of working with his family, Cooper had to leave to go into town, leaving Sam in charge, a challenge that Sam was not prepared for. He tried desperately to keep the slaves in line while Cooper was away. However, some saw him as a slave not worth rendering the respect that they would give to a white overseer.

Sam wasn't about to let Cooper down. He wanted to make him proud. He had every intention of resolving the challenges that he was facing. To do so, he stood from a distance, analyzing each of them, singling out those who were problems.

Micah was returning from his third water break of the day and was off to relieve himself of the fluid, again. Sam filled a jug with water and set it near Micah's workstation and waited for him to return. "'Dat be water 'dare for you. 'Dat mean you don't has to lees' the field to get it."

Micah looked at the jug, then at Sam. "Oookay."

Sam walked away feeling proud. "Problem solved. One down." He went to the twins.

"How you tell me how to use it, when you use it wrong?" Jalean yelled at her brother, Thomas.

"That be why it takes you so long to get things done, you using it wrong."

"I ain't ask for your help, Thomas. Why you bothering me?"

"Cause the less work you do, the more we gotta do to make up for what you didn't get done!"

"What you say?"

"I said—"

"I'on wanna know. Just leave me 'lone!" Jalean was aggravated.

Sam ran over and stepped directly in between the two, separating them. Big mistake!

"What you doin'?" Jalean asked.

"Break up 'dis here fight."

"Who you 'sposed to be," Thomas fussed.

"He thank he a white overseer. You too black to be white. You don't have no power to boss us around! You better get back on your horse and tell it what to do. That be 'bout the only thing you'll be bossin' 'round here!" Jalean said.

Standing in between them, Sam got an earful, making him extremely upset. Their voices, their words stung him terribly. He walked off murmuring, leaving them fussing at each other. "To thank, I sacrificed my freedom to purchase 'dees ungrateful slaves! I ain't never know Mister Cooper to be unkind, but 'um sure he ain't gone take a liking' to 'dey behaviors. 'Dey gone sure draw out the worst in 'em."

After lunch, Micah's wife, Sarah, and Cecil remained seated while the others went back to the field.

"Y'all gone get moving?" Sam had to ask two times before they got up and headed back to the fields, never answering him.

Sam had enough! He looked around and saw some talking, others moving slow, and a few not working at all. Only three were on task. He blew the break whistle, getting everyone's attention. "Ay...over here. Everyone over here 'rite now! Get over here where I be!"

Many seemed to be in no hurry, walking and talking, dragging along, making him wait for them.

"Everybody here?"

"You, blind? You see us here don't you?" Cecil joked.

The twins laughed.

Sam ignored them. "I want everybody to listen. 'Dis here farm started out from nothang, now it be somethang. Me, Yes'sa Man, and Remy, we not work 'dis here fields and make it prosper our own selves. Mister Cooper and Missis Suzanna work the field too. 'Dey worked hard, harder 'dan us and 'dey treat us not like slaves, but like folks should be treated. Now, you won't fines better white folks in 'dis whole world 'dan 'dees here white folks."

"These white folks," Thomas mocked.

Cecil leaned over to Thomas, "He done trick them good."

The whispers and snickers did not stop him. "'Dees white folks, 'dey never beat us or talk mean to us. We be like 'dey family and y'all can be too. You treat 'em good and work hard and I promise 'dey'll treat you just like you 'dey family."

"Fam'ly. I gotta work hard buh'fo I can be treated like fam'ly?" Cecil questioned.

Sam looked at Cecil. *I can see he gone be the trouble maker.* "I was like you. I gave 'em a hard time too. But Mister Cooper, he worked harder 'dan me and treated me good, taught me how to 'preciate a good Massa."

Again, Cecil tested Sam. "So, he the Massa, and we the slaves?"

"Cecil," Bertha whispered, "don't make no trouble. Of course, he be the massa."

Cecil looked at her. "Massa?"

"Yeah, he 'dah Massa. What kine' of question 'dat be?" Sam asked.

"'Um just wondering if we gotta call him Massa Cooper or Mister Cooper," Cecil said.

"He fine wit' Mister Cooper. I never had to call him Massa, and he never treats me like no slave. We respect each other as men. Now, we done talk long a'nuff. Like he said, y'all take orders from me. Now, if y'all want 'em to change 'dat and make 'em get a white overseer, y'all keep givin' me a hard time and 'dat be 'xactly what gone happen. He be back soon and I want 'em to see 'dat we work hard for 'em. So, let's get movin'."

"Lord, he got slaves rulin' slaves," Jalean said

"Ain't nobody payin' that fool no mine'," Cecil said.

Forty-three

*T*he work day was just about over when Cooper returned to the farm. Without delay, Sam went out to meet him and explained his challenges. Which slaves had given him problems, and which hadn't? Listening and nodding, Cooper was relieved to learn that Nina was not one of those who had compromised his kindness. After the day's work ended, Cooper told the entire family that he would meet them in their cabin after dinner.

The family gathered, waiting for Cooper. The unknown contents of the meeting were weighing heavily on the mind of Cecil, who after only a month of being on the farm, disliked the arrangements that Cooper had set in place for the family. He paced the parlor floor, arguing his point to the quiet room.

"...Why his own flesh and blood gotta eat in our cabin when Sam them 'lowd to have supper wit' them? And instead of us being over him, he makes Sam over us and let Remy work in the house while our women work the fields. I 'spect 'um not the only one who see that this here Cooper ain't no Jesse. This Cooper ain't no different than a white Massa who works his slaves from sunup to sundown. Anybody ever wonder why he ain't buy us our freedom? Stead, he buy us as slaves and make us work his fields. I'll work his field like ah proper slave if I hads my freedom. Wouldn't you, Thomas?"

Thomas dropped his head.

Cecil looked at Nina. "Then he buy his slave wife and make her watch how he treats his precious white wife. Nina be his wife, not that white woman! He no better than none of us, his skin just be white. He still be a black slave and if he makes me real mad, 'um gone tell that white wife of his."

"Tell her what, Cecil?"

Cecil turned to the sound of Cooper's voice. "What you 'spect? For us to come and work for you like we slaves?"

"Pardon me, Cecil, but that is what you are. A slave. Am I wrong?"

Cecil walked over to Cooper, who was standing near the door, bold and tall, a daring look dressed his face. He kept his eyes on Cecil. "Reah?"

She quickly stood.

"Have John stand outside and make sure he understands to not let anyone come in without my permission."

Reah took John's arm, guided him outside and made sure he understood the strict order.

Not waiting for Reah and John to exit, Cecil continued, "How you gone purchase yo' fam'ly as slave 'stead of just buy us our freedom? You no different from the white massa, 'sept you worst, 'cause you our own brother, our own blood who making us work like we dogs. Why you goes and play the white massa wit' the white wife in the big house."

Cooper's gaze remained on Cecil. "Are you finished?"

"No, I not! Why you treat Nina like that? She yo' wife, not that white lady. That be what I wanna know. And who be this Sam, Yellow'man, and Remarrow, whatever they name is? They be slaves just like us be but you let this Sam act like he the overseer over us blacks. We yo' fam'ly, it should be us ruling him, not he ruling us."

Cooper's eyes were fixed on Cecil when Reah returned. Thoughts of anger fought to speak on his behalf, but he remained calm. His eyes, on the other hand, showed the hostility that wanted to burst free from his lips. It took a smile to free him from the tension. "I thought I explained this upon our first meeting, but I suppose I failed to make things completely clear."

He stepped around Cecil and walked to the center of the floor to address everyone. "I appreciate those of you who did understand and worked without giving Sam any problems."

He returned to Cecil. "Sam...you're right, Cecil. He is a slave just like you. So are Remy and Yes'sa Man, but they didn't have to be." Again, he turned to the others. "You see, when I first moved to this farm, it was only Suzanna and the slaves. The farm was much smaller and this cabin that you all share did not exist. The helpers, as we prefer to call them, lived in a shack so small, it could only be sectioned off by thin pieces of cloths. The three barely had enough room to expand their arms without touching the others.

"Suzanna and the helpers worked the fields alone, trying relentlessly with failure to build it up. When I came along, they each were open to learning and through their unselfish submissions, we all worked together and turned this fruitless land into a harvest of prosperity. We worked before the sun came out and when it was long gone, sacrificing sleep and our bodies, working hard to assure the land's success.

And those slaves that you speak of, Sam, Remy, and Yes'sa Man, they sacrificed the finances of their freedom so you could be here today. The money that was saved for their freedom, they allowed me to use to purchase you all. And to answer your question, Cecil. Why did I purchase you as slaves instead of buying your freedom?" He walked over to Cecil, who was now sitting. Bending over, he looked directly into his eyes. "Because I had no reason to purchase your freedom."

Standing, he addressed the family again. "What reason would I, a white man, have to purchase the freedom of an entire slave family? Slaves I didn't know, whom I've never met, with the money that is needed for the benefits of the farm? Now, that makes no sense. But if I were to purchase slaves for the purpose of this farm, I would rather purchase my family and Nina and give them the opportunity to live decent lives. And just like Sam, Yes'sa Man, and Remy, who are not my family members appreciate the given opportunity, I was hoping that my family would see that unlike other slaves, they now have the privilege to be purchased as slaves, but treated like human beings and not like the properties of the Hartford's. And one day, life will grant them the opportunity to have their freedom without having to run to get it as I did."

Turning his attention to Cecil again, "And as for Nina, as you said, Cecil, she is my wife. That means she's *my business,* and I never want to hear your concerns about our business again! You got that?" Not waiting to hear Cecil's response, he bid them goodnight and exited the cabin.

The truth was, he didn't know how to handle the "Nina" situation. He had thought about it and thought about it, but never found a solution. From the moment he saw her, he realized that he loved her more than anything in the world, but he knew he couldn't act on those feelings. Now that she was on the farm, his feelings for her had gained strength. The more he felt he couldn't touch her, the more he wanted to.

Yet, his feelings for Nina didn't change the way he felt about Suzanna. She was such a wonderful and giving woman, *how can I not love her?* The situation allowed him to be in love with Suzanna but restricted him from showing his love to Nina. Circumstances that put him right back where he was on the Hartford Plantation, restricted to be with the one he loved. *Slavery has once again controlled my freedom to love her, and I hated it!*

After Cooper left the cabin, the family was torn down the middle. One half understood Cooper's efforts to help them and vowed that they would not give him any more problems, while the other half thought like Cecil.

"Cooper don't need for us to be slaves!" Thomas said.

"Just like he pretendin' to be a white man, he could've purchased us our freedom, and we can pretend to be slaves," Mark added.

"He using the white woman's money, what he gone tell her? That he wanna buy his black fam'ly when he white?" Micah questioned.

"He not be white," Cecil said.

"But she don't know that," Bertha jumped in.

They went back and forth, one side against the other, while Nina just sat there, not voicing her opinion, not saying a word. And when asked to choose a side, she said, "I trust Cooper."

"You mean Jesse," Jalean corrected. And the argument continued until family members stormed off to their rooms.

The next day revealed to Cooper which family members would comply and which would remain in defiance. He had created their purpose for being there, established a method to get them there, and prepared for their arrival, but he didn't expect the problems they were causing. And life was in a hurry to show him the outcome of his decisions.

Cecil's behavior in the field was intolerable. When Cooper gave him an ultimatum to perform his work duties or work the entire day without stopping for lunch, the twins Thomas and Jalean and her husband, Mark, interjected, threatening to expose him. They said it loud enough so that Sam could hear. "And if you don't start treating us like this so-called 'fam'ly,' we gone tell everything."

From a distance, Sam suspected that the slaves were giving Cooper a hard time, but he couldn't make out what they were saying. When he asked them, Cecil said, "It's a fam'ly matter."

Micah urged them to get back to work. "If y'all mess it up for Cooper, y'all mess it up for all of us."

Jalean answered, "But Jesse gone feel it the most since he be the one passing as white."

Weeks, then months went by and things were not any better. Cecil and his group were taking breaks whenever they felt like it. Fights between him and Micah, verbally and physically continually had to be broken up.

Cooper tried to work alongside the defiant group, hoping to motivate them as he had years prior with Sam and Yes'sa Man, but the more he worked to lead by example, the less work they did. He threatened to sell them or to hire a white overseer to keep them in line, but every warning he gave received threats of exposing him in return.

Not only about him passing, "...but I'll tell that white wife of yours that you been bedding Nina," Cecil threatened and walked off the field feeling empowered, headed to the cabin an hour early before knock-off time.

‡‡‡‡‡‡

Cooper walked into the house one day and met Suzanna's wide smile.

"Darling." She grabbed his hand and led him to the dining table. "I have great news. You are going to be a father."

"That's...that's wonderful. I'm so...you've made me a happy man." Forcing a smile, he was still soaking in the news he'd received earlier that week.

"What's wrong?" he'd asked Nina, whose head had hung low.

Haunted by guilt, she was unable to look him in the face. "I'm pregnant."

Cooper wrapped her in his strong arms. "Everything is going to be fine. Don't worry."

Now, after hearing Suzanna's news, concern was on his face, although he tried to hide it behind a smile.

"Aren't you thrilled?"

"Of course, I am," he said and grabbed his wife, squeezing her, he rubbed her stomach. "We are going to be parents. You've made me a very happy man."

Cooper was everything but happy. His siblings had been introduced as Nina's cousin, leaving him no explanation that would explain her pregnancy. And then there was the issue of her losing their first child while laboring in the fields. He had to find a way to get her out of the fields.

"How are you feeling, my love?" Cooper asked Suzanna.

She looked up at him. "Excited, afraid, nervous. But the emotions I'm experiencing are all normal according to my sisters. I really hope that I will be a good mother. I can recall watching slave mothers caring for their babies. They were such little humans. So innocent, needing a mother to do everything for them. To protect them, to love them. Oh, darling, I just want to be a good mother for our child. I must be." She fell into his chest.

"And you will...You know if you think that the task will be overwhelming, maybe you should select one of the slaves from the field to be your maiden. To care for you and the baby."

"How could I even consider such a thing? There is so much work in the field, Sam needs all the help he can get. No, we can't afford to take one away from him. Remy can help, she's in the house more now that we have field help."

"But Remy can't feed a baby. You need a nursing mother."

"Feed the baby? I can nurse my own child, Cooper. As I should, I'll be its mother. And who of them would be able to feed the baby? That would require a nursing mother and none of the women are pregnant, are they?"

"Of course, you're right. Only a new mother can nurse a baby. I meant to take care of the child while you rest. Your body will need to recuperate after you've given birth."

"Recuperate? Are you calling me fat?"

"No. I was only saying—"

"Is that's why you hardly touch me anymore. That explains why you leave our bed in the middle of the night."

When sneaking away to be with Nina, Cooper thought he'd assured that Suzanna was sound asleep before leaving and after returning to bed. *Has she been pretending?* "Suzanna, I don't...of course, I don't think you're fat."

"I'm pregnant, you know. It's normal to gain weight, I have a life growing inside me."

"Suzanna, I don't—I didn't know you were pregnant. Remember, I'm just learning of this."

"So, you thought my weight gain was me just getting fat. You're disgusted by me." She turned her back to him.

"That's absurd. Honey, look." He turned her to face him. "You have always...you are, and will always be beautiful to me."

"Beautiful, but fat."

"I did not say such a thing. You're barely pregnant, and inside of your belly is our most precious life. I love you. You are not fat. You are beautifully pregnant." He kissed her. "Here, let me help you get to bed."

"Help me? You're not joining me?"

"I will... Shortly. I 'um...I need to go speak with Micah. I have some cropping plans I want to go over with him."

"Why not go over them with Sam?"

"Micah has the ability to communicate well with his family. Poor Sam, he's still finding his way with them." He laughed.

"Oh, okay. Well, how long will you be?"

"I wish I could be accurate, my darling, but that depends on questions he may have. Here, let's get you undressed and all cleaned up."

Cooper took his time bathing Suzanna, fully relaxing her. After getting her into the bed, twenty minutes later, she'd fallen asleep while he massaged her scalp. He covered her and went straight to the barn.

‡‡‡‡‡‡

Wrapped in his arms felt so good. It was where she belonged, even if only for limited hours, a few nights a week.

Relaxed in the aftermath, they'd just made love. Feeling her naked body so close to him, he could go a second round. He kissed her forehead.

The secret room in the barn was small, hidden behind stacks of hay. On a beautiful handcrafted table, a lantern sat. Next to it was a burner that expelled an expensive fragrance of aroma oil to alleviate any stuffy smell. The room's temperature was perfect that pre-winter month.

Cooper rolled Nina on her back and rubbed her stomach. "How do you feel?"

She knew why he asked. "I've been feeling fine."

"I won't risk you losing another child." Cooper held her hand. "I will find a way to relieve you of your field duties without drawing Suzanna's suspicion."

"How do you plan to explain my baby?"

"I have something in mind. You don't worry about that. I don't want you to worry about anything."

As the days passed, Cooper slowly worked on Suzanna. Pushing suggestions on her, carefully persuading her of his reasoning. "Have you considered our last discussion?"

"I don't need her help."

"But don't you think that it worked out perfectly. We were recently discussing you having help with the baby, then we learn that she's pregnant."

"Yes, how convenient. But her pregnancy has nothing to do with my pregnancy."

"It's a common practice for nursing slaves to nurse the first lady's baby."

"I'm not your normal first lady, and I do not require the need of those privileges."

"But you are my first lady. I don't want you burdened by childcare. I want you lying beside me at night. I don't want our lovemaking spoiled by the cries of our child. I don't ever want anything interfering with that. And I don't want any lips sucking your breast but mine."

"Will you be jealous?"

"Yes, very. At the very thought of it."

She smiled bashfully. "Well, you'll have to get over it. I will be nursing my child. Our child." She walked away leaving him standing with a dropped head.

Forty-four

With a mind loaded with problems, Cooper sat quietly at the breakfast table, oblivious to his surroundings.

"Darling."

He jumped, almost hitting Suzanna's swollen stomach. Stress was written all over his face.

He'd never spoken to her about the problems he was having in the field, but one evening while Remy cleaned after dinner before going home, Suzanna overheard a conversation she was having with Sam. Her bedroom, in close proximity of the kitchen, did have its advantages.

The very next day while preparing dinner, Suzanna worked to ease the information out of Remy.

"Hmm," she said to get Remy's interest.

"What's the matter, Missis Suzanna?"

"It's Mister Cooper. I hate seeing him this way, Remy. He always seems so worried."

"He got a lot on his mind. Sam said some of them slaves giving him trouble."

"What kind of troubles?"

"Sam said…"

Suzanna listened intently, down to the very last word.

"...He just need something to help him get his mind off it, that's all," Remy concluded.

"I got it. I'll host a social."

"A social?"

"Yes. Invite my sisters and their husbands over for dinner. Perhaps they can lend him some advice on how to deal with problem slaves."

Remy looked at Suzanna.

"What?"

"You think that's a good idea? Mister Cooper has his own way of dealing with problem slaves. He done fine by us."

"You all were susceptible."

"Sus-ses-cept—"

"Susceptible. Open to learning, being taught. These slaves, I don't believe they were worth the money. Especially that Nina."

"Nina? Sam says she's a good slave."

"Yes, I'm sure she is."

They continued preparing dinner.

A month later, Suzanna's family visited, and Nina, Remy, Bertha, and Yes'sa Man served the couples who all sat at the dinner table enjoying their conversation.

During dessert, Suzanna's eldest sister shared a story about a slave owner. "This man was always away on business trips, leaving his wife home alone. Upon returning after one of his long travels, he entered their house and called out to his wife. They only had a few slaves, who by that time of the night had returned to their quarters, so she would be in the house alone. His call went unanswered, he called again while checking their bedroom. She wasn't there. He searched the entire house for her, but to no avail. It was as if she'd vanished.

"Afraid for her life, he nervously searched the house again, looking under beds, in closets, in and out of the house. He thought for a moment, then went toward the end of the hall near a small storage room in the back of the house. While going to it, he noticed that the ladder to the attic had been drawn. It confused him. He'd known his wife to be terribly afraid of dark tight places, she would never go up to the attic alone, he thought. He climbed the steps, slowly creeping upward.

"Suddenly, he heard sounds and stopped. Frightened for his wife's life, he rushed up the stairs in a panic, following the sounds that grew louder, kept increasing, getting faster. Then he heard the sounds of clapping."

"Clapping?" the youngest sister asked.

"Yes. The sounds that two bodies make when hitting one against the other," the sister said with a mischievous look on her face.

"Oooh, clapping," the youngest said after understanding.

"Yes, the clapping together of body parts. I suppose I should have chosen a better word. Anyway, the husband rushed around a corner and found his wife on her back, a slave hovering over her."

"Choking her?" the younger sister asked.

"No. Engaged in a hot steamy sexual act."

"I don't understand. With another man while the slave watched?" the youngest sister said.

"She was having sex with the slave," Suzanna corrected.

"No," the younger sister said.

"Yes. Can you imagine? She was having intercourse…with a slave," the eldest sister said while clutching her pearls. "The poor husband was beside himself. Well, the very next day he marched into town and got the authorities. They hung the slave in the middle of the town for all the townsmen to witness."

"What happened to the wife?" the youngest sister asked.

"The husband beat her blue and dragged her off. They left town, and no one knows where they relocated," the eldest sister answered.

"She deserved it. I mean I love our niggas because they've been very faithful to us. None of them have given us any problems because they know what will happen if they defy us. But to have a slave put his filthy hands on me—I would just die of disgust!" the youngest plump sister said.

Without moving her head, Remy's eyes beamed in on Cooper and Suzanna who were quiet during the story. She paid special attention when the eldest, prettier sister asked, "What about you, Suzanna? What would you do if one of your slave men were to touch you?"

"I love my slaves, but never in that way."

That's reasonable, Remy thought. *There have only been a few white folks I loved. But just like Suzanna said, I have never loved any in that way.*

The husband of the youngest sister spoke. He was a little fellow whose baby face made him look much younger than his red-headed chubby wife. "Any slave who put their hands on a white woman should be beaten to death. Hanging would be too good for them. They need to be tortured. I say light a fire to them and set them ablaze."

"Or even better—castrate them for putting their hands on our precious gems." The husband of the eldest sister was tall and handsome. He grabbed her hand, causing her to blush.

Cooper sat quietly, listening to their laughter that erupted after thinking of creative ways to "torture" a slave man for touching a white woman.

"I say give to him what he gave to her. A thick stick, right up his cavity." The little brother-in-law followed with a belting laugh.

The taller brother-in-law picked up his glass of wine. "Since he wants to be a big man, I say cut him down to size. Every limb of his body and let the husband do it." He sipped.

"Pluck his eyes out. Then he won't be able to lay eyes on white women. Or better yet, feed him to the hounds." The thicker sister chuckled.

Cooper looked ahead of her at Remy, Bertha and Nina, who were all standing behind their guests, dutifully waiting for their next command, while those they'd served were having fun by throwing out suggestions of how to torture a black man. The cluster of sadistic jokes and laughter amongst the group caused Cooper's anger to boil over. "Tell me...how do you all feel about a white man touching a slave girl?" His clear baritone voice quieted the room. Their laughter ceased. Their eyes all turned to him.

Cooper picked up his wine glass, gazed upon it while teasing the rim with his fingertip. "Have any of you considered the nightmare, the horror that she must endure? Her innocence being violently stripped away from her young, immature body by an overbearing powerful white man. The nonconsensual sexual attack on her would be a traumatizing experience. And while dealing with the shame of the abuse, she learns that she's bearing the offspring of the vicious rapist, who will consider her child by him as nothing more than a piece of property." He looked at each of them, including Suzanna. "What are your thoughts on that matter of humanity, hmp?"

Quiet pierced the room, impounding their words and confiscating their laughter. Nothing else was said. No remarks, not one comment. The undisturbed silence offered Cooper the space to excuse himself from the table. He did not return that night.

Everyone at the table felt uncomfortable, especially Suzanna. "He's had a rough week. Half of our new slaves have been such a challenge for him."

"What do you mean?" the taller brother-in-law inquired.

"Well...some of our slaves are very unruly and Cooper, well, he is such a kind-hearted soul, he finds it very difficult to punish any of them. Now, I don't care to put a whip to the back of any human being, but this group...well, they deserve it."

"He does seem to have an unnatural compassion for the blacks," the handsome husband said.

"Suzanna, I don't see how you bear it? Unruly slaves could become a physical threat. He should have each of them beaten into submission for your protection," the thick younger sister said.

"I agree. You own them, they don't own you, and God didn't intend for it to be any other way. They have to be punished to make them obey. You can never spare the rod, even the bible says so," the eldest sister added.

"What you need is a non-tolerance overseer to straighten them out and I know just the fellow. The plantation he worked for was recently sold after the owner died and now the gentleman is out of work. You just say the word and I'll send him right over," the taller brother-in-law said.

"Why I...I could never make such a decision without my husband. Cooper manages the farm and the slaves. It would be inappropriate for me to decide something like that without first discussing the matter with him."

"Cooper's choices are putting your life in grave danger, and I for one, will not hear of it. When it comes to your safety and the security of your unborn child, the decision is yours to make," the eldest sister argued.

Suzanna didn't respond.

"Well, it's decided. I will send Abraham over tomorrow. Just try him out for a month and see if things don't improve in the niggas' attitudes. If not, then they are not worthy of life. I mean, we feed them, clothe and house them. The least they can do is show appreciation by obeying our orders, for God's sake!" The tall brother-in-law tugged on his waistcoat and smooth it out. "And if it doesn't work out, I will pay his wages myself. But if it does, well, we'll just consider it as a favor owed." Pushing his chair out, he stood and drank the last of his wine. "It's time for us to depart. We don't want Cooper feeling uncomfortable in his own home."

They said their goodbyes with hugs and kisses and Suzanna retreated to her room, not expecting Cooper to join her that night. Recently, he'd slept on the lounger when he was upset or burdened. At least that's what she assumed after finding him there a few nights and mornings.

However, that night, Cooper didn't return to the house until the next morning to get ready for the field, and she never knew. For the first time, he spent the entire night in the barn with Nina, and the feeling was contagious. He was finding it harder to be without her.

From the moment he'd laid eyes on Nina; he fought hard to resist his craving for her. He tried to stay away from the farm by taking trips into town. When he was at home, he found reasons to keep his distance from the field by giving Sam authority, so he wouldn't have to be near her. But Sam couldn't handle the insubordinate family members, so Cooper had to get involved, putting him in direct contact with Nina.

He tried to calm his urges by making love to Suzanna in hopes that the burning sensation that he felt for Nina would extinguish. But it only ignited the lusting flame that continued to soar.

When he made the decision to purchase Nina, he was madly in love with Suzanna and thought that his love for her would repel any feelings he had for Nina and help him to remain faithful to Suzanna. But the first day he met them, and she rushed into his arms, he knew he was in trouble. She had an untarnished beauty and a sensual body that was hard to resist. And her innocent love was so pure, he couldn't help but to naturally gravitate to it.

As Nina slept on the full-size bed in the private location of the barn, Cooper placed his hand on her stomach to feel their unborn child. Thinking of an inactive baby in time past, he was afraid, but he did...slowly, delicately...he smiled. It was a strong kick.

How can I be a father to you? Suzanna must never know. Then it came to him. The only solution that would contradict Suzanna's suspicions. "Yes'sa Man."

Forty-five

"*N*iggas, darkies, smuts, blacks, bastards, sons o' bitches... ah whipped, beat, amputate, burn. Even lea thaim oot in th' sun fur wild animals tae maul 'n' sloch alive."

"Sloch?" Suzanna questioned.

"You say eat, we Scottish say sloch? 'N' ah don't hing 'em, ah strangle 'em tah death wi' mah bare hauns, ah dae." His Scottish accent was almost harder to bear than his punishments. With a wild swing, Abraham Luke Williams sliced the ground with his whip. Showing all twenty brown stained teeth with an atrocious laugh.

Cooper was appalled that his brother-in-law would hire anyone to take charge of his slaves without first speaking to him. He looked at Suzanna with angry eyes.

"I didn't agree with this," she rushed to explain.

"Then what did you say to him to make him feel that he had the authority to send him over?"

"He was only mentioned and said to be sent over to see if we would be interested in hiring his services. I never agreed to hire him, my dear, I promise."

Abraham broke up their conversation. "Ye hire me, 'n' ye won't regret it. Ah guarantee that if ah punish yin, ah wull ne'er hae tae punish anither." For his resume, he opened what he called his case of punishment. Reaching inside, he picked out his most prized punishing tools. "An ax that ah uise tae cut aff th' foot o' ony slave wha attempts tae run 'n' mah gey pointy claymore that ah used tae methodically cut oot th' tongue o' ony slave wha talks back."

Almost heaving, Suzanna's hand went to her mouth. Cooper pulled her into his chest. "Leave at once. Take your case, and your filthy mind off of my property!"

"Who 'dat be?" Cecil asked.

Yes'sa Man told all that he heard.

That evening, Cecil held a family meeting, telling everything Yes'sa Man told him. "He gon' hire sum'body to beat us, he own fam'ly. 'Um tellin' y'all, 'dis not be the Jesse we know. 'Dis be a whole nother person."

Sarah spoke up, "I was there. Cooper wanted no part of it. He wasn't even in the room when they talked about that man."

"It don't matter, Sarah, I saw 'em talkin' to the man. The only reason he didn't was for his self. He sca'ed we gone tell that he a slave. He worse than any white Massa I know. Y'all gone fine out who this Cooper person is. 'Cause he ain't no brotha' of mine."

Everyone listened in quiet while he went on and on. Bashing and belittling Cooper. Making threats that would cause them all to be returned to the life of slavery that stripped them of their human dignity.

Nina looked around the room. Reah was hugging her son, John. Micah pulled Sarah's head to his chest. Thomas' lips and eyes were squinted nearly closed in shock. Mark was shaking his head in agreement. Jalean shook her head in disagreement. Tears were running down Bertha's face.

Nina had enough! "Massa Ordell would have beaten several of us many times over if any one of us treated him the way Cooper is being treated."

Cecil turned to her with disgust in his eyes. "You think you somethin' cause you talkin' like them now. He teach you proper words and suddenly you a proper nigga. But when he hires that white man over us, he gone show you your rightful place."

"There's not gonna be a white overseer, Cecil. I was there too when that man was mentioned. Cooper wasn't there and Suzanna never agreed to it. Cooper spoke against slave cruelty even though there be more of them than him. Cooper ain't did nothing but help us and all he gets back from some of y'all is ungratefulness. He's much kinder than I'd be after y'all act like that when all I did was help you have better lives."

Cecil became outraged. "Woman, who you talkin' to? You ain't nothing but a weak fool. Cooper spends a few nights wit' you in the barn and give you a belly and that's 'sposed to make things right wit' us? He throws us a few pieces of meat, and we 'posed to bow down to his feet?"

And the argument in the room broke out... Splitting again, twin brother, Thomas and Jalean's husband, Mark, continued in Cecil's persuasion, but twin sister, Jalean had taken the views of Micah and his wife Sarah, Bertha, and Nina.

Reah and her son, John, didn't take sides. Reah's only concern had always been for the care of her son. She privately appreciated all that her eldest brother Cooper had done for them and showed it by doing anything he asked her to do. She was so proud of what he'd accomplished after running.

Reah's husband was a part of a group of slaves on the Hartford Plantation who tried to escape, but they were caught and severely beaten. He was the only one of the group to survive the brutal punishment, but later succumbed to wound infection.

After his death, Reah, who was pregnant at the time, was strung up in the midst of the slave quarters and not fed for days. When Missis Annie Bell learned that she was being punished while pregnant, she was furious. "We need that child born healthy. The husband has left us one slave short. Take her down immediately!"

Overcome with grief due to her husband's death, Reah barely consumed any food. Her baby came prematurely, and it was obvious from the child's battle to sit and take his first steps that he would be a child of mental challenges. She'd always blamed herself for his mental dysfunctions and dedicated her life to protect him from any other harm.

John trembled as the verbal ruckus of his family escalated to shouting. Reah squeezed him tighter to calm him, but it didn't work. "'Um gone take John to the room. All 'dis arguing upsets him." They left.

The arguments were intense. Neither side gave in to the persuasion of the other. Soon they were up in each other's faces, shouting loud ugly words, having to be pulled apart by the women.

"Y'all keep at me, keep on. I'll tell everything," Cecil threatened.

"And if you do, it'll mess us all up," Jalean said.

"Let it! I don't care. Cooper needs to hit the ground anyway. He up to high."

"What's wrong with you, Cecil? Why you hate Cooper so much?" Sarah asked.

Cecil stopped talking. Caught off guard by the unsuspected question.

They all stared at him, trying to figure out the source of his malicious and misguided anger for his brother.

"He's jealous," Nina said.

"Jealous of who, Micah?" Cecil responded, standing directly in Micah's face.

"No. Cooper."

He looked at her. The spoken words exposed him like a husband caught in the act of adultery. Some truths that are hidden behind a large stone are never meant to be exposed. But there he stood, the stone split by lighting. The truth now visible for all to see.

Forty-six

"Push, Suzanna, push…Just a bit more, the head is approaching," the doctor urged, and after a few more pushes, grunting and screaming, Suzanna gave birth to a darling baby boy.

The very next day, life repeated itself with Bertha delivering Nina's beautiful baby girl. A few days later, Suzanna watched with a fake smile as Bertha helped Nina move out of the family cabin into their home to prepare for her new duty as the nursing mother of Suzanna's and Cooper's son.

Nina was afraid to live under the same roof as the wife of Cooper. She wondered if she would become suspicious. If she would figure out that the two of them had the father of their children in common.

Cooper had hired carpenters to work on their home prior to the baby's arrival. Their bedroom had been expanded to a much larger room, adding a breakfast nook that looked over the farm. The center bedroom was now their son's nursery which included two adjoining doors. One entry led to Suzanna's and Cooper's room and the other door led to what would become Nina's room, which had been Cooper's old room.

Because she was a new mother, Suzanna was allowed to sleep in late, was served breakfast in bed or at the breakfast nook, bathed and received assistance getting dressed.

Because she was a new mother, Nina woke up all through the night to feed and tend to the babies, she ate alone in her room, and her suckling breasts were in constant demand. She'd functioned on a lack of sleep until Remy taught her how to put the babies on feeding and sleeping schedules.

‡‡‡‡‡‡

"Yes'sa Man is the father of the child," Cooper told Suzanna.

The lie was a convenient excuse for Cooper, but for Cecil, he stored the explosive secret on a mental timer, waiting patiently to detonate it. For Suzanna, the answer left her deeply suspicious.

"Nina's baby girl is quite light, isn't she?" Suzanna asked Remy one morning while being served breakfast in her room.

"Yes, she is." Remy continued arranging the utensils in the order that Suzanna preferred.

"Who knew that Yes'sa Man and Nina was sleeping together?" Cradling her son, she looked up at Remy. "Did you know? I mean, he works with you a lot and you two live together, surely he must have mentioned her once."

"Can't say that I can remember him saying anything about it, ma'am."

"It's Suzanna. You know I hate when you address me that way. We're friends, Remy. You don't have to be so formal when it's just the two of us."

Remy stood up straight and cupped her hands in front of her. "Ma'am, it's just not you in the house no more."

"Anymore."

"Yes...anymore. I have to make sure not to slip up around other folks. Now, let me take this fine boy from you." Remy took Cooper, Jr. Smiling, she thought of her daughters. It had been a long time, but the memories came back as though they were yesterday. "Enjoy your breakfast, Miss Suzanna. I'm gone, I mean, I'm going to take CJ to be fed... Hey there, little Cooper. You are one fine boy," she said to the chunky baby while walking away.

‡‡‡‡‡‡

Cooper's and Nina's indiscretion had led to her becoming pregnant, having a baby girl, and now the nursing mother to Suzanna's baby. Knowing the child would have light skin, months earlier, Cooper went to the only person on the farm who could provide the excuse for the child's lightness.

"You know I consider you a friend, Yes'sa Man?"

"Yes'sa. You and me friends. You teach me how to work."

"Yes, I taught you how to work. Now, I need a favor from my good friend."

"Yes'sa."

"Nina is pregnant, but she has no father for her child. I need you to be the father of her child."

"The baby's Pa?" Yes'sa Man asked.

"Yes. Her child will need a father. I think you would make a wonderful father."

"I'll have my own baby?"

"Yes. You will tell anyone who asks that it's yours. But you must never mention this conversation...to anyone. Do you understand?"

"Yes."

"Tell me what I'm asking of you?"

"Have a baby with Nina. But don't tell nobody."

"No...share a baby with Nina. Become the father of her child after its birth. When others ask, you are to tell them that you are the father, but that you don't want to talk about it. You don't like talking about it."

"I'm the pa, but I don't wanna talk about it."

"Yes, exactly."

"Yes'sa. It's my baby."

"You cannot provide any additional information."

"It's my baby. That's all I tell 'em."

"Right."

Yes'sa Man did as he was instructed and when the baby was born, they had him over. "I even got to hold it. For a long time," he proudly told Sam.

The relationship was quite peculiar. Not to Cooper's family, they knew that he wasn't the father. But to Sam, Remy, and Suzanna, they all wondered.

"When you taken a liking to that woman? I ain't seen no signs of you liking her. What, y'all planning on getting married or some'thin?" Sam quizzed.

"I ain't like 'it'. I don't wanna do it no mo'."

"Sam, are you harassing Yes'sa Man?"

"No, sar'. I just ask him a question 'dat he don't wanna answer."

At thirty-six-years-old, Yes'sa Man stood 6'2, and weighed around two-hundred and twenty pounds. But with the vulnerability of a childlike mind, he attempted to hide in the eclipse of Cooper's thinner, but muscular body, peeking around his frame at Sam and quickly pulling back.

"Stop pestering him, Sam. You're making him uneasy."

Sam left him alone, but not the question. He shared his thoughts with Remy. "So how you thank 'dis 'it' happen?"

"You mean, 'who' happen. 'Cause it sure wasn't Yes'sa Man who did the happening."

"What you say? You thankin' that's Mister Coop—" He looked around and out the back door, making sure no one was within earshot of their conversations. Whispering, he continued, "You saying 'dat's Mister Cooper's child, ain't you?"

"I'm not saying that it is or it isn't. I'm saying it's not Yes'sa Man's baby."

"Oooh. So 'dah massa done been in 'dah slave girl's bed. I should've figured."

"Masters have been sneaking into slave girls' bed for years, Sam. Mister Cooper ain't no different. And it's not our place to care."

"You sho' right 'bout 'dat." Sam shook his head. "Po' Miss Suzanna."

"Poor Nina! Miss Suzanna has a choice. Slaves don't."

"Ain't 'dat be the truth. We don't have no choice. The white man has the best of both worlds. But Mister Cooper, I just don't believe 'dat he forced Nina like the others, dough."

"Probably didn't. Nina is a sweet person, you can't help but like her."

"And she gotta body, too."

"Sam!"

"Well, it be 'dah truth? 'Um a man, now. You can't help but notice her unless you blind."

"So, Mister Cooper was probably just attracted to her," Remy said.

"You think so?"

"I don't know. But I don't think it was forced. Mister Cooper isn't like that. I heard how he feels about white men raping..."

"What?"

She lowered her voice. "He put those white folks in their places. No, he didn't force it. Those two had a relationship. I don't know if it's still going on, but when it happened, it was consensual."

"Look at you and yo' proper big words," Sam said.

"I sound smart, huh?"

"You sho' do. Just like white folks."

Remy handed Sam a large basket full of sandwiches she'd prepared for the slaves' lunch. As soon as he exited the back door, she resumed her housework, leaving his last conversation about Cooper, Nina and their child behind him, never to speak of it again.

Forty-seven

Months after the babies' births, Cooper closed the front door behind him and stopped on the porch. The sun was making its morning introduction. He looked over the property as far as his eyes could see and proudly shook his head. He was having better days lately. His in-house situation was working out fine and in the field; his family was performing their duties well, successfully helping to put the farm back on track. Even Cecil had become less of a problem. Sure, he continued complaining and making threats, but he and his crew worked the fields without being forced.

The lightly blowing wind didn't cease, making the day pleasant, almost perfect, a defining metaphor of his current life. But as he stepped off the porch and headed for the field, he wondered when the amicable weather would turn into a vengeful storm, tossing and stirring up trouble, ruining everything in its path. His inquisitive thought would soon find its answer. "Nothing good last forever."

That day in the field continued with its deception of better days to come. The family sang songs, they laughed and joked so hard, that Bertha fell over, hitting her knee on a tool.

"Mr. Cooper, Bertha done fell," Yes'sa Man yelled.

Cooper and Cecil ran over and helped her into the house.

"Thank you," Cecil said to Cooper.

"No need to thank me. I was happy to help."

Was the day being misleading? Had Cooper gotten it wrong? He wondered when Remy returned to the field to help out and brought slices of cake with lunch.

At the end of the day, Cooper headed for the house feeling optimistic about the days ahead. He cleaned up and got ready to have a late dinner with Remy, Yes'sa Man, Sam, and Suzanna. Although Nina lived in the house, she did not eat with them.

That would be crazy to dangled curiosity in Suzanna's face. He and Nina had discussed it. She would always feed and bathe the babies at dinner time. That way she would have that as an excuse if the invitation came up.

Because of Bertha's injury, the workday ended a little late, and Nina wasn't aware of it. She'd already fed the babies and put them to bed. And just as she was about to sit, she heard a knock on her door. "Come in."

Remy stuck her head in. "Are the babies asleep?"

"Yes."

"Do you mind helping me with dinner? I had to help out in the field after Bertha fell. So 'um a little behind."

"Is she alright?"

"Yeah, Cooper thought it was best for her to stay off that leg for a few days to keep it from getting worse. I been in for a minute, but I'm still behind. I just need help finishing up."

"Sure."

As they were setting the table, Sam and Yes'sa Man walked in. Cooper and Suzanna followed. After the entire dinner was set out, Nina headed for the kitchen to fix her a plate as usual and take it to her room where she ate.

"Why can't she eat wit' us?" Yes'sa Man blurted out.

Cooper's eyes shut; he slightly shook his head.

Sam cleared his throat.

Remy perfected the table, unnecessarily moving plates and silverware.

Nina stopped, still facing the kitchen.

Suzanna seized on the given opportunity to learn more of this so-called "relationship" that she'd been fed. "It makes sense. I don't see why not. She's a part of the household. He and Nina had some kind of relationship. He's the father of her child."

Yes'sa Man innocently waited for Cooper to answer, but he was at a loss for words, "Um—"

"I prefer eating in my room." Nina scurried out of their presence.

The dinner conversation that evening was non-existent.

Although Suzanna had never questioned Cooper about Nina's daughter, silent words didn't mean that she wasn't thinking loudly. Now, her thoughts had turned into mumbles.

On another evening, Cooper returned home after a long business trip. Suzanna had just dressed for bed.

"How was your day, dear?" Cooper asked and gave her a kiss on the cheek.

"Not as exciting as your day, I'm sure," she mumbled.

"I beg your pardon?"

"Oh, excuse my mumbling. It was wonderfully relaxing as usual."

"You have been speaking to yourself quite frequently lately. Is all well?"

"Yes, I have. I suppose it's normal behavior for those of us who have no social life and nothing to do around the house. We tend to communicate with ourselves."

Cooper felt a fight coming on. A fight that he wished to avoid. But being the forever fixer, he neglected wisdom for trouble. "Why don't you go visit your family for a spell?"

"And why do you continue to try to get rid of me? What would it benefit you if I wasn't here?"

Regretting that he'd ignored wisdom, he sought wet words to extinguish the rising fire. Taking her hands, he kissed every finger. "My dear and beautiful love, I don't like that you are moping around the house with nothing to do. I only want what's best for you. It would benefit me greatly to know that my wife is happy. Maybe getting out of this house would help."

"I'll go to my family if you join me. I know you can't stomach them, but perhaps you can change their ways of thinking."

The fire was increasing, his words and actions would have to match its growth to put it out. He bent over and kissed the left side of her neck. "I only want to change your mind." He stepped back, removed all of his clothes.

She turned away from him. *We're in the middle of a discussion, for heaven's sake.* But how could she resist? He was standing in front of her with a full salute ready to honor her. Taking her hand, he guided her to bed. His mission, to put out the fire once and for all.

For the first time, Cooper performed sexual acts on Suzanna that he had only embraced with Nina, who was an erotic lover. Just the opposite, Suzanna mannered herself as a proper lady in bed, submissively allowing Cooper to have his way. But not that night.

Feeling liberated, she embraced the heat of passion, moaning words of enjoyment for Nina to hear. But she need not fake it, he was whipping her into euphoria with fits of pleasure that she loudly announced. Her pulsating body told him when she'd released, but he was not finished with her.

Taking her in every position, her unfiltered screams traveled rooms away, just as she'd planned, passing through her son's room, landing in Nina's ears.

The cries of her son came. Nina rushed to comfort him.

Knowing Nina was in the next room, Suzanna's concerns as a mother were disregarded. She became a vengeful lover. "It's so good," she screamed over and over again. "I love it! Harder, harder! I love it...I love every inch!" she clamored with a vindictive smile.

Cooper was also aware that Nina had rushed to his son's aid. He grunted and fell over, pretending to have reached a climax.

"Don't stop. Pleasure me madly!"

"And I shall. After I've recuperated." He had no plans to resume.

Suzanna mounted him, taking him as she never had before. Wild, untamed, her animalistic moves demanded that he loudly exclaim joy.

He tried to restrain. Grunting through his teeth, his face intensified, his jaw bones flared, his face grew flushed as he released a loud, hard grunt that immediately brought on guilt knowing that Nina, who was still in the next room, would recognize the sounds that she'd drawn out of him on many occasions.

Suzanna threw her head like a possessed lover, smiling satisfactorily, she dropped forward. Peering at him, she went up and down, laughing, screaming, speaking dirty. Every moan he subconsciously released energized her as she bounced, pounded against his thighs. He couldn't hold back any longer. Forced sounds of pleasure filled Nina's ears. And as tears traveled down her face, a big grin came across Suzanna's.

Cooper weakened with curled toes. His hands gripping her waist, lifting her up with his hips, he let out a deep dull moan and slowly lowered her back to the bed.

Suzanna fell over, drenched in sweat, breathing hard, exhausted!

Five o'clock the next morning, Cooper eased out of bed. That morning, he was quieter than usual. Carrying his shoes and some of his clothes, he twisted the doorknob to avoid its click.

Nina heard when the door opened and felt his presence over her.

He was sure she'd heard Suzanna and him the night before, undoing all the other times he'd made sure to be as quiet as possible to avoid breaking her heart. He reached to touch her but decided not to. It was as if he'd committed the ultimate marriage sin. Adultery.

She'd never complained, waited patiently to be in his arms, ate alone in her room, took care of his son, helped around the house, but she'd been treated like the slave girl who the master took when he wanted. And she'd given her body so obediently.

He'd freed her from the fields, but not from slavery. Just as she sniffled, the door closed. He was gone.

‡‡‡‡‡‡

A couple of days later, Cooper returned to the house to grab a quick lunch. After eating, he put on his working gloves before heading out the door.

A door opened, the pattering of feet came closer, arms wrapped around his face, hands covered his eyes. It was a guessing game that he was unwilling to play as he went for the hands that blinded his sight.

Suzanna's hands were pale pink. Nina's hands were smooth chocolate. One used expensive oils and wore lovely smelling fragrance. The other used the floral smells of natural ointment cream created by Remy. He tried to pull them from his eyes, but she resisted with a tighter grip.

Cooper felt the fingertips, the fingers, examined the hands, stopping at the wrists. *Suzanna's wrists are thicker than Nina's.* Using the intellect of his nose and the sensation of his touch, he smiled. "Nina."

The pale pink hands released, he opened his eyes and quickly turned to face an angry Suzanna.

"Nina?! Why would you suppose that it was her?"

"I...I played the same game with her just the other day as I have with Remy, Sam, and Yes'sa Man. And the smell of that lotion. I recall smelling it on Nina when I took our son from her one day. It was so pleasant. I asked her about it, she explained that Remy had made and gifted it to her as a birthday present," he lied.

"Remy also gave some to me."

"Well, it smells great on you." He gave her a kiss. "I have to return to work now, my dear." Cooper rushed out the door.

Suzanna stood with folded arms, frowning.

┼┼┼┼┼┼

She was becoming unsettled with each rising sun. The feelings of insecurity were shadowing her days and stirring up suspicious notions. She had never questioned Cooper when he used to come to bed late. And when he'd purchased all the slave women gifts for Christmas. She'd watched quietly as he gave Nina a necklace and charm with her daughter's initials on it.

"It's a gift for first-time mothers," he said when turning to Suzanna and putting one similar around her neck.

As if we're equal. Suzanna had initially resisted having another woman care for her child but finally gave into Cooper's pressure. "It's normal for a nursing slave girl to care for the master's child. I need your body in perfect shape for your husband," he teased while lying in bed behind her, rubbing his stiffness against her butt. Now, his urging had turned to another attention. Coercing Suzanna to visit her family.

"He doesn't even care for them. Why is he pushing me to be in their company? Something is definitely going on," she said to herself, sitting alone at the breakfast nook, staring out the window. Yet, she had no proof. No 'caught in the act', 'slip of the tongue', or 'off guard' moment to verify her mental claim. The constant suspicion was wreaking habit on her kind personality, creating an irritable, snappy, downright bitchy woman.

Cooper had done everything he could to settle her imploding suspicions. Less time with Nina, more time with her. He even skipped days from the field to help her start a garden, temporary fixes that often led to opportunities for her to throw subtle hints about Nina.

"Since they have a child together, maybe we should allow them to get married," Suzanna said out of nowhere.

"Who?"

"Nina and Yes'sa Man."

"Suzanna, we don't force our slaves into relationships. Yes'sa Man explained that it happened only once. Who knows how or why, but I doubt if it will occur again. We will leave it at that."

"But you will agree that she needs a man. Her own man."

"And what do you mean by 'her own man'?"

"You know, someone she can love and who can love her. Her own man."

"When we purchase more slaves, maybe she will find someone at that time. Look, my angel…I couldn't care less about what she needs in her life. My only concern is what you need in your life and in your bed."

A round of sex normally changed the conversation for days. And if he pleased her several times over, it lasted for weeks.

"Enough of this gardening, I have something else I would like to plant."

She smiled and followed him to their bedroom.

Weeks passed without Suzanna even mentioning Nina's name. But a new day was dawning.

Forty-eight

The farm was improving, and the need for Cooper to travel further away for longer period of times to gain more business opportunities became essential. In his absence, Suzanna managed the farm with Sam's assistance in the field and Remy in the house.

As she'd seen Cooper do on many mornings, Suzanna walked outside and looked over the property as far as her eyes could see. Taking notice of the slaves in the field, she acknowledged that Sam was effectively supervising them and didn't need her interference.

She went to her bedroom, opened a large old trunk, pulled out her old work clothes and fluffed them. "It's not proper for the first lady," she mocked, recalling Cooper's words. Sighing, she laid them on the bed and went into the nursery where Nina was sitting on the floor playing with the babies.

"CJ." Bending over with stretched out arms, Suzanna waited for her son to come into them. "CJ, come here, darling. Come to mommy."

On hands and knees, CJ crawled in her direction, but stopped and sat. Nina's daughter, Alexandria had dropped the ball she was playing with. It rolled towards her brother. Falling to his knees, he went after the bright red object.

"Come here, baby boy," Suzanna called again, still bent over.

Both CJ and Alexandria went for the ball. Swatting at it at the same time, giggling, enjoying the round object that had zapped CJ's attention from his mother.

Exhaling, Suzanna stood and looked at her son, who was paying her no mind. Tears welled in her eyes. She left the nursery through her bedroom and dried her watery eyes before going to the kitchen. "What are you cooking? It smells absolutely delicious."

"It's already done, Miss Suzanna. You wanna taste it?" Without waiting for an answer, Remy scooped up a sample of soup and put the spoon to Suzanna's lips.

Slurping it, Suzanna's eyes rolled back as she wiped juices that fell on her chin. "Oh my, this *is* delicious... What else needs to be done? I would love to help."

"Everything is done."

"What about your chores—"

"The chores are already finished too. I'm about to change clothes and help out in the field. See if we can't make Mister Cooper proud by the time he gets back." Remy took off her apron and headed towards the door. "You just relax, First Lady. Have yourself some of that tea I made." She left Suzanna alone.

"Everyone has something useful to do except me." She felt bored, worthless. She'd complained to Cooper about it but was tired of his same old answer. "Visit your family," she mocked.

Suzanna went to the front porch and sat. But after a few minutes, she went for that glass of tea. Returning to the porch, she sat sipping and reminiscing of her days working in the field, working alongside the field hands, forming a special relationship, bonding with them. "If only things could go back to where they were before the new slaves came. Hmm...maybe..."

Leaving the glass of tea on the porch, she went into the house. Snatching her field clothes from the bed, she got dressed and went to the barn, grabbed a tool and marched to the fields. She began laboring without as much as a greeting to the others who were in shock to see her.

"What she doing?" Sarah asked.

"Child, I'on know," Bertha answered. "As long as she mines her business, um'ma mind mines."

The long time away from the field quickly revealed the momentum that she no longer had. But she was determined to get it back. She dug the shovel deep into the soil, tussling to pull it out. One hard tug and back she went, leaving the shovel stuck in the soil. She huffed, got up and dusted off. Spitting on her hands, she rubbed them together, got a good grip of the shovel and pulled. Left, right, forward, back, struggling, fighting, tussling with her foot on the shovel's shoulder.

The field hands watched as she grunted, giving her best efforts, but failing miserably to lift the tangled shovel.

"Should we tell her that's the raggedy hoe?" Sarah asked Bertha.

"Nope. She'll figure out it's busted I reckon. She probably got it caught up on some weeds."

"Well, how long you think it'll be buh'fo she give up on that raggedy hoe and gone back in the house where she buh'long?" Sarah asked.

"By the time it tears up her soft precious hands."

Suzanna hit the ground for a second time; her stubbornness was deliberate. With weak muscles fighting against her endurance, she convinced herself that she had to push past it. She balled in her lips, grunted, tensed every muscle in her body, gripped as hard as she could and gave the shovel one good yanked. Her hands slipped, her feet went back and did not stop until they were no longer on the ground, replaced by her butt. FLOP!

Sam, who was returning from urinating, saw Suzanna fall and ran to help her up. But due to his past injuries, one misfortunate pull caused him great regret.

Micah ran over and carried her into the house where Remy immediately took over looking after her.

Bright and early the very next morning, Cecil looked up. "Well, I'll be. Ay?" He got the attention of the twin, Thomas, his baby brother, who turned to see Suzanna with a different tool propped on her shoulder, wearing a wide brim sun hat and fresh new work clothes.

"I guess the first lady's not scared of work," Cecil said. He and Thomas giggled and went back to work.

She'd humored them enough the day before. "I ain't got no time to waste on her. I gots work to get done," Thomas said.

In a few days, Suzanna was back in stride. Many times the slaves took notice of her drive and were quite surprised by how hard she worked. She was a strong worker but periodically would require help to learn new things or be taught how to use new tools.

Although they were impressed by her efforts, no one was in any hurry to offer her assistance. Especially Cecil, who got a kick out of watching her trying to use the scythe Cooper had purchased just before leaving. He smirked and continued working.

One late afternoon, the wind that had taken forever to visit, blew nicely on the day that was heading to an end. Everyone had done their share of work, fulfilling the daily goal put in place by Cooper. They worked in quiet, focused, waiting to hear the sound of Sam's whistle to relieve them from the field.

All of a sudden, a scream broke their concentration. They stopped, looked around to see Suzanna acting crazy, batting the air, squealing. She dropped her tool and ran right into the plow Cecil was pushing. He rushed to help her.

"Did you see?" she yelled.

"No, ma'am. Can't say that I did. See what?" He helped her up.

"Some huge, *enormous* bug attacked me." She dusted her clothes and went to take a step, but still a little shaken, she tilted over onto Cecil who caught her.

"You be alright, ma'am?"

"Yes, I'm fine. I guess I'm still a little shaken."

"Maybe you oughts to go in the house."

She turned to him, looking him right in the eyes.

He immediately lowered his head. They had new lives, but some behaviors never die, like staring a white person in the face.

She reached up and lifted his chin. "You can look me in the face. In my eyes. Thank you for your help, but I'm not going into the house. I'm returning to my work details." She smiled and went back to work, leaving him with a smile.

Forty-nine

"*H*e be a good man!"

"What you in love wit' him or some'thin?"

"Yeah, I loves 'em, he be fam'ly"

"Mine, not yours. I the reason you here, not him."

"None of us would be here if he didn't purchase us."

"And we still slaves, ain't nut'thin changed. We still slaving the fields why he gets to go off being the white man. Living the white folks' life, wit' the white wife, in the big house. We his slaves, Bertha, and he the massa." Cecil stormed out of their bedroom and didn't stop until he was sitting on the porch, staring at the dark sky.

Bertha looked around their bedroom. Sitting on the full-size bed, it was nothing like the hard, narrow beds they were used to on the Hartford Plantation. "How can he not 'preciate this." She dropped her head as soon as she felt tears coming.

Cecil never returned to their bed that night but slept on the lounger. And before the others were out of their bed the next morning, he had made it to the field working off the stress. The moment he looked up and saw Suzanna carrying a scythe on her shoulder, wearing her sun hat and dressed in fresh work clothes about forty-five minutes after everyone's arrival, he smiled.

Bertha noticed him staring at Suzanna. Later that day, she watched as he taught her the proper way to use the tool. She saw him giving her water and carrying her tool from the field when the workday ended.

That night in their bedroom, they were at it again.

"I be hot and thirsty, you don't offer me no water!"

"Bertha, there be a white woman in the field working, slaving wit' us slaves. That be a extra two hands, a extra body working side us slave. A white woman workin' the field! And I gone do everything in my will to make sure she keeps helping us."

"You don't fetch Cooper no water when he out in the hot field using his two hands and his body to slave with us slaves!"

"Cause he ain't white!"

"You lower your voice."

"For what? Everybody in this here house knows that he ain't white. He a slave! He ain't got no white wife, 'cause his wife be black. He ain't white, he passing fo' white. And his name ain't Cooper, it be Jesse!"

As if his words were heard over the entire farm, Bertha looked on in shock. Once again, she watched her husband storm out of their bedroom. And again, she was left crying.

In the field, Cecil continued his attentiveness towards Suzanna. The more Bertha protested at night, the more attention he gave Suzanna in the day.

Suzanna was thrilled about her achievement. "Oh, Remy, I think everyone is finally coming around to me. Especially Cecil. Cooper will be so impressed with how I've won him over." She squeezed her left side.

"You sure he'll be alright wit' you working the fields. You know he said—"

"I know, I know. A first lady shouldn't be in the field, but I love it. I did work in the fields before he came, you know?" She tried her best to massage her achy back.

"Hey, why don't I draw you a bath and wash your back for you?"

"Oh, you don't have to—"

"Oh, hush, now. You deserve it. You the only white woman I seen in all my days who work in the field alongside slaves. You help us, we help you. That's how it goes."

A few more reasonings and painful tension convinced Suzanna that she needed the soak.

She leaned back in the perfectly warmed water with soothing bath oils. Remy dipped the sponge into the water and started on Suzanna's hair.

"Mmm. That feels amazing."

"Good."

"You know, when you get to know Cecil, he really is a sweet man." She giggled. "Oh, you should have seen him the other day..."

Remy listened as Suzanna went on and on about the most rebellious slave on the farm.

"...He's so much fun. Keeps me laughing. He's making my time in the field quite enjoyable."

Mmhm. "Sit up, so I can get your back."

Remy was well aware of Cecil's behavior towards Suzanna. She'd seen him rushing to get her water without being asked. He moved faster, pushed harder, ran instead of walking when Suzanna worked the fields. On the few days she didn't, he made everyone's life miserable. Arguing and complaining, taking long breaks, wasting time talking to his brother, Thomas, and brother-in-law, Mark.

Sam had to prompt and coerce him, even beg him at times to return to work. And although Bertha didn't work near him, he always made his way over to nag her. But Suzanna never saw that side of him, the real Cecil, who everyone knew, but her.

All she talked about was how nice he was, how hard he worked, and it was all due to how she'd treated him. Using Cooper's practice as a model, Cecil was now giving the same performance as Remy, Sam, and Yes'sa Man when Cooper worked alongside them.

"Cooper is a genius. Who needs a mean ole overseer? Slaves normally return what's been given to them. Kindness and hard work beget the same behavior."

"All through, Miss Suzanna."

"Thank you, Remy. I'm going to rest here for a few more minutes." Finally, she succumbed to being treated like a first lady by the slaves. She closed her eyes and leaned all the way back. "You're dismissed, now. You've been a great help. The pain is gone."

She'd never dismissed Remy before, at least, not in that way. '*You're dismissed, now.*' "Yes, ma'am." Remy felt as though a curtsy should follow. Looking at Suzanna whose eyes were still closed, Remy smiled. *I think I'm making too much of it.* She left.

Fifty

Cooper got on a train destined for Louisiana. But prior to his train trip home, he'd stumbled on several business investments. One, in particular, sparked his interest, and if it proved to be successful, he would become a very wealthy man.

"Investment, my dear friend, that's where the money is. But you have to prove your worth. To date you have. My partners and I are very impressed. We could use your drive, that go-getter energy on our team. If you fulfill your promised order, we would love to have you on as a manufacturing investment partner. We invest in some of the largest industries in the northern regions of the United States and some overseas. We're looking to expand in the near future."

Once they said their goodbyes, Cooper was off to pursue that venture. Of course, he shared this information with no one and risked all of his money to secure his future endeavors. The new business opportunity caused his trip to be delayed. He'd sent a message to Suzanna telling her that things were taking a little longer than he'd plan.

"...I love you dearly. Your husband, Cooper." Suzanna ended the letter and placed it on the breakfast nook table. She was disappointed but delighted. His delay gave her at least a few more days in the field.

She woke up very early the next morning, wanting to be the first in the field, just as Cooper used to do. She found herself looking forward to the fields and relishing her time with Cecil. He had given her all the attention her husband had failed to do when he was home. And more so, now that he was often away on trips.

Suzanna turned on her side in the big empty bed and stared out the window recalling her sister's words. *But to have a slave put his filthy hands on me—I would just die of disgust!*

"I concur, sister." She closed her eyes and slept in that day instead of going to the field.

‡‡‡‡‡‡

"...I shall arrive in three days..."

After receiving Cooper's latest postcard, Suzanna went around the house making sure that everything was perfect. Wash this, fold and store that. Her work clothes, shoes, sun hats, and gloves, anything that had the field's residue on it, she wanted it cleaned and out of sight.

She had Sam gather the slaves. "You mustn't mention to Mister Cooper my time in the field. He says it's no place for me, but it has been my pleasure working with each of you and I hope that I've made your days a little easier."

On the day of his return, Nina made sure to be in CJ's room nursing the babies. She knew Cooper would want to see them as soon as he returned. He always did and Suzanna also knew.

The nursery door swung open and in walked Cooper. Nina smiled as soon as she saw his face but lost her joy when Suzanna entered behind him. Both babies crawled to him, but he only picked up CJ.

Nina reached down and picked up her daughter, Alexandria. With a lowered head, she stepped away as soon as Suzanna stepped forward and grabbed her son's hand while in his father's arms. They were in portrait form. *The white woman, her white child, and white husband.* Nina immediately began fighting tears. "Excuse me, ma'am, sir, may I be dismissed?"

Cooper opened his mouth to speak, but Suzanna spoke first. "You may."

Nina went to her room with no hope of spending any time with the man she loved. *Suzanna will see to that.* And she was right.

Cooper woke up the very next morning expecting to make up for his absence but was surprised to see the accomplishments which coincided with his new business promise. He gathered everyone together. "...If you all continue working as you have, your hard work will seal the new business prospects I have in place. If that happens, I will give you all a weekend off and host a celebration, including a new outfit especially for the celebration, a feast, and wine."

Cheers came from them, laughter, obliging words filled the air.

Later that evening, he visited his family in their cabin. "If all goes well and based upon the perfect timing, each of you will have your freedom granted to you. I need your full commitment on this project in order to see that through."

The news privately excited Cecil. He wanted to concede to it, but he mentally instigated his heart to loathe Cooper no matter what good he did.

Cooper had to leave again for another extended trip to seal his deals. As soon as he was off, Suzanna immediately resumed her time in the field.

In the months that followed, Cooper went back and forth on business trips. But when he stopped to take a look over productivity, he knew he needed more acres, inventory, and slaves to meet the dedicated date. Then there was the issue of purchasing the helpers from Peter, Suzanna's father. But his rising interest kept increasing, making the pursuit to purchase them almost impossible.

"He'll never let us buy them," Suzanna said.

"Everyone has their breaking point. We'll only need to discover his. For now, we need more money to complete the business orders I have lined up."

"How did your business go with the landowner?"

"I hit an impasse. He's increased the land's price." Cooper said while looking over their books to see if he could make any sort of sacrifice for the land's new value. "What's this? The numbers aren't accurate."

He went back and forth, paying attention to every entry. With further investigation, he looked up at Suzanna.

"He said he would pay it back," she explained.

"First, you allowed your brother –in-law to send an overseer without my permission, now you're lending them money without my permission? Do you understand the position you've put us in?"

"I'm sorry—"

"I'm sure you are because now we don't have the needed funds to purchase supplies to fulfill the prerequisite orders that I've made. You've risked our success for your brother-in-law, a man whom the banks don't even trust. And you did so without my knowledge. When were you going to tell me about this?"

"I...I was—"

"When are they going to pay back the loan?"

"They said—"

"With interest, I'm sure? If they are going to use us as a bank, we must treat them like banks treat borrowers."

"We didn't discuss interest. I didn't think it was necessary."

"You didn't think? Well, when did they say they would pay it back?"

"A week ago."

"So, they did pay it back?"

"No, they are a week late. I told them that the loan must be satisfied prior to your return, but they don't have the money."

"Suzanna, this is not good. I have deals set in place depending upon money that we no longer have. You and I just spoke with your father about purchasing the helpers. You knew we didn't have the money to do so, but you allowed us to go to him with no honor in store."

"I'm sorry, I was trying to help them. He promised to pay it back before—I'm sorry."

"It's alright. It's alright. Come here."

She went to her husband who gave her a strong gripping bear hug. "Don't worry, I'll figure it out."

"We can always borrow the money from my father."

"Never... It's alright. I just need to readjust some things. Hey...look at me." He released his hug and lifted her chin. "Don't worry. You were only trying to help family. I understand that."

Cooper found himself in a familiar situation. They had enough money to increase their land territory and some inventory, but he couldn't afford to purchase or lease any additional slaves to work the land.

Unbeknownst to Suzanna, Cooper had a northern bank account. Money he'd earned from her prior to their marriage. He kept the account and continued adding to it, made wise investments that were separate from the farm and it had grown substantially.

In the past, when they would be in financial binds, he'd used his own money to bail them out, but that would not be the case this time. His money was tied up in his new business endeavors and more equipment. He was in a bad place financially and with orders already in place, he had to try to move a mountain with limited resources.

He went to the property owner as he had done in time past. "Please, sir. It would help us out greatly if you would be willing to subdivide the land."

"Hmp. I've been watching you, Mister Cooper Edwards. And what I did not see, I've heard. You have been able to do great things with the land I've sold to you. You probably have more money than I do. You're smart, but I won't be taken advantage of by someone who is trying to outsmart me. It's all or nothing. Decide soon, I have other interested land buyers. People who can pay before sunset if I give the word," he lied and Cooper figure as much, but he couldn't take the chance and gamble with 'what ifs'.

"What about a bank loan?" Suzanna asked

"Out of the question. That would be financial suicide. Life doesn't give us guarantees, and I would never want to be in danger of losing all that we own because of a bad year of unexpected challenges."

With limited choices, he stood in his siblings' cabin, explaining the situation as he had a few years prior to Remy, Sam, and Yes'sa Man. "We have enough to purchase the land and some inventory, but we can't afford to purchase more slaves to work the fields. We would need each of you to pull double your loads."

"So, let me get this right. You want us to do the work of two men for you and your white wife?" Cecil questioned.

"I work hard a'nuff as is," Mark, Cooper's brother-in-law said.

"Whatever you need, Cooper, I'm in."

"Of course, you would be, 'cause you a fool!" Cecil told Micah.

"'Um smart a'nuff to know I gotta help the person who helping me."

"Well, 'um in too," Sarah said.

"Us too, Cooper. Anything you need us to do," Reah spoke for her and John.

"Y'all can do the job of three people. 'Um not working myself crazy for them to be rich, leavin' me a po' black slave fool."

"This order is not the normal order, Cecil. It will change all of our lives. This is not about making us rich, it's building the type of wealth that will grant each of you your freedoms and enough money to set up a better life for you all outside of slavery. We'll all be making major sacrifices to reach this very important goal."

"I ain't seen you out in the field working from sunup to sundown. It be us. Yo' fam'ly slaving in the fields why you off on this so-called business. Everybody on this farm works but you."

"If what you doin' while on business gone get me my freedom, 'um in. Only a fool would turn that down." Micah looked at Cecil.

"You see. You see how he tricks us, and we go for it. He turnin' us against each other. He not settin' up a better life for us. He settin' up a better life for he and Suzanna. And whoever believe different is a fool!"

"Cecil, Cooper done did everything he said. We eats good, we sleeps good. He never had a whip put to our backs, and he's never called us boy or our women gals. I gots me a soft bed to sleep on. Look around here. We gotta a real settee to sit on, our own kitchen out back. We have working and dress clothes. And he throws us celebrations. We never had that on the Hartford Plantation. It's time we show our thanks. Now, me and Jalean been talking and she right." Thomas walked up to his eldest brother. "Thank you. Thank you for everything you did and gone do. Whatever you needs from me, for freedom or not, 'um in. I don't feel like no slave no mo' cause you don't treats me like no slave. And it's like Jalean said, if I was up north, I'll have to work just like 'um doing now. 'Sept, I have to take care of myself. Who can say if I'll have it better than what I have here? And I ain't have to run to get freedom, like you said. 'Um grateful, brother. It took me a time to see, but now my eyes be open." He shook his brother's hand.

"You are welco—"

"Thomas, you be a fool!"

Mark, Jalean's husband jumped in. What Thomas said had made him think. "How, Cecil? What Cooper gone do, start treating us bad? Micah's right. He could've bought other slaves and treat 'dem like he treats us. I bet 'dey would 'preciate it. N'all…'um in, too. Freedom or not, 'um in, Cooper." He looked at his wife, Jalean, and Thomas. He turned to Reah, Micah, Sarah, and then to Bertha. "I not blood fam'ly, I be lucky a'nuff to marry Jalean. I sorry for givin' y'all trouble." He turned to Cooper. "But you won't have no more troubles out'ta me."

"Me either," Jalean said.

Cecil looked around the room at the *dumb smiles on they faces.* Even his wife Bertha. "Y'all fools. All y'all fools, and he gone prove me right."

There was no one left on his side. Cecil felt unaided in his hostility towards Cooper. *He done turned everybody against me.* Vengeance grew and never stopped growing on that day.

Fifty-one

"**D**o you see how she smiles at him? She wants your husband and if you are not careful, she's going to seduce him." Suzanna had become fast friends with a little devil that constantly sat on her left shoulder whispering in her ear.

After a visit to town, she returned home and found both babies asleep and Nina nowhere in sight. "Remy, where's Nina?"

"She went near the river—"

"To the river. She left the babies alone?"

"No, ma'am. I told her I'll watch after them if they wake up."

"*To the river. You know that's Cooper's favorite place to sit and think,*" the little devil whispered.

To-the-river...hmm, "You're right," Suzanna answered her invisible friend.

"What, ma'am?"

"Oh, nothing, Remy" Suzanna raced out the front door, prepared a horse and took a ride *to the river.*

While on her way there, her little shoulder sitting devil was in full effect, convincing her of what was happening on the riverbanks.

"*At this very moment, his hand is traveling up her thigh and under her clothes, making its way to her dark breast that he will squeeze and kiss.*"

Furious at the thought, Suzanna squeezed her heels into the horse's side to hurry it *to the river.* She pushed the horse faster and faster, knowing this would be the day that would bring answers to her question.

Looking ahead, she could see the spot where Cooper would often visit, but there were no signs of them.

That doesn't mean that they aren't somewhere out here. She got off the horse and quietly listened for any sounds of human voices and even harder for the sounds of moans and groans, but she only heard the sounds of the river.

Suzanna stood silently, her thoughts interspersed between being thankful to have not found them and wanting to in order to prove that she was right. She got back on the horse and went home, rushing pass the kitchen going directly to her bedroom where she did not find Cooper. From there, she tried to pass through her son's nursery to Nina's room, but the door was locked. She hurried out the nursery and nearly busted Nina's bedroom door open. And there they were, Nina and Remy playing with the babies.

Seeing the look of distress that Suzanna wore, Remy worried. "Are you alright, Miss Suzanna?"

"Yes. Yes, Remy, I'm fine. Have either of you seen Cooper?" she asked them both but was looking directly at Nina.

"He went into town. Said he had some business to tend to," Remy answered.

Suzanna folded her arms and walked up to Nina, who was sitting in a rocker with CJ on her lap. Suzanna looked at CJ, then Nina. "Did you have a nice visit *to-the-river* while Remy performed your duties and hers?" Her tone was quite tense.

"Ma'am, I didn't go to the river, I went to find these pebbles to make a rattle for Alexandria."

"But Remy said…Remy, I thought you said she went to the river."

"No, ma'am. I said near the river. Miss Suzanna, you sure you're alright? You need me to make you some tea to help calm your nerves? You look upset."

"My nerves are fine!" Suzanna went to the door of Nina's room that adjoined the nursing and look back at Nina. "This door is to remain unlocked at all times!"

"Yes, ma'am."

Suzanna slammed the door behind her, causing both babies to cry.

"I better go see after her. I'll fix her that tea. It normally settles her nerves."

Later that day, Remy was cooking when the back door opened. Cooper walked in. "Smells delicious, Remy."

"Dinner'll be ready in a spell. You gone like this, Mister Cooper."

"I'm sure I will." He went into their bedroom where he found Suzanna sitting on the bed seething.

"Where have you been?"

"In town to place an order. We needed more fertilizer. I had to make sure there would be enough before leaving for my business trip. Why, is all well?"

"You told Remy you were going into town. You should have told me you were leaving."

"Darling, since when do you require knowing of my every whereabouts? If I'm not here working, I'm out doing business or taking care of business related to the farm. What's going on? You've been edgy since my return."

Suzanna dropped her head, her hands rested on her lap. "It's just that when you are away on business, I feel lonely. There's nothing for me to do and no...I do not want to visit my family. I feel so neglected, darling."

"But I'm not always away."

"Yes, I know. But when you are here, you're either in the field working or in town on business. Aside from our honeymoon, we've had no real time together except in bed at nights."

"Dear love, I'm always working to improve our lives."

"I know, but why can't I go with you? At least once or so. My mother accompanied my father and my sisters their husbands. But—why haven't you included me on your business trips?"

Cooper sat and wrapped his arms around her. He lifted her chin and turned her to face him. Knowing that sex always calmed her, he gently kissed her lips. She didn't return the kiss. No sex this time, it was not what she needed or wanted. She'd become a lonely wife who was afraid of losing her husband to a slave. She needed to feel special.

"Will you accompany me on my next trip, darling?"

"Really?"

"Yes. I would love to have you by my side."

Cooper took his time making love to his wife and for the first time in a long time, she felt loved. There was nothing left to prove to the woman two rooms away. She relaxed her legs that were out to his sides and accepted his forgiveness of neglect with sheer pleasure.

Fifty-two

Although they would not be leaving for a few weeks, Suzanna was thrilled as she prepared for the trip. But Nina on the other hand...

"It's only to smooth things over with her. You've acknowledged that she was beginning to suspect something between us," Cooper whispered in the privacy of their secret room in the barn.

Hours earlier, he'd been awakened by CJ. Hearing Nina tending to him, he got out of bed and sat at the breakfast table watching Suzanna, assuring that she was sound asleep before sneaking outside of Nina's window. Tap-tap-tap...tap...tap...tap-tap-tap.

The special signal left her no doubt that it was him. Nina checked on the babies before stuffing pillows in the shape of her body underneath the bedspread and tipped-toed out the house to the barn where she found Cooper waiting.

"She's feeling neglected. The only way to remedy this is to have her accompany me on a business trip. I assure you that it was not my idea, but I can't ignore her needs. As her husband, I can't—"

Nina stopped his explanation with an intense kiss. She was a slave, his slave. She could not stop him from taking his wife on a trip, but she could make him think about her while he was away. She climbed on top of him and took him aggressively, erotically, draining every source of his energy. Leaving every part of him limp.

Sexually weakened, Cooper could barely climb back into bed with Suzanna after being so passionately loved by Nina. Not even a minute after his head hit the pillow, he was sound asleep, but still in ecstasy. His mind could not escape Nina's erotic love moves as she crept into his dreams. Her sensual body, perfect breasts, spread thighs that drape his torso like divided curtains hanging perfectly on a window.

"Mmmm," he moaned, disturbing Suzanna who slept next to him. Waking up, his moans of pleasure heated her cold body. She climbed on top of him, rubbed and caressed his sleeping vessel, but it remained slumped over on his thigh.

Suzanna fell over and stared into the darkness. "That's never happened before. Even in anger or in a deep sleep, I'm always able to make him respond," she whispered.

That following day, Cecil entered the kitchen carrying a basket. "I got some fresh corn from the field, just like Miss Suzanna like 'em."

"Put them over there, Cecil." Remy was getting their lunch ready. "I'm glad you came. You can take the lunch to the field for me. Save Sam a trip."

"Okay. Where's Miss Suzanna?"

"She's in her room packing."

"Packing?"

"Yeah. She's going away with Mister Cooper on his business trip. She's been giggling like a little girl since he asked her."

Remy turned around to the unexpected sound of a dropped basket of corn and the slam of the back door. She picked up the basket. "I guess we'll have this for dinner. He could've at least taken the lunch with him."

Hearing the slamming door, Suzanna walked into the kitchen. "What was that?"

"It was Cecil. He bought you some corn. I'll get it ready for dinner."

"That would be great." Suzanna went to the front room where Nina sat on the floor with the babies. "Nina, after you put the children up for their naps, come to my room. I need your assistance packing."

"Yes, ma'am."

About an hour later, Nina knocked on Suzanna's door.

"Come in."

She entered.

"Oh, there you are. I've been packing for days, and I'm just about done. Look in my top drawer and get my chemises. Pack them in the bag on the bed. My sisters gave them to me as wedding presents for our honeymoon. I don't believe I wore them for a second before Cooper ripped them off me. I imagine this vacation will be a repeat of our honeymoon. He's planned for business, but there will be little business in our room." She giggled. "He does have a hard time keeping his hands off of his wife."

She took one of the chemises from Nina. "Yes, this is my favorite." She held up the lingerie to her body. "Oh, yes. This is going to be perfect. Let's see, now...I have one for Monday, Tuesday, Wednesday. Looks like we will have to do some shopping for Thursday, Friday, and Saturday." She passed the chemise to Nina, who packed the sexy lingerie with Suzanna's other things.

Nina looked around the room and noticed the toiletries on the bed. "You need me to pack these things up as well?"

"No, I can manage."

"It's that all, ma'am?"

"Yes, that's all."

Nina left the room knowing why she had been asked to come. With her head down, she sped up.

"Nina, you wanna help me with dinner—Where she going?"

She closed the door and sat in the rocker near the bed. "I can't let her break me." Her bedroom door came open by way of the nursery room.

"Oh, Nina, when I return, I will need you to wash my chemises. This is between you and me. Sometimes, he takes me before I can remove them from my body. They will surely need washing upon our return."

"Yes, ma'am."

Suzanna left the room smiling.

Fifty-three

After their trip, Cooper returned home alone.

"Where Miss Suzanna?" Sam asked while helping to carry the luggage into the house.

"Her sister met us at the train station. It's quite interesting actually. It seems whenever we go away together, their father becomes ill."

"He alright?" Sam asked.

"No. It appears that his health has declined greatly. I wasn't able to be with her this time. I needed to make sure that all is well here. It's getting closer to the time of fulfilling that production obligation."

It was also time to fulfill another commitment he'd made. His obligation as a husband to Nina.

"Remy, Suzanna's not here and I'm tired from the field. To assure that everything is going well with that order, I have an awful lot of paperwork to tend to. It's quite tedious honestly but requires a lot of attention. I was thinking that it would be best if you all eat at your cabin. I don't require a fancy meal and would rather spend the time with CJ and working."

"Oh, okay. Let me kiss CJ good night. I'll fix you a plate before I leave."

"That won't be necessary. You do so much. I can manage."

"Good night, my big man." Remy tucked CJ in and left with her suspicion. *No Suzanna. He might be working, but that's not all he'll be tending to I'm sure.*

Each night after Remy returned to her cabin, Cooper and Nina enjoyed romantic evenings together. They shared candlelight dinners and talked about one day being free to show their love to the world.

"Remy, can you watch the babies for me? I'm going to find some more pebbles to make Alexandria another rattle. She's broken this one." Nina held up the rattle she herself had broken to prove her need to leave. She went directly to the river.

Cooper helped Nina sit on a blanket in their hiding spot by the river. "Here are the stones I collected while on my business trip."

"They're so pretty."

"I tried them in a hollow container, I think they'll make a unique sound."

"Alexandria will enjoy the sound of her new rattle."

Staring into her eyes, he could never resist her. "And I want to enjoy her mother." Minutes later, her arms and legs were wrapped around his body as he grinned until she could take no more.

In Suzanna's absence, Cooper spent every night in Nina's bed, holding her in his arms and each night she fell more in love with him. It was the freedom of love they had never had and one that she never wanted to end.

Fifty-four

A woman's intuition. It is that thought that propels a woman to put everything aside and trust her gut instincts. It tells her to trust the thought that she's having and to know when to act on those thoughts and follow where they lead. And that's exactly what Suzanna did.

While visiting her ill father, out of the blue and in the middle of the night, Suzanna pulled herself from bed, went downstairs and left out the door. After preparing a horse, she rode non-stop until she reached the road that led to her farm. Tying the horse in the stable, she walked across the wet moist grass.

The dark night limited her sight, but familiarity led the way home. Opening the back door that was never locked, she didn't hear a sound, only the beating of her heart. She tried to ease the door closed, but it was difficult, her hands trembled terribly.

Calm down, Suzanna. One final deep breath before continuing on to her bedroom. She was able to open the door without it making too much noise. The room was too dark to see. In silence, she walked over to the bed and felt around for Cooper. Her heartbeat sped up. He wasn't there. Tears started building. An overwhelming effect of trembles took over.

She turned to her bedroom door, then to her son's room, unsure of which direction to take to get to Nina's room.

As calmly as possible, she took gentle steps on the wooden floor. She was extremely nervous, wanted to cry, but held herself together and continued on her quest. She took slow steps, one foot in front of the other, but the slow pace in the dark made it difficult to keep her balance. Swaying a little, she managed to continue without falling.

Every step brought her closer to her destination, but one misplaced foot on a squeaky floor, and the wood screamed. Suzanna stood as still as possible, listening for any movement, any sounds, any voices. But the squeak failed to reach sleeping ears. She slowly twisted the knob and entered. Getting his attention, her son rotated his small body and fell back to sleep.

Suzanna resumed, her legs shook, her body trembled, overwhelmed, she had to stop halfway in. She could no longer stand the anticipation. She rushed the remainder distance, twisted the knob, and opened.

The room was dark, the window was opened, the light of the moon pierced through the window panes and stopped on Nina's bed where she slept peacefully, her back against Cooper's naked body, his arm wrapped around her. The shock was too much to bear. Suzanna closed her eyes. Her limp body hit the floor. FA-THUD!

Cooper and Nina rose up, he jumped out of bed completely nude, picked up his wife, and carried her to their room.

Nina just sat there on the bed, not knowing what the discovery might mean. But whatever the cost, she was happy that their relationship was out in the open.

Fifty-five

Cooper had always been well-reserved with his thoughts and for that reason, everything he'd planned had always worked out. There were a few bumps like falling in love with Nina, being discovered by Ben, the challenge of Remy, Sam, and Yes'sa Man, getting his family to the farm and overcoming the problems with Cecil. But there had been nothing so challenging that he couldn't recover.

He had changed his life's fate and learned that the color of his skin was no longer a curse, but became a blessing. But as he sat at the breakfast table in their bedroom, the color of his skin had no relevance to what he was now facing. This was a matter of the heart, what was on the inside had become his greatest challenge ever.

He had been caught, and now his reserved thoughts that he had protected so carefully had been exposed, and life hadn't taught him much about his truth being exposed. He didn't know what it meant to him or his situation and all the lives that would surely be affected by his unearthed secrets.

Cooper stared at his wife, who was asleep after Remy had given her a homemade remedy. He was afraid for her to wake up, fearing to see her eyes staring upon him as if she would be able to look into his soul and see all of his truths.

No longer did he feel reserved. He was more vulnerable than ever before. His hands rapidly trembled, so much that he had to take them off the table and rest them on his lap. He sat straight up, hoping that would help calm his nerve, but it didn't. He dreaded the questions, the look of disappointment, the pain that he knew she would display, and the weapons of attack that she would surely use against his guilt.

He didn't move from the room or that chair. He had to be there when she awakened. It was all he could think about...*when she awakens.* What was going to happen when she awakens?

÷÷÷÷÷÷

Suzanna sat at the river, her tears dripping into the water. Feeling a presence behind her, she turned to see an indiscernible image. In its hand was a bouquet of flowers for her.

Standing, she came face to face with the distorted figure. She leaned in, then pulled back. It was Cooper. She looked down. The aroma of the flowers entered into her nostrils. "Mmm...they smell so... Who's there? ... Cooper?"

She heard laughter. "Is that..." Distinct voices she'd heard many times as a child. Those of her sisters ruined the joy she felt after receiving the flowers that were now withering away. More laughter came, that of a feminine and manly voice, adding to her misery.

"Cooper, why are you laughing at me? And who is that laughing with you?"

The laughter ceased, but only for a second. The humorous sounds of Nina and Cooper became louder, draining her sisters' joy.

"You must allow her to be his mother," Cooper said.

Suzanna turned to see her son in Nina's arms. The three looked so happy.

"Bye, Mommie," the child who'd never spoken a word said.

"Nooo...give me back my son. Give me back my son." She attempted to run away.

Her sisters returned, pointing, laughing as she ran in place. Belting, loud laughter as she popped up from her sleep. Sitting in her bed, covered in sweat, her eyes were full of tears. She turned to see Cooper sitting at the breakfast table staring at her. A look of guilt covered his face. He dropped his head.

She realized that the reality was just as bad as the dream. "GET—
OUT!"

He stood and looked at her for a second. "I have to go into town to
take care of some business. Would you like me to pick you up
anything?"

She laid down and he left.

✂✂✂✂✂✂

On the night Suzanna caught Cooper and Nina in bed, Cooper scooped
her up and carried her to bed. He rushed to the helpers' cabin and
returned with Remy who took care of her.

While she slept, he went to Nina's room. Sitting beside her, he didn't
know what to say.

"I know, I should leave," Nina said, breaking the silence.

"I think it will be for the best. Just for now, until I figure out what
happens next."

They heard a soft knock on the door.

"Come in," Cooper answered.

The door crept open. Afraid that it was Suzanna, he stood.

It was Remy. She noticed the relief on his face. She looked at Nina and
her daughter who was still asleep in her small bed in the corner of the
room. The room was oversized, like every room in the house. Tall
ceilings with his and her closets. It was Cooper's former room when
he had first moved in. When they remodel the house, the room had
been repainted with softer colors. Although not elaborate, it had a
mother's touch. Nina was allowed a small allowance to fix it up, and
she wanted to assure that her daughter, Alexandria, appreciated the
pastel colors.

In the darkness of the night with only one lit candle, it was dim and
so was the atmosphere between the two.

"I came to see if you need anything. Miss Suzanna is sleeping. I gave
her something to help her sleep for a while."

Cooper looked at Nina. "Yes, I appreciate the offer. Nina will need help packing her things. She'll be moving back to the slave's cabin until I figure this all out."

"What about CJ? How will she tend to him? It might not be a good idea for her to come here to care for him."

"You'll have to add dropping him off and picking him up to your duties. Just until—"

"I know, Mister Cooper. Let me get some crates to help with your things." Remy left, allowing them the space they needed to say their goodbyes.

╪╪╪╪╪╪

Now that Suzanna had awakened, they were all afraid. The farm had had its share of problems with nature and noncompliant slaves, but this was a different kind of problem. Cooper had been caught in bed with a slave. What would happen next was anyone's guess. And his family worried about their fate.

After getting dressed, Suzanna sat at the breakfast table looking out the window. Remy had served her hot tea that was now cold. CJ had been taken to Nina for nursing and to play with his sister.

"His sister," Suzanna wondered aloud. She knew that white men sought the company of female slaves, her father included. So much so that he'd lost his desire for his wife in bed.

Suzanna recalled seeing the misery on her mother's face when she was young. By the time she reached her teenage years, her mother's sadness was a normal part of life. Whenever she'd smiled, it would confuse her children. When Peter moved out of their bedroom, their marriage changed for the worse.

"Why? I am your wife, Peter! Why do you not find me attractive?" With eyes full of tears, Suzanna's mother begged her husband for an answer.

"Marion, please."

"No, Peter, I demand to know. I demand to know why you sleep beside a slave girl every night and not the woman whom you swore to God that you would love until your death."

His eyes grew surprised.

"Did you think I would not know? How could you? I'm your wife! What is it that they have that I don't? What is it about their dark skin that makes you crave them?"

"Marion, I can't—"

"Peter, I demand to know!"

"I can't...I won't!"

"You can and you will!"

"Marion—"

"Tell me!"

"Curvaceous."

"Curvaceous?"

"It's their voluptuous body, their sensual breasts...full lips, full of sweet addictive juices that I find hard to resist. I've tried to stay away, I have, but every time I see a beauty pass me, I burn with desire. It has nothing to do with you, my love. It's me and my weakness that pulls me from our bed." He looked into his wife's eyes. "I'm sorry, Marion. I'm so sorry. I will always love you, but I've become obsessed."

"I don't care to hear the description of their anatomy. What must I do to get you to speak of me in that way? Must I stand in the sun and darkened my skin?"

He looked directly into her eyes and damned her with his lips. "You are how God made you, and they are how God made them. And you can never compare."

He turned, reached for the doorknob, but stopped. Looking down at it, his conscience told him to go back to his wife and make things right, but lust twisted the knob and made him exit the room. It guided him into his bedroom where Dottie, one of his regulars, awaited him.

She rushed out of the bed into his arms. Tearing his clothes off, she satisfied him like she knew his wife never could, in hope of gaining the promise he'd made to her which was to see her mixed daughter from him. A child he'd given to his barren sister as a gift.

The moment Peter left their bedroom, Marion broke down and cried. Depression encompassed her. Desperation for his attention left her dysfunctional. She threw herself over the staircase of their home, three levels down onto the floor. The fall left her in tremendous pain from several fractures and made her pay dearly for seeking death.

Peter went to his wife's side, faithfully nursing her back to health. He bathed and read to her underneath a tall oak tree. She fell asleep in his arms at night and was served breakfast in bed by him each morning. But once she healed, he was sharing his bed with slaves again.

Marion had learned how to get his attention and just as he was addicted to slave women, she became addicted to his affection. Suddenly, she was suffering from unexplained seizures, periodic stages of collapsing with uncontrolled convulsions. The doctor declared that she could not be left alone.

"Marion, this is Dottie, your sitter," Peter told his needy wife.

Marion despised being taken care of by her husband's lover, the mother of his child. And as strange as her compulsive episodes of fits and faints had come, they left, inadvertently sending Dottie back to Peter's bed.

Marion couldn't take it. Self-abuse was no longer an option. She loved her husband's attention during those times but hated the pains of broken bones more. A substitute took its place. One slice to her wrist and it was over. She'd bled to death and was found in her bed the following morning, finally receiving the attention of her husband she'd longed for.

Peter's obsession was replaced with guilt. He was never with another woman, slave or white, after his wife's death.

A knock on Suzanna's door took her mind off her mother's death, but not off her pain. "Come in."

Remy pushed open the door, carrying lunch. After setting it up, she left her alone. About an hour later, Remy eased the door open and found the untouched food sitting on the breakfast table and Suzanna in bed, sound asleep, traces of dried tears staining her face.

Fifty-six

*D*o *it...pick it up and do it.* Suzanna stared at the steak knife lying beside her full plate of food. *One slice and it will be all over. Your mother's haunting suicide, your father's disappointment, the death of your first love and his family, the laughter of your sisters who speak ill of you behind your back, and the pain that Cooper caused. One swipe will end it all.*

A quick grab and the knife was in the palm of her hand. On the table lay her wrist, palm up, purple veins pumping pulsating blood.

DO IT!

Tightly squeezing the knife handle, her fingernails stuck deep into her palm.

DO IT! DO IT NOW! END THIS PAIN FOREVER!

Lifting the knife, it was within inches from her veins. Suzanna flinched the moment the bedroom door opened.

CJ was placed on the floor, his hands and knees rapidly pattering against it, moving in pursuit of his mother's arms.

Seeing the steak knife, Remy locked eyes with Suzanna whose palm was turned up, the knife only needing pressure to carry out the deed.

Breaking free, Remy rushed to pick up CJ. "I'm sorry. I knocked a few times, but I can see why you didn't answer." She went to Suzanna and made the exchange, CJ for the knife. Looking around the room for any other sharp objects, Remy took the full plate of food and utensils, and left CJ with Suzanna and rushed to the kitchen.

Returning to the room, Remy didn't bother to knock. Yes'sa Man followed her. Taking the baby, he left the room and closed the door behind him. Remy sat in the chair across from Suzanna and smiled. "Here, Miss Suzanna, drink this." It was a potion to help her fall asleep.

Suzanna drank the glass of tonic and allowed Remy to help her to bed. Remy looked at the woman who was once so vibrant and happy, but who had now become desperately sad. After tucking her in, she sat in the rocker by the bed minding Suzanna whose eyes stared out the window. No tears, just her eyes glued to a tree outside.

Before meeting Cooper, her entire life had been dying while she fought hard to find a reason to live. The farm that had once given her life had been stained with the death of her husband and in-laws. In honor of them, she'd worked vigorously to keep it running, but their deaths had left her empty. The days of laughter had been quieted by pain and required no joy to keep it thriving.

One fateful day, Suzanna had taken a knife from the kitchen drawer, put it in her pocket and walked near the banks of the river where she'd planned to take her life.

DO IT! It had been the first time she'd heard the manipulating voice that was too loud to ignore. *DO IT!* She turned her palm up, tightly securing the knife, placing it to her wrist, and applied pressure. She dropped to her knees, losing the battle to take her life.

You can do it. You have to live free of sadness. Suzanna put the knife back to her wrist, pressed down and continued pressing until her pale skin turned burgundy.

And that's when she heard it...him, his voice, his words that saved her.

"Madam, I do not wish to frighten you and will only present myself upon your permission."

Cooper's voice had come from nowhere and with only a few words, he turned her moment of hopelessness into the possibility of 'what if.' With one quick hand movement, she tossed the knife and walked towards a reason to live. Now the man who'd given her hope had reneged on his promise.

Drowsy, Suzanna's eyes remained on the tree outside of her window. "My mother took her own life. She left her children motherless. I understand her now...what she must have felt. How could she possibly be a true mother to her daughters without being true to herself? And the truth was that she hated her life and the pain it always offered. Do you know that after killing herself, the very slave named Dottie whom my mother resented became our caretaker?"

Still looking out the window, her eyes blinked slowly, taking longer periods to reopen. "He forced her on me. He took away my motherhood and gave it to her, just as my father had done to my mother. I didn't want her in my house, but he kept insisting. He wanted her here. He always wanted her here. Because she had given birth, she could nurse...my...child." Fighting against the relaxing influence of the potion, Suzanna's eyes swung open.

"What's the matter, Miss Suzanna?" Remy asked.

"It makes sense now. Nina's child belongs to Cooper." She was barely audible. Her eyes suddenly grew heavy with slow, long blinks. She mumbled. Every word grew further and farther apart. "He...tricked me... This.....can't......be happening. It's.........a...........dream." *Maybe if I fall asleep, I will awaken from this horrible dream.* One final blink and she was out.

When Cooper returned, Remy sat him down and told him how she'd found Suzanna. She gave him a stern look and spoke with authority. "Mister Cooper, I know white men like the company of a slave woman, but in that room in there is a young beautiful white woman who loves you to death. She's your wife, the mother of your son. It's your duty by law and God to take care of her!"

Without protest, Cooper got up, went to their bedroom, and lay next to his wife. She opened her eyes and tried to push him away, but he gripped her wrist and forced her head onto his chest. She stopped fighting, laid still and cried herself back to sleep.

The following morning, Remy served Cooper and Suzanna breakfast in their bedroom. The two sat in silence, he at the breakfast table and Suzanna sitting in bed, staring at the breakfast that she had no desire to eat.

Seeing her disdain, Cooper got up and sat on the bed. He picked up the fork, filled it with eggs and put it to her lips. "Suzanna... You must eat, my dear."

She glared at him, but he did not falter. "Suzanna, I understand that you are angry, and you have every reason to be. I'm angry with myself. I don't know how I allowed that to happen. But not eating is not punishing me, it's punishing you and our son. If you don't eat for yourself, eat for CJ. You need your strength for him."

Suzanna took the fork from him. "Leave."

"I'll sit at the table—"

"No, get out! I want you out of here."

Cooper stood, looked at her and left, taking his empty plate with him and giving it to Remy.

"One plate? How's she doing?"

"No changes."

"She'll come around. Keep trying!"

"I will, but—"

"No but. Keep at it!"

Days went by of the same behavior, but eventually, Remy's words came to fruition. Cooper didn't give in at winning her over and after a while, his remorseful actions gave Suzanna comfort.

Not knowing what tomorrow would bring, Cooper was holding his breath. But slowly, she'd she allowed him to breathe, starting with a hand touch, then letting him hold her while she cried. He brushed her hair, bathed, and massaged her. She slowly allowed him to love her as she deserved to be loved.

In their bed, Suzanna sat between Cooper's legs, her back against his chest while he rubbed her shoulders. The night was quiet, the wind blew in the room, relaxing them both.

"Do you love her?" Suzanna asked.

The truth hurts, a lie is only a pacifier, and somewhere in the middle lies the words, "It's complicated." His faithfulness to Nina had become protected and would not permit him to deny his love for her, even though he needed to convince Suzanna that she was the love of his life.

She got up and lit the lantern. "What did you say?"

Cooper scooted back to the headboard. "It's not what you think."

"Then tell me what it is." Her words came off like a threat, but the real danger lay in her facial expression.

"It's complicated," he repeated.

"It's complicated? I can't begin to imagine what that means. Do you love her—yes or no?"

Cooper didn't know what to say but being that close to a woman who not long ago had wanted to kill herself was not the safest place to be. He got out of bed and walked to the window to think. After returning to the bed, he got on one knee and pulled her to the edge. "I love you, Suzanna. *You* are my wife and it is *you* whom I love and will always love. And no one can ever change my feelings for you." Getting off his knees, he sealed his words with a long seductive kiss.

Her hands pressed against his chest, trying to push him away. But squeezing her upper arms, he refused by pulling her closer.

"No." With his 'it's complicated' words still lingering in her mind, she tried again to resist.

Cooper's arms wrapped her into his seduction. His tongue slipped into her mouth, making her helpless to its moistness. But he was unworthy of her love, and she was determined to rebel against the man who'd betrayed her. She beat his back. "Nooo."

He looked into her eyes; she into his. So much came to mind, words that she wanted to use to hurt him, words he wanted to say to beg forgiveness. But he settled for a different approach, something that she could not or would not resist.

He tore away her clothes, turned and bent her over onto the bed. Like a beast, he took her in her favorite position, and she gave in, relaxing her body, enjoying his sexual apology while tears fell upon her bed.

A knock on the bedroom door went unanswered. Concerned, Remy set the platter that carried two breakfast plates on a nearby table. She gripped the doorknob and gave one last listen before entering without permission. With an ear pressed to the door, she twisted the knob, but the sounds of pleasure stopped her. Smiling, she picked up the tray and headed for the kitchen. "I'll make some lunch. They'll be good and hungry by then."

On the second day, neither Cooper nor Suzanna left their room. Remy gladly took and collected used items left by them on the table outside of the bedroom, where she placed their plates of food.

Fifty-seven

Nina walked to the window to see if there were any signs of Cooper. Throughout the days, she had sat by the window hoping to see him, but hadn't since the night they were caught. Suzanna made sure of that by controlling his every move.

The door opened.

"Hey."

"Hey, Bertha. You seen Cooper today?"

"He passed by the field the other day. I think he was headed to town."

A week later, Remy met Nina at the front door to pick up CJ. She remained in the open doorway hoping to see Cooper, but again, there was no sign of him. She closed the door and returned to her room. *Three days and no sign of him. Maybe that's it for us. Maybe he loves her more.*

She picked up her daughter and held her close to her heart as tears rolled down her face. She had been without Cooper and had been confused about his feelings for her before, but this was different.

Had he used her as his unauthorized concubine like a master would use a slave girl? If he truly loved her, why had he hidden her underneath a rock and not proclaimed his love for her to the world? He'd never fought for her love but took it freely.

The white people have always been so much more important. First Massa Hartford and now Suzanna. He never genuinely loved me but had toiled with her emotions. Never did she ever want to feel used again or that she wasn't number one in his life. Nina lay her daughter back in her bed and sat in the rocker, tense, fed up. "She can have 'em."

The following day, Nina met Remy on the porch, passing her CJ.

"There's my big boy." Remy took the chunky baby.

Her words landed on deaf ears as Nina looked over her shoulder where she spotted Cooper getting on his horse. He rode to the field, spoke to a few people and rode away. Nina went into the house saddened.

Not long after, the front door opened. "Hey, Nina," Reah said. "Cooper sent for you to meet him at the river. He said for me to watch after Alexandria while you gone. Let me wash up first and put on a apron, so I won't get her dirty. Gotta get this grime off me."

"Thanks." Nina left out the back door, going through the woods until she made it to their private place where she found Cooper resting on a blanket with a bottle of wine, a corkscrew, and two wine glasses. She stopped. So absorbed in the moment, her feet would not let her move.

He looks so handsome. Here I am, a slave woman in slave clothes with nothing special done to my hair. And there he is in the finest of clothes, clean shaved, and he's requested me to come to be with him. Smiling, she felt special again. *Maybe he does love me. He's just in a bad situation. But he's not getting off this easily.*

From behind his back came the reason he'd gone into town weeks prior.

Tears welled in the corners of her eyes. Her thick, full lips curved up forming a smile.

Cooper held out a small box.

She closed her eyes, releasing thick tears that housed all of her pain. She had always been so in love with this man whose love had always been limited to her. Her undying love for him had caused her tremendous suffering.

When Cooper left the Hartford Plantation, they strapped Nina up, but after receiving two lashes to her back, Missis Anna Bell put a stop to it.

They tried to couple her with another man, but her faithfulness to Cooper was too strong. Resisting, she refused to have another man inside of her. "I would rather die," she told the overseer after her new husband complained.

"Force her!" the overseer ordered.

"Nina, I want you I do, but you won't have me. The overseer said to force you, but I won't do to a slave woman what white men do to them," the man said.

"'Um sorry, it ain't got nothing to do wit' you. But, I don't want nobody but Jesse."

"Death might come buh'fo he do."

"And 'um fine wit' waiting."

The next day, the overseer questioned the man. "Well, y'all started on them babies, yet?"

"Sir, I tried, but she won't have me."

The overseer sent for Nina. Her stubbornness caused them both to be beaten. But for Nina, the whip sliced over and over again. And when her clothes fell apart, the lashes continued mercilessly. Against Missis Anna Bell's protest, Massa Ordell's order was to beat her into submission, but her heart was too foolish to give in. She would rather be punished to death than betray the man who'd run off and left her without even a word and not knowing if she would ever see him again.

Now standing before him with a wrapped box in his hand that he had especially for her, she was confused.

"Nina...please take it."

What choice did she have? She was a slave. *What choice does he have? After all, he's a slave too. It's not his fault that life for us be the way it is.* She had to learn how to make the best of it. She released more tears.

"Nina, please. I'm begging you, take it."

She took a deep breath and ordered her feet to move, but her perplexed heart made her afraid. She didn't want to be a willing concubine.

Understanding her pain, Cooper went to her and slowly put his arms around her. She broke down and cried, shedding all the pain he caused when he had run off and left her, the pain she felt when watching him with Suzanna, and the pain of never having all of his love.

He squeezed her as tight as he could without causing pain. The rhythmic beats of his heart were symbolic testimony of his love for her. For the first time since crying for the loss of their son, he cried too.

Nina wrapped her arms around him, holding him while he released life's unfairness through droplets of wetness.

Life was so discriminating to their love. He hated that he couldn't be with her as he wanted to. But he was determined to let her know that he loved her more than anything in the world. Slowly releasing her, he took her hand, led her to the blanket, and never taking his eyes off her, he helped her to sit and waited patiently until she was comfortable and only then did he hold the box in front of her again.

She stared at it for a moment and with a slight smile, she took it. Her beatific expression brought him joy.

Removing the item and putting the box aside, she gazed upon its attraction and noticed the engraving. Reading it, she looked at Cooper, her eyes hypnotized by love.

"Let me have it," he said.

Giving it to him, she could barely control her excitement that was masked with confused love and pain.

Cooper held the item from its top and bottom and turning it inward, he read, "To my true wife, I love you, Jesse."

Tears fell, first from him, then from her as he slipped the ring on her finger midways and said, "With this ring, I, Jesse Cooper Edwards, take thee, Nina Edwards, to be my wedded wife. From the beginning, to now, for always." He pushed the ring in its respectful place, and there on the blanket, in the woods, by the river, secluded behind a huge rock that was hidden behind a blanket of bushes, she gave her body to her husband, Jesse Hartford, who was now Cooper Edwards. She took him, he took her, their bodies intertwined, wined, and danced and made music like never before. A brand-new song, they created.

Drenched in moistened passion, Cooper looked into her eyes. "My wife, Nina Edwards. No matter what happens this day forward, no matter what it seems like, I love you more than anything and any other...and nothing, nor anyone, will ever change that. One day, I will force the world to consent to our love. Until that time, I need you to trust me. Do you trust me?"

"I always have. Seeing how you ran...but came back for me, that taught me to trust you even when I don't know what you're planning." The moment she spoke the last word, she recalled the pain he'd left her with when he had run. She'd felt betrayed, unloved, used, and heartbroken. But those thoughts never removed her love for him. She knew what he was about to say required the same strength.

"In a few days, Suzanna and I will be going away to celebrate our anniversary." The pain that quickly grew in Nina's eyes crushed him. He rushed to explain. "It's just to ease things over. I have to—"

Nina sat up.

He pulled her arm, forcing her to face him. "I need her full trust again, Nina. I've caused her a lot of pain...pain that was no fault of her own. I know my request of your faith while seeking another woman's trust is unorthodox, but I do need you to trust me. It would burden me so if I didn't have your trust. Will you grant me that, my love?"

Nina sat there trying to grasp how she should respond. Before, she had never complained about his relationship with Suzanna. Slavery justified it and as he explained to them all, his relationship with Suzanna had allowed him to purchase them. Because of his marriage to Suzanna, she could now be with her husband, even if that meant she had to share him with another woman. But there had never been any verbal acceptance from her to him that she was comfortable with his relationship with Suzanna.

She couldn't make meaning of how she was feeling. No thoughts entered her mind whether she would or could be alright with it. She'd always tried to put his relationship with Suzanna far in the back of her mind. But now, having him to ask her to allow him to be with his wife, to make love to his wife, to be alright with the two celebrating their marriage was extremely hard for her heart to consider.

Cooper waited to hear her feelings. Good or bad, at least he would know and could help her to understand the need to go along with the idea, should she contest. But she provided him with no clue of her thoughts.

She got up. "I need to get back to the baby." She grabbed her clothes that were so simple, it took no time to put them back on.

Cooper quietly watched, searching for the right words, dumb to her thoughts, knowing she needed the space. When she began walking away, he reached over to grasp her hand but was barely able to take hold of her fingertips as she pulled away and continued walking. He wanted to go after her, but he knew her mind had settled itself, and he didn't want to know what it had settled on. "I have to make things right."

The next day, Nina stood looking out the window. With tears, she watched as Cooper and Suzanna packed up and rode away. She hadn't given him the chance to tell her that they would be leaving the very next day and the reality of it all came rushing in. And it was not that she couldn't handle it, it was that she didn't want to.

A flood of emotions tore at her like a lion that came out of nowhere with no growls to warn her of the attack that would rip her apart. Every pain he'd made her feel, every thought of not having a normal marriage from the beginning ate away any contemplation of justification.

A loud burst of pain dropped her to her knees. So much hurt, so many tears, so overwhelmed that she was not able to control the pain that abruptly awakened Alexandria. She exchanged loud cries for moans, but that did not stop the baby from crying. Too weak to stand, she tried to crawl to her room to see about her daughter, but she began hyperventilating.

When seeing Cooper and Suzanna loading up to leave, Bertha decided to check on Nina. Immediately after opening the door, she rushed to Nina, who was still on the floor trying to force out air. She sat next to her, and pulling her into her bosom, she rocked, rubbed, and hummed until Nina was quiet. Only Alexandria cries filled the house, but she would have to comfort her later.

Nina awakened in her bed. Not knowing how she'd gotten there, she went to the front room to search for her daughter. Her cries were the last thing she'd recalled. Seeing Bertha sitting on the settee watching Alexandria, who was playing on the floor, Nina remembered the pain.

"She's the sweetest thing," Bertha said of Alexandria, then let out a loud breath while getting off the settee. "Ooooh. Well, let me get back out here to this field fo' Sam come lookin' after me." Bertha started walking towards the front door.

"Bertha?"

Stopping, she turned and face Nina. "Yes, ma'am."

"I'm pregnant."

Fifty-eight

Not long after Cooper and Suzanna had returned home, he was off again on business. Before leaving, he tried to see Nina by sending messages through Bertha. Although she was nowhere near showing, her state made her ashamed. She knew it would cause him more problems, so she refused his request every time.

Waving goodbye to her husband, Suzanna went into the house feeling emboldened. Kindness, she felt, had made her too vulnerable. It had caused her to be used, taken advantage of. "I'm too strong for this and it's about time that I take my rightful place. I've been much too lenient with these people. What has it awarded me? My husband was seduced by a wench, and I receive no respect from any of the people *I own*. Things are about to change starting now! Remy?" She went into the kitchen. "I need you to get Sam from the field. Tell him to prepare the carriage. I'll need him to take me to my sister's first thing this morning."

"Yes, ma'am."

Suzanna watched as Remy stopped what she was doing and washed her hands. "I would like for him to start preparing the carriage immediately, Remy. You might want to move a little faster."

"Yes, ma'am." Remy removed her apron and rushed out the door.

"That's better." Suzanna gave a satisfied smile. "No more of that friendship thing. Everyone will take their rightful places. Everyone!"

A month later, Cooper was back from his business trip, but before he could get a day's rest, Remy was repacking his bags with fresh clothes.

"You'll have to leave immediately, darling. It's imperative that you're there not a day late. My brother-in-law has taken care of everything and said that this business venture will make us quite wealthy."

"But the farm—"

"You mustn't worry yourself about the farm. This will enrich our farm. You're so brilliant, I'm sure this is going to go greater than we can imagine. And while you are away, I'll oversee the farm. You wanted me to find something to do, this will fulfill my days perfectly. I'm really looking forward to it."

Keeping him away from the farm meant it kept him away from Nina. "It had to be her who used her beauty to seduce him." Nina was a sensual threat. Even in slave's attire, her curvy body gave sex appeal to the demeaning clothes she wore. "How could Cooper resist her? How could any man resist her bewitching beauty? She is the worst kind of female slave. One who wants a white man. And I'll be happy to grant her desires."

Suzanna sat listening to her eldest sister and her tall, handsome brother-in-law while having dinner at their home. "How does this work?"

"Slave owners sell or trade their problem female slaves to these slave owners at a very low value to get rid of them," the brother-in-law answered.

"It's also punishment for the women," the sister added.

"How is that punishment?" Suzanna asked.

The husband and wife shared a glance and smirk.

"The slave owners rape the female slaves as soon as they arrive and continue until they produced sons and daughters," her sister answered.

"Children they then sell to other owners. This buy-and-trade slave system is the way these owners finance their plantations," the brother-in-law explained.

"I have just that kind of slave."

Fifty-nine

Cooper didn't complain about Suzanna sending him to pursue new business. Although the venture set up by his brother-in-law was more of a fool's run, he used the time wisely, setting up things to spend the rest of his life with Nina. For the first time, he wanted to share his thoughts with her, but she'd denied him that. "I have to show her."

His trips were branching farther up north where he had found and purchased over a hundred acres of land with four houses on them. He also purchased the livestock and inventory needed for the land to prosper.

Cooper was still in contact with Darwell Lingston, the slave purchaser. He contracted him to purchase the rest of his family members at a fraction of the cost due to their ages and because the Hartford's was in financial trouble due to Massa Ordell's bad business practices. With most of their slaves sold to keep the plantation afloat, they desperately needed the money to survive.

Cooper met Darwell in the wilderness. Just as before, Darwell remained on the wagon while the family sat around a campfire on a cold winter's day. Cooper briefly united with his mother, stepfather, and his baby sister, May. He met his nieces and nephews and greeted Nina's and Bertha's mother with welcoming hugs. Both of Sarah's parents had passed away. He learned from Darwell ahead of time that his brother-in-law, Mark's family had been sold off.

Cooper put his family on a train for the first time in their lives and had them transported to Pennsylvania where he'd purchased the property. He taught them how to work the land, but it wasn't easy. They were either too young, too old, not strong or wise enough to work the land in his absence. With a scratching head and set to leave,

Cooper tried to leave them encouraged. "I'm not expecting perfection, just progress. Soon, I'll be returning with the rest of our family. If we all work hard, we can turn this land into something very profitable." He hired three knowledgeable black men to teach and assist them, then he left.

The train pulled into the station in Louisiana. Cooper was back in town, but he didn't go home immediately. He hired a carriage for the day, and his first stop was to see Peter, Suzanna's father.

"Does my daughter know you're making this deal behind her back?"

"I have Suzanna's best interest in mind always, Peter. I speak on behalf of us both," Cooper said while being served a glass of brandy that he had no plans to drink. He had to be sure to be in his right mind while dealing with his crooked father-in-law.

Sitting before the ailing crude businessman, he sized him up. Understanding what attracted his attention, Cooper laid out his proposition. "After your death, Suzanna will be part owner of your estate, and I have no doubt that her sisters will allow her to purchase, if not give her the three slaves without charge or at a lesser value than what you're proposing. Money that will go to them, not to you. I've always thought you to be one of the wisest investors I know. Surely your business skills have taught you when to sell. And I would guess that you would want to benefit from their sale while you are alive as opposed to after your death."

With a crossed leg, Cooper looked into the eyes of his sick father-in-law and saw a well-aged, weakened man who'd cheated death two times too many. "With a sporadic heartbeat, who knows how many more days you have left to make a wise financial decision? Sell them now while you can rejoice in the profit."

"Not at that offer."

"It's my only offer, Peter."

"Never!"

Cooper stood. "Well, I guess my business with you is over. I'll make the same offer to my sisters-in-law proceeding your death. That's if they don't give them to us at no cost as one of your daughters is in our debt."

"Sit down, sit down. I'm sure we can come to a figure that will work for both of us."

"The offer remains the same, Peter." Cooper looked at his pocket watch. "In fact, the dollars are diminishing with time, just like the ticking clock of your heart."

Peter laughed. "Sit down, man! I'm sure we can work something out."

Cooper sat in the hired carriage reaching into his satchel. He took out papers and with the daylight shining through the window, he smiled while gazing upon Peter's signature. Cooper was now the new owner of Sam, Yes'sa Man, and Remy at half the cost of his first offer. He stopped by an attorney's office before heading home to have their freedom papers drawn. He'd done everything without Suzanna's knowledge. He wanted to make sure that the law was on his side when she found out.

Needing to think, to go over all of his documents before confronting her, he didn't go home that night. Instead, he got a room in town for the night. A few months later, he was off on another trip that would be his last without his family.

‡‡‡‡‡‡

Suzanna's plans were set into motion, but there was a problem. She learned through her vindictive desires that Cooper was the only owner of the family of slaves, which gave her no ownership or authority to sell them.

"Remy, I need Sam this instant," Suzanna ordered.

"Yes, ma'am. I just put the food on. I'll—"

"You shall do it now!"

"Yes, ma'am." Remy rushed out the door.

Forceful and demanding orders had removed all niceties. The word "please" had been replaced with "now...this instant...immediately, and...you will regret it if I have to repeat it again."

Remy, Sam, and Yes'sa Man noticed that after returning from their anniversary trip, Suzanna was no longer the loving and kind woman who viewed her slaves like family members. She'd become her father's daughter, a slave owner who reveled in the role. Her hate for one woman had seeped into her heart and poisoned the entire vessel.

Some days, Suzanna would be happy, other days, she would be sad. But most days, she would be predatorial.

"Why she be like that?" Sam asked Remy one evening after Suzanna had told them that they would be eating in their cabins from that moment forward.

"She can't get over Mister Cooper being with Nina."

"So, she makes us suffer for it?"

"I suppose she'll come around. For now, we gotta do our best to not make her worse," Remy answered before they all went off to their separate bedrooms.

The next day, Yes'sa Man was on the receiving end of Suzanna's attack. "Do as I say and don't ever question me again or you'll regret it!"

Dropping his head, Yes'sa Man was still confused about the command she'd given. "Yes'sa."

"It's *yes ma'am*. I am not a man! How many times do I have to tell you that?!"

Tears welled in his eyes.

Remy waited for Suzanna to leave before taking the needed time to explain the order to Yes'sa Man. He looked up, his eyes full of water, thick teardrops fell. He'd been her victim lately, an easy target while inching closer to her real adversary.

Remy had paid close attention to Suzanna's erratic behavior of late. Her obvious metamorphosis was not only unpleasant to watch, but it was also uncomfortable to be on the receiving end of it.

One morning, while preparing lunch, Remy was cutting homemade bread. "This knife too dull. It won't even cut through water. Where's that sharpener? Oh, I let Sam use it. I bet he left it outside when he cleaned fish the other day." After laying the dull knife on the counter, she went outside and returned with the sharpener. "Sam don't ever put things back where he found them," she fussed, looking at the countertop. She frowned. "Where's the knife I just put here." She looked around. "Did he move that too? Couldn't have, I just laid it down. I know I left it here—" The worst thought came to mind.

Remy hurried to the door and pounded. "Miss Suzanna, I need you to open this door, now." Twisting the knob, it was locked. She ran out of the house, running as fast as she could, rushing up to Sam, barely able to breathe. "Miss Suzanna done locked herself in the room. I think she took a knife with her."

"You knock on the doe'?"

"Yeah, but she's not answering."

Sam raced to the house on his horse. Rushing in, he pounded on the door. "Miss Suzanna, 'dis be Sam. Open the door now." His wide-eyed stare frightened Remy, who'd finally made it in with Yes'sa Man behind her. "Move."

Remy and Yes'sa Man stepped back while Sam rammed into the door with his shoulder and belted out a painful moan.

Yes'sa Man moved him aside and collided against the door several times, forcing it open.

Passing between them, Remy rushed to Suzanna who was sitting on the floor, leaning against a wall with an empty wine bottle between her legs and the long, dull knife in her hand. She was covered in vomit.

"Come on, let's get you cleaned up. Sam, y'all come help me."

Suzanna's sluggish body was not much help; her arms dangled as if her limbs were broken from the joints. After cleaning her, Remy got Suzanna dressed and in bed.

"I hate her. I really hate her. She'll pay for the pain she's caused. I promise she'll pay with her life," Suzanna muttered before falling asleep with three sets of fearful eyes and ears that had heard her menacing promise.

Sixty

*H*er eyes were full of tears as she stared into space. *How could he betray me?* "How could he love another?" She sat on the porch searching for hope in the dark full clouds that predicted rain. And as soon as the sky's hanging fog released its fullness, so did she.

Maybe it was just a phase. A moment of pathetic weakness. She had to think that way. It was the only explanation that she could provide for what he no longer cared to hide.

Bertha's husband, Cecil, was obsessing over Suzanna and there was nothing she could do or say to sway his behavior.

Once, Bertha had been the center of Cecil's world, but now another woman had taken her place. Bertha swiped tears that continued to fall while thinking of the unfamiliar challenge. A white woman, the farm's first lady, her brother-in-law's wife, their owner had become her competition. How could she contend with such a rival?

Her face grew serious when she pondered the thought. Her tears ceased, leaving trails of dried pain. She would fight for *her* man, *her* husband, the father of *her* children. "He's mine, and she can't have 'em."

Bertha stood and looked into the skies. The clouds had no more water to offer the dry lands, and she had no more tears to lend to her pain. Trying to feel any hope that existed, her lips curved up just a little to form what looked to be a smile. She went into the house.

Going into their bedroom, Bertha laid beside Cecil, who was laying on his side, making wheezing sounds that turned into growling snores. She placed her hand on his arm and lightly stroked up and down. His caramel skin was so smooth. With every caress, she felt his muscles' definition and projected veins. *He was always so strong. And he used to love me so hard.*

Bertha loved that man with every ounce of her being. The two had been inseparable. When she started a sentence, he would finish it. He would not take a fork to his mouth until she had taken one to hers. It was as if they were joined at the hip, but now she felt like they had been amputated and the imbalance was causing her to fall apart. Her heart was splitting right down the middle, and *he don't care. Ain't no woman gone take you from me. I don't care if she white or black.*

She kissed his shoulder, slid her hand to his stomach and tugged. *I refuse to let you go.* She gripped tighter.

As the days proceeded, Bertha worked towards the unfair challenge, and Cecil provided her much practice for the fight of her life. Since the entire family's position leaned towards Cooper, Cecil was alone in his vendetta. Bertha felt sorry for him. *I gotta be on his side, no matter what.*

Cecil stood another night in the front room arguing with his family. "Y'all be a fool. Cooper don't love nobody but he'self. Look how he treats Miss Suzanna. A good woman like 'dat d'serves better."

"Cecil, let it go. Cooper treats us good. I never thought I'd see good days like these until he gets us," Thomas argued.

"He got us, so we can slave his fields, Thomas. That not be a good thing, he using us."

"Here we go again. Yeah, Cecil, Cooper, our brother treats us like we his slave and makes us work his fields. But what else he do? He makes us live in this big house. Us all have bedrooms and beds to rest on at night. Shame on Cooper for making sure our bellies stay full. That man makes us work to help get our freedom. Yeah, I can understand why you gotta problem wit' that. We had less wit' Massa Hartford and I ain't never hear you complain and freedom be nowhere in sight."

"Massa Hartford ain't our brother."

"And our brother didn't have to get us. We thought maybe he be dead. We wouldn't've ever known until he came back to get us," Jalean said.

Bertha listened to the exchange, wondering when or if she should intervene on his behalf. What could she say? Everything in her told her that Cecil was dead wrong.

"If you hate it so much, then go back to the Hartford Plantation. I bet you'll miss Cooper then," Micah suggested.

Say something now, Bertha. "Cecil, baby, it be alright—"

"Y'all notice how Cooper don't work the fields no mo'? He too good now. And Miss Suzanna used to help us, but he don't want her helping cause he know how she be treating me."

He'd cut Bertha off and said something that left her with no defense for him. She never used the word hate. Even as a slave at the cruelty of her Massa's anger, she'd never even pondered on the word. But there it was, right there in her mind and heart as she listened to her husband argued the rights of another woman. She lost her interest to defend him. Any thoughts or signs of sympathy were removed as she considered him loving Suzanna, a woman who would never allow Cecil's "filthy hands" to touch her skin.

Sixty-one

As soon as Cooper went away on another business trip, Suzanna returned to work. And each day, her presence in the field pushed Bertha's and Cecil's relationship further into the past.

"Look how she lookin' at me. She wants me to know how weak my man is for her," Bertha whispered to herself.

Suzanna looked at Bertha and the others and then turned to Cecil. "Cecil, can you help me with this?"

Cecil dropped his tool and rushed over to her, *glad to be her little pet.*

Bertha was burning up inside. *It ain't a'nuff that the white man force his'self on black women, now this white woman's playing man husband like a fool.*

Bertha used to look forward to leaving the field on the days Suzanna worked. The evenings provided an escape from Cecil's wretched behavior towards Suzanna. And every now and then, he would act like a husband, reminding her that he still loved her. Giving her hope that they would survive the Suzanna storm. But lately, the storm had turned into a five-category hurricane that had just reached the already sinking island that their marriage rested upon.

Cecil had begun sneaking out of the house in the late of night.

"Where he gone?"

Cooper was away, he didn't like the helpers, and all the family members lived in the cabin with them. And at that time of night, most of them had retired to their rooms. His whereabouts made no sense to Bertha, who woke up and found her husband missing from their bed.

"She said she wouldn't let a slave put his 'filthy hands' on her. But she is lonely these days. Cecil can be charming." He was a very handsome man.

Back on the Hartford's Plantation, he could've had any slave he wanted. But Bertha's personality was far more attractive than any other woman's body or face. And that's what he loved about her. Instead of considering her fat, to him, she was soft and cuddly. *Where's that old Cecil,* she pondered.

Bertha's thoughts were working overtime, only taking breaks when she was asleep. Always incorporating new thoughts about Suzanna's behavior towards her husband. Wondering if Suzanna had given way to her game of tease, especially since Cooper was away on business. Perhaps she had sent him away, so she could be with Cecil. There was that possibility. Just as he'd tried to send her away to be with her family, so he could be with Nina, maybe she'd sent him away, so she could be with Cecil.

Bertha looked at the empty spot on their bed and wondered whether Cecil was filling the empty spot on Suzanna's bed.

Sixty-two

Cecil was beside himself. There he was, a slave, getting the attention of the white woman who owned him. She wanted him and he knew it. But he understood why they couldn't be together. It was an abomination for a white woman to be with a slave.

He wondered if he told her that she had already been with a slave, would she realize that they were no different from a white man when it came to pleasing a woman, perhaps even better.

He envisioned the two of them sneaking away for private, intimate rendezvous where their two bodies would become one. He craved her and was not able to conceal it. At first, he shrugged it off when Bertha accused him of having feelings for Suzanna.

"No! You crazy! 'Um'ma slave. Ain't no sense in wanting a white woman that owns me. I got no interest in nobody who considers me as they property."

Now, he didn't care who knew. The most exciting part of his days was when she'd call for him to do things for her when she was in the field.

"Cecil, can you help me with this?"

Sure, she looks around to see if anybody notice her feelings for me. She don't want them knowing that she wants me. But that's all changing. The more she calls for my help, the more she becomes the victim of my charm. Let me go see what she wants.

Cecil dropped his tool and rushed over to help Suzanna. He touched the lower part of her back while trying to teach her to use the tool. "Turn this way. Hold it like this to get a good grip. Now put your foot right here." Making her face him, he wanted to draw her in with his mesmerizing hazel eyes. Sweat traveled down his gorgeous caramel skin onto his chest, giving a vision of the spectacular specimen that was beneath his shirt. He knew he was handsome. Bertha and other slaves had always told him that. *How can she resist me?*

She bold too. She don't care who knows she wants me. The thought made him feel special, free to lavish his attention on her regardless of his wife's sad eyes. *And she likes it too. Seeks any reason to get it.*

Face to face, they locked eyes and he smiled. She returned the gesture before looking down at the tool.

"So, I hold it like this?" She leaned over, showing cleavage that he took a peek of.

She knows what she's doing. "Yeah, like that." *Look at her, all ripe and ready. I bet she full of sweet juices too.*

When the days ended, so did Cecil's time with Suzanna. He pressed the hours to bring on the next days. Some went without Suzanna in the field. It was getting hard to not be in her presence. He'd gotten addicted to their teasing each other, touching each other.

One day went by, and there was no Suzanna. A second day and still no Suzanna.

Cecil was going crazy, finding reasons to argue with his family about Cooper. Every little thing Bertha did seem to get on his nerves. Anything he could do to get out of the house, even if it involved hurting and angering others, he did it and always left a slamming door behind.

Bertha climbed into bed one night and while rubbing him, she accidentally awakened him. Wrapping her arm around his stomach, she tugged him close to her. His eyes swung open, his mind became full, his desires flared, making him want Suzanna. He waited until Bertha fell asleep and left. "I gotta see her," he mumbled while walking outside in the dark like an addict in search of a fix.

Standing in the dark against a wall next to her opened window, Cecil watched as Suzanna undressed. Dropping her dress, she stepped out of it and eased into the tub one leg at a time. Leaning back, her nipples pointed upward as she closed her eyes enjoying the nice warm water. Dipping the sponge in, her body shined from the oil Remy had added. His view of her body was limited until she stood, her nude body in full view as she stepped out of the tub and dried off before slipping into her gown.

"Red hair," he whispered. He heard a door close. Considering the time, he thought, *must be Remy*. He crept around the front of the house and waited until she was completely out of sight. Easing back to the window, the lantern had been put out, he couldn't see anything, so he listened until she snored. Walking away, he could not release his mind from what he'd seen. Her naked body, pubic hair, nipples, he smiled. The visual seduction became the first of many nights that he would slip away to enjoy. He wondered if he would ever get up enough courage to go in her room from the window and *give her what I know she wants.*

For now, it be a thought. But one day, it'll be me and her.

Sixty-three

*H*atred had become her vice and alcohol her instigator. More and more, Suzanna consumed large amounts of it. But there had to be another way to free herself of its magnetic addiction and the emotional turmoil that lured her to the wine bottle's obsessive grip.

Often left alone, she was easily drawn to the toxic liquid. Snatching it from the wine cabinet, she filled herself with it until she was left holding an empty bottle that blessed her hate. Unhealthy thoughts were getting out of control and turning her against the wrong people. Remy, Sam, and Yes'sa Man, who ate and worked with her, had become the victims of what fueled her misguided pain.

She recognized her wrongdoings and tried to cleanse herself of both the alcohol and the hatred. She needed to silence the demon who daily whispered new ideas of vengeance. Work was needed. *It will take me away from this loneliness.* But after learning that she'd returned to the field, Cooper forbade her to ever do so again. However, she needed work to occupy her idle mind. To rid her of the spells of anger that possessed it.

One evening while sitting at the breakfast nook pouring another glass of wine, the feelings of uselessness and boredom hyped up her pain with thoughts of death and betrayal. The memories gave her all the reasons she needed to self-medicate herself with alcohol until she reached an intoxicated numbness.

Suzanna looked out the window at her thriving farm. Since meeting Cooper, her land had gained such prosperity. And after marrying him, life had seemed so promising. She had never imagined the pain that would follow. "Life was so much better when I was poor. I guess you have to pay with pain to be wealthy. Isn't that right, mother? Here's to you, me and the slave-loving men we married." She raised her glass, toasting to the air, spilling wine. "I suppose I'll give the field another try tomorrow."

Early the next morning, Suzanna dressed for work and headed to the field. Her presence caught the attention of Micah, who nodded for his wife Sarah to take notice. John, Reah's son pointed, getting his mother's attention. Reah quickly glanced over and turned back to her son. "Get back to work."

Her fussing got the attention of Jalean and her husband, Mark and her twin brother, Thomas. When they stopped working to turn around and look, Sam shifted in the direction of their stares and saw Suzanna as soon as she entered the field dragging a new tool behind her. Bertha had already noticed Suzanna, but her attention was on her husband, Cecil, who was smiling.

Suzanna examined the tool she'd grabbed from the barn. She'd never used it before. She looked around to see who else had the same tool. Bertha had one similar. *Should I ask her for help?* She turned to the others. *No one else has a comparable tool.* She turned back to Bertha to ask for help but noticed that Cecil had the exact same tool.

"Cecil, can you help me with this?"

Cecil dropped what he was doing and rushed to aid her.

"This thing is new. I don't have the faintest idea how to use it."

"I'll show you." He tried to tell her how to use the tool, but she was still confused.

"Show me what you're talking about. Which way do I turn to hold it properly?"

He shifted his body in the direction that she should turn, and with his hands, he explained, "Hold it like this."

"I...I still don't understand. Put my foot and hand in the positions that they should go. Physical teaching works best for me." It's how she'd taught Yes'sa Man in the past.

Cecil smiled inside. He'd been given permission to touch a white woman. He went for her back but had to move lower, almost touching her butt to put her in the right position. He stepped in front of her to position her hands on the tool. She looked directly into his eyes. *Their hazel, like Cooper's.*

Every motion he made showed his masculine frame. *Wow, what a physique. Slave men are usually so strong. I suppose he was forced to marry Bertha. She's plump and he's handsome. They are so physically unequal.*

"Put your hand here."

"Oh, okay. Right here?"

"Yeah."

"So, I hold it like this?"

"Yeah, like that. Now, swing."

"Ugh! I still can't get it." Although instructed, Suzanna found it difficult to use the new tool. It was discouraging. Standing right beside him, she dropped the tool and walked off the field. No explaining why she'd given up so abruptly. She lost any interest in ever returning.

⁜⁜⁜

A few evenings later, Remy laid CJ in his bed and checked the house to make sure everything was taken care of before leaving. She went to Suzanna's bedroom door. "I'm leaving, Miss Suzanna." She didn't wait for a response. They had become non-existent lately, and Remy didn't expect that evening to be any different as she closed the back door behind her and headed home. "Something's coming. Something really bad is coming." She shook her head while walking across the lawn dwelling on the strange feeling she had.

She'd been paying close attention to Suzanna after a meeting she had with her brother-in-law a week prior. Remy couldn't make out their entire conversation, but what she heard concerned her.

"I'll need one who can nurse CJ." Suzanna made sure that her order was completely understood. "An unattractive girl. A thick one if possible."

"Oh, I'm sure that won't be a problem. The slave wenches on his little camp are often knocked up or have recently given birth to one of his bastards, and he's god-awful hideous," her brother-in-law said.

"So, how soon can this be arranged?"

"Immediately. I can take care of it in a day's time. Do you have her ownership papers?"

"Ownership papers?"

"Yes. All I need you to do is sign over her ownership to him, and he'll do the same with the replacement."

"Yes, about that. Cooper stored all of our documents away, you know, in case of a house fire, or God forbid, a tragedy like the one that took the life of my first husband, God rest his soul. I would have to wait for Cooper's return to gain access to the documents, but I was hoping that we could have this done before his return. Something like a trade agreement. Is that at all possible?"

"I see," he said suspiciously. "I don't see why that should be a problem. Many wives have found themselves in your predicament. Meet me in town later this week. I'll have all the necessary documents ready and in a week's time, your problem will no longer exist."

Suzanna smiled. "Wonderful. That's absolutely wonderful." She refilled their empty wine glasses. The two raised them and drank to their business deal.

"Now, if you will just compensate me for my time, I'll be on my way."

"Come again. Compensate you?"

"Yes. Why, Suzanna, there is a lot of work involved to carry out your will. Surely you do not expect me to take time away from my business to handle yours without being financially rewarded for my work and sacrifice, do you? Of course, you wouldn't."

He still owed them for the money she'd lent them a few years prior, but she didn't bring that up. "Of course, not." She smiled.

Remy was around the corner from the dining room where they sat, taking in bits and pieces of the conversation.

"Expect to see him this coming Saturday," her brother-in-law said after being paid.

"Wonderful. I will anticipate his arrival."

Saturday morning, Suzanna awakened after only getting a few hours of sleep. Within hours, she would be ridding herself of one problem that would surely bring on many to follow. She deliberated, second-guessed herself, talked herself out of it, then back in, and finally settled on the authority that belonged to her.

Angered by deceit and the discovery of Cooper's deeds while initiating her own, she felt justified. "It will be for the best for all of us. He'll see in time. Temporary sorrow for a lifetime of happiness shall follow."

She got out of bed, walked over to the breakfast table and picked up the wine bottle, she finished off the remnants left from the night before. Sitting the empty bottle back on the table, she stared out the window.

In the depths of her eyes was a vision of no return.

Sixty-four

*T*he day had just begun, but before the sun could rise, the heat had already begun walking to and fro upon the earth. There was not a wind blowing to be felt. Dirt laid still, not even a speck of grain lifted from the ground except in the fields where weeds were pulled and seeds planted by those who labored. Mules pulled wagons and sweat was wiped off faces.

The field hands momentarily ceased working to follow the sound of rolling wheels from a creeping wagon traveling on the dirt path to the house. An old white man sat tilted on the driver's seat.

Suzanna rushed out of the house to meet the man as the wagon came to a halt. After a brief conversation, she took a few steps back and waited for him to step down.

Getting off the wagon, the man went to the back, tugged the arms of a young chubby black girl, and her body flopped onto the ground. She didn't bother to dust the dirt from the side of her face, ear, hair or clothes as she struggled to stand. Taking a rope from the wagon, the man followed Suzanna to the family's cabin with the plump girl trailing behind them.

The family consumed themselves with work. No need to worry about what Suzanna was doing. She'd been acting strange lately. Her erratic behavior was of no concern of theirs. The chubby girl had to be a newly purchased slave, they assumed. Perhaps to take Nina's place, so she could return to the field. Suzanna's grudge for her had not ended. It was no surprise to them that she would be replaced and sent to the field while Cooper was away.

Not long after entering the family's cabin, they heard howling and screams. They all stopped and turned in the direction of the cabin when its door flew open.

The old man exited the cabin dragging Nina behind him. Her hands pressed together, tied with a rope. Her hair was mingled, blood spewed down her face from a blow to her head. She fought, kicked, screamed, and cried, but nothing stopped her from being dragged, yanked, and pulled.

Gearing up his horse, Sam jumped on and rode to the scene ignoring his pains. "What's going on?" He got off the horse.

"You mine yo' business, nigga!" the old man ordered.

"Miss Suzanna, what—"

"Get back to the field! This is of no concern to you," Suzanna said.

"But what about Mister Cooper? He won't be happy 'bout 'dis."

Suzanna turned to Sam with a stiff face. "I own this farm, these slaves and you! It's my money, my land, my rules and don't you ever forget it."

Not knowing what to do, Sam walked away pulling his horse.

"Sam!" she called out.

He turned to face her.

"Don't you ever question me again, or I will hire a real overseer and have you beaten."

Sam looked into her eyes and saw a woman he didn't recognize. "Yes'sum." He walked away as the devastation of Nina's cries continued to sadden his ears and anger him.

Scuffled trails led to the wagon. Like a wild animal fighting against being caged, Nina fought to be free, begging for the help she knew would not come from the slave mentality of the others who were as helpless as she was.

The old man yanked the rope that restrained Nina to him. He tried to grab and toss her on the wagon, but she hit him. A hard punch to her face knocked her to the ground where he stomped her until she was motionless.

Tugging the rope, he dragged her closer to the wagon, lifted her limp body and with a loud grunt, slung her in the back. He climbed in, cuffed her to chains, and a moment later, the wheels of the wagon creaked, tossing dirt into the wind that twirled around like a storm, demonstrating the chaotic tale of what was left behind.

Remy, who'd been watching from a window of the main house, rushed back into the kitchen when she saw Suzanna headed her way.

"Remy! We have a new girl. She'll be taking Nina's place. See to it that she's cleaned and settled in."

"Yes, ma'am. What about the babies?"

Her question told that she'd seen Nina leave without her daughter. "She's a nursing mother who just gave birth a couple of weeks ago. Now, go. CJ will need to be fed soon."

"Yes, ma'am." Remy went to the family's cabin.

The young girl quickly stood with a lowered head.

Looking her over, it was obvious that her breasts were full of milk. The arrangement had been made; she would nurse CJ and Alexandria and Nina would nurse her newborn that she had been forced to leave behind.

As Remy helped clean her up, she noticed how chunky the short girl was. Her looks were the total opposite of Nina's. Remy recalled what she'd overheard Suzanna say to her brother-in-law. "An unattractive girl. A thick one if possible."

"Oh," Remy thought out loud.

"What?" the girl asked.

"Nothing, child, just mumbling to myself." *That's why she chose her, so Mister Cooper won't be attracted to her.* "Turn your head this way," Remy instructed while combing the girl's wild hair.

"Ouch!"

"Sorry, but I gotta get you fixed up. Can't have you scaring the babies with this wild hair."

The next day, Remy confronted Suzanna, even after Sam had made her aware of her threat to him. "But, Miss Suzanna—"

"No, Remy. Mister Cooper hasn't been honest with me. I've learned that he's been very deceitful. He went behind my back and purchased the family of slaves with him being the only owner."

"If that's so, how did you sell Nina without ownership?"

"She was a trade. One nursing mother for another. There are no ownership papers required for such a transaction," she lied. "Now, go draw my water. I want to take a nice hot bath."

"Yes, ma'am." *There's no way this will be alright with Mister Cooper.*

Sixty-five

*A*fter signing the business contract, a stern handshake and laughter finalized the business deal. Cooper Edwards was now an investment partner. On his way to becoming a very wealthy man. It was time to return home to retrieve his family, but first, he headed up north to take care of some planned business and meet with his ma and pa.

"When I return this time, I will bring the entire family with me," he told his parents.

"I can't wait to see my childrun." His mother cried and fell into her husband's chest. He wrapped his arm around her back and pulled her in. She was still so pretty despite the years of slavery that had aged her well beyond her years.

"I'm sure proud of you, son," his stepfather said. He'd been chosen especially for Cooper's mother to darken the color of her children's skin, but the white man's blood still seeped through. Although their skin was either medium tan or caramel, they all had their mother's hazel eyes and dark wavy hair.

"The life you made for yo'self and not forgetting yo' family, God gone surely bless you for that." His stepfather reached out his hand.

Cooper gripped it tightly and shook.

He smirked. "And I be glad when the family comes too, we needs they help real bad. You done bought all this property. We gotta make it prosper, just like you want. I been working it hard, us and the men you hired. Can't let you down, son."

"I know, Pa. But it's our family business, not mine alone."

A hug to his mother and another handshake to his stepdad and Cooper left his family, headed for the city a few miles away. Walking out of an attorney's office after finalizing a purchase, Cooper was the brand-new owner of a huge home that set on twenty acres of land and had a corner general store. A gift for Nina.

Headed back home, he sat on the train in route to face his greatest and latest challenge that was less than an hour away. The very thought gave him anxiety. Leaving with his family wasn't going to be as simple as loading them up and riding off into the sunset. And the hope of a peaceful transition did not preside in his mind. Because Suzanna was no longer that docile, humble woman she had been when they first met. She was now mad as hell.

Cooper rested his head on the wall as the train drew him nearer to home. He recalled meeting Suzanna, making love to her for the first time, their marriage, his son. Had he not gotten his family, their life may have been perfect, at least for her. He knew his heart would have always longed for its true love, making his dream life with Suzanna a big lie.

She deserves the love I am no longer able to give her. Words he planned to tell her, *perhaps start with. Despite all that has recently happened, she'd been good to me.*

He had no plans for leaving her life in ruins. While away, he used his own money to order more slaves with her as the owner to replace his family. It was their account that he used to purchase more inventory that was scheduled to be delivered the day after their departure. He'd planned to stop into town before going to the farm to have his name removed from their estate and accounts and to open a bank account for his son.

Maybe I should tell her what I have done before explaining what I'm about to do. Perhaps that would be a more acceptable approach. He constantly thought of ways to soften the blow, but no matter what came to mind, the outcome would be the same. He was leaving with his family, *and she is going to be very angry about it.*

Cooper had committed adultery and fathered a child with a slave woman, but leaving Suzanna would be the ultimate betrayal. And he had no idea how she would handle it. However, he was about to be on the receiving end of a valuable lesson. The prediction of pain, tears and heated words, even a physical attack was inevitable with every thought.

Prior to his unfaithfulness, Suzanna's words had always been kind, sprinkled with *dear heart, my love, my husband*. Now her words had turned into vices that cut deep and left bleeding wounds that started on the first day of their anniversary get-away and never ended.

"You would be nothing without me...
I made you...
I financed your skills...
The only thing you had was a poor man's ability to run nothing...
I afforded you the land and substance to refine your skills...
You were a bum when I met you!"

"You're right, dear, I made a terrible mess of things. I wish to make it up to you in any way I can," he would often offer in various ways.

But Suzanna had become a woman controlled by anger. She harvested malevolence that was perhaps born from years of seeing her father betray her mother and what lead to her death. No matter what Cooper said or did, he was due to pay for the true root of her anger, her father's sins.

Feeling that he deserved all the pain he'd made her feel, he put up with the abuse, but there was something about haranguing him that fed her worst impulses.

He realized that the more he apologized and begged for her forgiveness, the more he was feeding her need to victimize him. She became hateful, trying to break him in every way. He'd combated her brutal assaults with kindness, accountability, and humility until she finally found the words that tore at his soul.

"When I met you, you had nothing but the clothes on your back. I clothed, fed, and housed you. You were no more than a slave in need of an owner. And you chose to run away from my kindness and bed a wench. You chose a nigger over me! You are unworthy of the life I've given you. If you want to remain in my house, in my bed, you will treat me as your master. You will do as I say, when I say so, and however I tell you to do it. You will become my white nigger!"

Who knew those words would ever come from such a kind-hearted person? You never really know someone until they are broken. Although they are put back together, they will never be the same again. And she wasn't.

The thought of her words came to an end as the train stopped. Before going home, he stopped by the attorney's office and the bank. He signed documents, picked up others, and went over the maps and instructions he'd created to give to his family. He left nothing to chance. Everything was planned down to the very last minute and included a plan A, B, and C.

Over the last few months, he'd cautiously routed their trip from one location to the next. Traveling by wagon, then train, meeting people who he had put in place to assist his family in case he could not be with them. Friends of Darwell Lingston.

"Now, all I have to do is figure out what to say to Suzanna." He needed to think of something fast because the farm was just ahead.

The slaves were in the field when the wagon pulled up. The driver of the wagon who was well in age slowly got off and helped Cooper with his bags.

Sam left the field the moment he saw Cooper, in a hurry to meet him before Suzanna did. "Mister Cooper—"

The front door opened. Suzanna stepped onto the porch. "Cooper, darling."

Sam looked over at her, then back at Cooper, he walked faster. "Mister Cooper. I sure be glad you back, sar'. Let me help you with your bags. I gots a lot to tell ya'. I was hoping I could speak to ya' buh'fo you go into the house."

"Sam, I'm quite tired from my trip. Can this wait?"

"No, sar'. It be mighty important that I speaks to you now."

Suzanna plunged into Cooper's arms, forcing a hug in return. "It's wonderful to have you back home. I have Remy preparing you a wonderful meal. You'll need it to work up an appetite before dessert," she teased.

"Sam, this will need to wait. I promise to see you later."

"But, sar', I needs to speak with you now."

"Sam, my husband just returned home. It's husband and wife time now. Take the luggage in the house and get back to the fields this instant."

Sam looked at her, then at Cooper who slightly nodded. Lifting the luggage, he carried Cooper's things in the house. Suzanna and Cooper followed. Sam stopped, looking puzzled. "Where you want 'dees."

Suzanna pointed, "You can leave them there."

He set the luggage in the front room and headed towards the front door.

"Sam, the back door, like servants do. It's the door you shall use from this moment forward."

Sam headed for the back door with a hung head.

"Sam...do you understand?"

Sam dared her with a stare. "Yes'sum!" He left.

Suzanna quickly turned to Cooper and went for his lips, but he turned his head, causing her lips to land on his cheek.

"What's wrong?"

"Just tired. It was an awfully long trip." He started to smile but quickly dropped it. He didn't feel like faking a smile.

Sensing his coldness, Suzanna wanted to demand an explanation, but under the circumstances, her dirty deeds humbled her. She tucked her arm in his and led him to the settee. "So, did you bring us any presents? Oh, pardon me, I'm getting ahead of you. I guess I'm just excited to have you home. How was your business trip? Did things go well?"

Cooper stopped walking. He was not in the mood for idle conversation that had nothing to do with his agenda.

Realizing his resistance, Suzanna sought to control his thoughts by asking more questions. "Tell me about all the money we are going to make?"

She sat on the settee and tugged his hand.

Raising an eyebrow, Cooper scratched his forehead and sat beside her. "So, what has happened during my absence?"

"Are you referring to Sam's business with you? Who knows what's on his mind?"

"I wasn't inquiring about Sam's thoughts. I was asking about the farm."

"Oh, the farm." She was relieved. "Nothing new, it's always the same."

He stood.

"Where are you going?"

"To see CJ."

She patted the settee. "You have plenty of time to see your son. Come on, sit, I want to hear all about your trip."

Although CJ wasn't quite a year old and not mature enough to understand, Cooper had things he wanted to say to him. He wanted to spend time with his son before leaving. He could only hope that he would see him again. The thought of leaving him behind was his biggest regret. He'd written a well-detailed letter to leave with Remy to give to him when he became of age. "Come and find me, I would love to see the man you've become in my absence" were words he'd included, along with his address.

"Your wife desires your company on the settee, husband."

Oh, now I'm your husband. Prior to leaving, I was your slave. He pushed the thoughts of her brutal words aside. It would only make his explanation to her more challenging to speak calmly. "Suzanna, I really want to see my son. Is he being nursed?"

*Nursed! The nerve of him. He'll use any excuse to see her. I'm terribly happy for ridding you of that cunt. I traded your sex whore for a fat wench. She wanted a white man. I granted her wishes! Now she's **his** sex whore!* She thought with a smirk on her face. "My, darling husband, you're home from what turned out to be almost a ten-month business trip. I missed you dearly. I want to be with you." Still holding his hand, she stood and met him face to face. A moist wet kiss on his neck led the way of her words. "My..." mwah, "body..." mwah, "is craving..." mwah, "you." She moved his hand to the spot between her legs and looked at him with lowered seducing eyes, "...it wants you, too. It's been missing you terribly."

Looking at her, he had to make a decision. Something was wrong, he knew it. *Possibly the reason for Sam's urgency.* But he had to keep her defused. He took her in his arms and gave her a long moist kiss that made her tingle all over.

She tore away at his clothes.

He smiled and grabbed her arms. "I will please you until the sun comes up, but only after I've seen CJ."

"You will see him later. Right now, you should only be thinking of your wife. I want you something bad." She took hold of his arms and wrapped them around her waist.

"Not now, Suzanna, I really would like to—"

"Bed your wife." Taking his hand, she pulled, leading the way to the bedroom.

He wondered if he gave her what she wanted, would she return the favor by allowing them to leave without reproach. He could only hope while allowing her to guide him into the bedroom where he made her shiver in pleasure.

Full of sweat, Cooper fell over onto his back. "I'm famished."

Suzanna rolled over onto her stomach and looked at her husband with a satisfying grin. "You just rest, I'll see if Remy has prepared dinner."

When she returned, she found Cooper getting dressed. Quickly placing two plates of food on the breakfast table, she rushed to him. "What are you doing?" She grabbed hold of his suspenders to stop him from tightening them.

He took hold of her wrists.

"Mister Edwards, you said you were famished. Now, come and eat." She stepped aside to allow him to walk to the table.

Cooper sighed and sat at the table. He picked up a napkin, fanned it, and tucked it in his collar. "Suzanna—"

"No...let me go first. I know I wasn't that polite to be around before your departure. It's just—"

"I know, Suzanna. I'm so sorry for the pain I caused."

"I know. It's just so hard to get over it. I keep seeing you and her lying in bed. Your arm wrapped around her nude *black* body." She closed her eyes and sighed. "Maybe I wasn't enough for you. Maybe...I don't know...I guess you needed more." She looked into his eyes. "I can be just as pleasing in bed."

"Suzanna, let's not do this. I've apologized. I've begged for your forgiveness. It's not your fault. It was me, not you, nor her."

Tears rolled down her face.

He wanted to get up and comfort her, but he'd already made love to her and didn't want to complicate her emotions further. He caressed her hand that was on the table. "I'm sorry. I'm so very sorry for any pain I've caused or will ever cause you. Suzanna, look at me."

She gave her attention.

"Time has a way of healing anything. I need you to understand that. Now, let's clear the table."

"Remy will take care of that." She grabbed his hand. Her hand landing near the steak knife, drawing his attention.

He dabbed his mouth with the napkin. "The food was great as always. I missed Remy's cooking. Now, it's time to visit my namesake. Is he being nursed?"

"Upon expectation of your return, I made arrangements for him to spend the night. So, yes, he's probably being nursed at this very moment."

He stood again. "Well, let me go and—"

A door knocked curtailed his words.

"Come in," Suzanna rushed to answer. "Sit. We have other things to discuss."

Cooper was getting impatient, but he sat without a fuss.

"Welcome back, Mister Cooper."

"Thank you, Remy."

There's no tellin' if he knows about Nina yet. Let me hurry up and get out of these white folk's way before—"

"Remy, do you know if CJ is being nursed?"

She'd helped Nina train the babies' feeding and nap times and had passed their schedules onto the new girl, so she spoke with knowledge. "Yes." Remy continued clearing the table.

"There, you see. I told you."

"Can you pick him up from Nina the moment he's done?"

Remy side-eyed Suzanna. *So, she hasn't told him. Now, I'm involved. If I answer "yes," he'll know I lied to him.*

"Will you please allow Remy to do her job?"

"Remy? Is CJ with Nina?"

"Um..."

"Why are you harassing her?" Suzanna turned to Remy. "You may leave, Remy. Forgive my loving husband. He's in a hurry to see his son, but it can wait. Now run along, dear."

Remy was pleased to *run along* and hurried to close the door behind her.

Cooper stared at his wife. "Suzanna, is my son alright?"

"Of course, he is. I only want to spend time with my husband. Is that so horrible?"

He remained as composed as possible. "Suzanna, what is going on? It's obvious that you are keeping something from me, and I will no longer allow you to conceal the matter. Now, please tell me what it is? And I will not have you continue to stall."

Prior to him going away on business, Suzanna had the upper hand. She knew her answer to him might take away her strength, but no matter what she'd done, she refused to lose her authority. She sat up straight and locked eyes with him. "Some changes had to be made."

"Changes? What sort of changes?"

"After your departure—ahem..." She hoped that clearing her throat would remove the trembles in her voice. "...a slave became quite unruly, and I could no longer bear it. Their behavior became so threatening that I feared for my life. It was in my authority to make a very important decision. I had to...I had to do what was best for me."

"What did you do, Suzanna?"

Her hands went out front; laying them on the table, she fondled her fingers. The authority she had tried to marry left her standing at the altar. She stared at her fingers. "Ahem..." She took a deep swallow. "I got rid of that slave."

Cooper leaned back. Her face eclipsed the room. He tried to make sense of her words. He knew she had no ownership of his family members and that without ownership, she could not sell any of them. But that also meant if she had "got rid of" one of them, she'd learned that he owned them and that he'd deceived her. He didn't concern himself with whether she knew, he wanted to know what she meant by "got rid of." "Cecil...you got rid of my bro-" Feelings of anger prevailed over his every word, influencing him to speak without thinking. "You got rid of Cecil...without my permission?"

"No."

"I don't understand. You said you got rid of Cecil. Now you're telling me that you didn't get rid of him. Which is it, Suzanna? Did you get rid of Cecil or not?"

"No, I didn't get rid of Cecil."

He rested his arms on the table. Gripping his hands together, he looked at her. No words, no facial expression that offered a hint of what he was thinking. Leaning forward, he brought his gripped hands to his mouth. Fighting for calmness was a challenge that he was quickly losing as veins popped out of his temples. He had to release the anger, for her sake, he had to. Keeping the same position, he slumped his shoulders to relax. "Suzanna...who did you get rid of?" he calmly asked but knew. Still, he needed to hear it but didn't want to. He didn't know how he would respond to her saying—

"Nina."

He dropped his arms on the table and sat up while questioning if he heard her correctly and answering his own thought out loud. "No." Quick side to side head shakes kept him in denial. He tried to smile to calm himself, but his tightened lips refused to turn up. "What did you say?!"

Frightened, Suzanna knew better to not repeat the name. Her water-filled eyes saw fury from across the table that froze her still.

Filled with enraged intensity, Cooper popped up, grabbed the breakfast table and slug it out the window, shattering the glass.

Jerking back, Suzanna stabilized her tilting chair.

Cooper walked over to her, the fullness of his stature encompassing her. Trembling, she looked up as he looked down on her. Forming a fist, his breathing inflated his need to punch her. In seconds, his hand was around her neck, restricting it like a python squeezing its prey.

Tighter and tighter, refusing to let go, a grip so inflated that it lifted her from the chair.

Burgundy-faced, Suzanna fought for air, her watery red eyes had reached their limit of growth. The pain was excruciating. The restricted grip left her limp. Staring into her glassy eyes, he saw Suzanna, the mother of his child. His sanity returned just before her eyes closed shut. He released and her weakened body landed on the chair that had fallen over.

She grabbed her throat and coughed, gasping for air, crying in between, while making it to her knees.

Although his hand was no longer gripping her, fury refused to let him go. He took steps back and stared at her. Face flaming red, tight-lipped, anger-eyes with hate in his heart, he turned, walked to the door, and slammed it behind him to avoid the unthinkable.

The large breakfast table thrown through the window had caught the attention of the slaves working in the field. They stood looking and listening for any other turmoil and finding the noise's clue when Cooper stormed out of the house. His every step raged against the dirt road as he pounded the ground, headed for the family's cabin. Crossing the dirt road, he yanked the door opened the moment he stepped onto the porch. "Who are you?"

"I Rosa, sar'." She stood, looking at the tall, handsome white man who was the complete opposite of her former owner.

"Rosa?"

"Yes, sar'. I been bought here as the nursemaid fo' the youngins."

"Where's Nina?"

"My massa, he trade her fo' me."

"Who's your massa and where is he?"

The chubby slave girl spoke away like an unstoppable chatterbox. Explaining what kind of "Massa" the man was. Telling why he only purchased female slaves. "He sells us for a profit to other slave owners. We don't like it dough, sar'. I glad to be gone. The others, 'dey say you won't force me like he did. 'Dey, say you a good massa. Nothing like him. I sorry to tell you, sar', but as soon as he gets Nina on his plantation, he gone rape her and give her a baby. And if she try to fight back, he'll beat her. If she keeps fighting back, he'll cut her."

"What's the name of the plantation?"

As soon as the name left her lips, Cooper was gone, rushing to his horse. Rapidly saddling it, he sped off.

Sixty-six

The sound of the broken glass infuriated him and learning where it came from made it hard to concentrate on work that entire day. Cecil dragged his tool over to Sam. "What was that?"

Nina was gone, Suzanna had gotten rid of her, Sam suspected that Cooper had just learned about it and figured he was taking his anger out on whatever had gone through the window. No need to panic, Remy would come and get him if things got out of control. "White man's business. Ain't no concern of ours. We gotta mind 'dis here field. Massa Cooper gots contracts to fill. Go on now, get back to work."

Cecil looked up at Sam, who was sitting on a horse, then over to the house. Sam was right, it was not his place to involve himself in the marital problem of others. Although Cooper was his brother, he was also his owner and at liberty to sell him if he was angry enough to do so. *But he bet'not hurt her.* Cecil dragged his tool back to the field and remained busy for the rest of the day. Minutes later, he saw Cooper leaving the farm on horseback.

Come lunchtime, he had no appetite, and while others ate, he marched to the house and went straight to the kitchen where he found Remy. "Where she be, Remy?"

Remy went about her task of preparing dinner. "Where who be?"

"You know who, Miss Suzanna."

"She's in her room."

He stepped closer to her carrying the smell of sweat and the field that instantly made her frown. "I wanna see her—go get her."

After Cooper had stormed out the house, Remy knocked on Suzanna's door at various times to check on her. First, she got a "Go away" response, then a "Leave me alone." After the third attempt, she didn't get an answer at all, only sobs and sniffles. It was alright, as long as she knew that she was breathing. All the kitchen knives had been accounted for. She'd taken and retrieved a full plate of lunch and had given Suzanna a nice warm cloth to wash her face.

"She doesn't want any company right now, Cecil. Especially no smelly company."

He looked down at his sweat-stained clothes. She was right, he needed to clean up first. "But she be alright, 'dough?"

"The last time I checked she was."

"And how long it's been since you last checked?"

Remy pointed to Suzanna's uneaten lunch plate. "Lunchtime. She'll be alright. She just needs to rest. You mind your wife, and I'll mind Miss Suzanna."

Although he didn't care what she thought of his concern for Suzanna, her words did shame him. He backed away and hurried back to the field just as the slaves were ending their lunch break.

The moment Sam blew the whistle that ended the work day, Cecil rushed out of the field, quickly cleaned up and headed to the barn with his mind fixated on the main house as he calculated the perfect time to make his move.

It was dark with no sun out, only the glow of the night skies that granted enough light for him to dash across the dirt paths onto the grass, running as fast as he could.

Remy stirred around in the main house, finishing up her chores before retiring for the evening. One final look behind her before opening the back door.

"Aah! You scared me. What you doing creeping round in the dark?" she asked Cecil.

"I just wanna check on Miss Suzanna."

"I told you, she's fine."

Cecil respected Remy more than he respected any other slave on the farm. She reminded him of his mother. "Yes, ma'am. I sure she is, but I'd feel better if I could see for myself."

Remy looked him over. He was looking very handsome in the clothes Cooper had allowed him to pick for their last harvest celebration. "Mmhm, I bet you would. But I can't let you disturb her. Miss Suzanna's resting."

He remembered she didn't touch her lunch. "She ate yet?"

"Where's Bertha, Cecil? You just as concerned about her too?"

"She fine!" Standing tall, staring down on her, he was too close for comfort. With tightened lips, he stared a moment longer before briskly walking off.

Uncomfortable with his behavior, Remy waited until he was no longer in sight before speeding across the field to her cabin. *Who knows what that crazy man might do?*

Cecil sat in the barn, watching as Remy closed the door to her cabin. He had to see Suzanna. Having no idea where Cooper had gone or when he would return, he had to move fast. "The window." He rushed into the house with eyes focusing on no other concerns.

Trotting softly on the L-shaped wrapped porch that extended to Suzanna's bedroom where the broken window was located, he careful to avoid the broken glass. He pulled back the curtains and glanced through, but was blind in the darkness, leaving his curiosity empty. "Miss Suzanna," he whispered.

The silence left him more concerned. "Miss Suzanna, you be alright?" He lifted the broken window frame and stepped through, one foot at a time. With both feet safely planted, Cecil prepared to make the next step. Having peeked into her bedroom on many occasions, he knew the arrangement of every piece of furniture, but a fight might have shuffled things around. He continued carefully.

"Miss Suzanna." He placed every foot with thought. "Miss Suzanna, you be alright?"

A sniffle stopped him.

"Miss Suzanna, 'dis here Cecil. I just come to check on you. Make sho' you be alright."

Another sniff and he quickly turned, following its direction, stopping when his foot hit something. He bent down and blindly felt until his fingers came across her toes. He maneuvered around and found a clean spot to sit next to her and was thankful that Remy had pointed out the scent of his clothes earlier, it made him feel comfortable enough to get close.

The room was dead silent, extremely dark. All the things he ever thought of saying to her vanished, replaced by whatever he'd imagined Cooper had done to her as her soft cries made her sadness known. He scooted closer, leaned her head on his shoulder and sat still, not saying a word, listening to her moaning pain and giving her all the time she needed to release it.

÷÷÷÷÷÷

Earlier, Bertha had walked out of her and Cecil's bedroom. "Thomas, you seen Cecil?"

"I saw him headed out the door a while ago." Thomas continued on to his room.

Bertha went to the porch and sat waiting for Cecil to return. She'd decided it was time for them to talk. Cecil was nowhere in sight, until... "There he be." Exiting the barn. "He ain't with Suzanna." She was relieved as Cecil continued walking towards the main house. Watching his direction, she grew angry, sad, and disappointed as he walked around the side of the house and disappeared from her view. "But that was a while ago." And still he hadn't emerged.

Stepping off the porch, she stampeded across the lawn, stepped up onto the porch and slowly moved towards the side of the house. Recalling the loud noise from that day, they were told that Cooper had broken the bedroom window. She carefully slid her feet to push away any glass until she'd reached Suzanna's window and attempted to see past the sheer curtains. Darkness denied her of any visual insight.

Voices got her attention, but she was unable to decipher the words.

"Mmmm. Awmmm. Yesss…"

Bertha's heart palpitated. She was too shocked to cry. Backing off the porch, she stepped on a piece of glass, breaking it beneath her feet. That got Cecil's attention. She leaped off the porch, her large body frame stomped hard, running as fast as her heaviness would allow her. Her heartbeat sped up, went faster and faster, pounding through her ears, racing out of control. Her hand went to her chest. She grew dizzy, light-headed. Looking up, the family's cabin was right in front of her. She stepped on the first step, then the second, and collapsed.

Sixty-seven

$\underline{M}$icah quickly raised up from his sleep. "What that be?"

Sarah also sat up. "I heard it too."

Their bedroom was right off the porch. After all that had happened lately, Micah couldn't rest after hearing the thudding noise that impeded his sleep. It was loud and vibrated the floors.

He jumped out of bed and ran to the front porch where he found Bertha, all two-hundred and fifty pounds of her laying on the porch. He ran back in the cabin. "Thomas, Mark, come help me! Bertha's laying out here on the porch."

The emergency woke up the entire house. The women followed the men to the porch and back in the house as they carried Bertha in and laid her on the settee. Stepping aside, they allowed the women to take over. About ten minutes later, Sarah turned to her husband, Micah. "She gone be alright. I think she was just shaken up real bad."

"What happened? Why she fell?"

Sarah took her husband's arm and pulled him into the hallway. "She said she heard Cecil having sex wit' Suzanna."

Micah looked down at his shorter wife. "What?"

"Yeah. Said it hurt her so bad that her heart went crazy like it was jumping outta her chest. The last thing she remember is tryin' to make it back here. What we gone do? This ain't gone be good when Cooper finds out. She done already sold his wife."

"I'on no. Cecil done made it hard for all us."

Taking both hands to his face, Micah wiped hard as if he was trying to remove the stress of the dangerous news.

They helped Bertha to her bed and went back to their rooms at her insisting.

The next day came and took its time passing. All the slaves had taken to the field, working hard without complaints to make up for Cecil, who was obviously absent. Laboring helped them to diminish the worrying of all that had happened. No tears for the field, it was all about the hope that lay ahead. The hope that was promised by Cooper for better days to come, for freedom, to leave the life of slavery behind and all the pain that it caused.

Sarah put her hand on Bertha's shoulder. "You be alright?"

Bertha reached back, patted her hand and forced a smile. "Best I can be."

Sarah returned to her spot in the field and continued working.

Micah walked over to her. "How she doing?"

"She gone be alright."

"I can't believe Cecil," Micah said.

"What got into 'em to be such a fool?"

"Her," Micah answered.

No explanation needed, Sarah knew that *her* and Suzanna were one and the same.

Concerned for his sister-in-law who had always cared for everyone more than herself, Micah looked at Bertha, who was swinging a tool, working hard to exhaust her pain.

✝✝✝✝✝✝

Just before evening, they were exhausted and ready to leave the field behind. But there were no guarantees of a peaceful recuperation, especially when they looked out into the pre-dark night and saw Cooper coming up the road on his horse.

"He pulling a horse buh'hind 'em. What's on it?" Reah tried to discern.

"What's that, Mo'ma." Her son John could never quite say the word *momma*.

"I'on know, baby. But I reckon we gone fine' out soon a'nuff."

As Cooper came in view, so did the horror of his condition.

"What's wrong went 'em," Sarah asked. "Micah..."

Micah dragged his tool for a moment, then dropped it. His walk sped up to a jog, then running towards the horses, one with Cooper, the other carrying something.

Cooper stopped at the well where he got off and went to the second horse and carefully removed a thick blanket from it. Laying it on the ground, he sat beside it and uncovered it just as Micah made it to him, in shock, stunned, saddened.

The others made it to the well, stopping when they saw the horrific scene.

Bertha screamed.

Thomas held her back.

Tears fell down Reah's face. She grabbed John and buried his face into her chest to shield him from the scene.

Mark comforted his wife Jalean.

Sarah went to her husband's side; his arm went around her shoulder as she leaned her head on the side of his chest. He covered his mouth.

Yes'sa Man dropped to the ground and wept when he saw Cooper covered in blood, uncovering Nina's bloody body that had been wrapped in the blanket. "What happened? Mister Cooper, what happened?"

Cooper put Nina'a head on his lap. Her beautiful dark skin and thick crinkled mane amassed in blood. Lacerations covered her entire body, her limbs dangled lifelessly.

Sarah looked up at Micah. He released her and went to his brother. "Cooper, let me help you up." He pulled on his arms that felt twice its weight and barely moved. Micah knelt close to Cooper. "Cooper...you gotta let me help you up. She gon—"

"Aaaaahhh." The wailing sounds of the most horrendous inner pain emanated from Cooper's breath, shattering the night that was barely holding on to daylight. Howling, Cooper snuggled his wife's body to his chest, her face to his. He rubbed her face, kissed her and cried. Her dangling arm removed any hope that he tried to cling to. Rocking her motionless body, he dropped his head back, declaring his pain to the heavens. Questioning God, begging him to exchange their places, pleading to be with his wife.

He looked down at her. "Wake up, Nina, my darling, my love...please open your eyes for your husband. I need you to wake up." He shook his head and let out a long-lasting grunt while rocking Nina back and forth.

So many tears, so much pain. He stared at her bloody face while tears flooded his. Rubbing her face, he kissed her lips that did not return the sentiment. He wrapped her dangling arm over his shoulder and rocked. It fell off.

Her dead body was not the outcome that he'd hoped for when pressing his horse as fast as it would take him a day earlier.

‡‡‡‡‡‡

After leaving the farm, Cooper had stopped in town to get directions. Once on the plantation, he jumped off his horse and immediately heard the noises that trapped his attention to the point of no return. Loud screams coming from a small shack not much larger than an outhouse. His body became one large muscle that was full of passionate rage as he recalled what Rosa had told him of the abusive master.

He ran toward the small, filthy shack where the loud horrifying screams came from, telling of an unimaginable scene that was occurring inside. Cooper looked around. Slaves were on all sides, some looking at him, others minding their own business.

Kids running, women walking, children playing, adults working, barely talking; many women, mostly children, both girls and boys who all seemed to be unbothered by the terrible screams of a woman only a few feet away from their activities.

Not knowing what he would find on the other side of the door, Cooper was mindfully careful. Maybe it was a woman giving birth. *It has to be.* What other reasons would there be for the screams and the normality of the others who ignored them? Whatever the cause, it was obvious that a woman was in torture.

He went closer to the door, wanting to be in a hurry, but clinched by the fear of the unknown. He extended his hand, reaching for the rope used as the door's latch. He pulled it but was stopped by a man's sadistic laughter and the woman's cries that told of her pains, fears, helplessness.

"Stop, stop, please, stop!" the woman cried.

Cooper's eyes grew with anger. The shouts of Nina's voice stung like an unsuspecting arrow plunging through his heart, jerking him into action. He yanked on the rope and forced his way in. In his sight, a tall, thin man hovered over Nina. Standing between her spread legs, he held a knife with a thick, long blade, the sharp end aimed directly at Nina. Before Cooper could move, he stabbed down, piercing the sharp end of the blade through Nina's chest and quickly snatched it out. Blood spewed, leaking and drenching her blouse.

To Cooper's left was a thick stick that was normally used to prop the door open. He picked it up and plowed the man on the back of his shoulder. He fell sideways onto the floor, tried to get back up, but fell again.

Cooper raised the stick again to take his anger out on the man but stopped. "It can't be."

The crooked nose overseer. He could never forget the man whose blood ran through his veins; the man who had forcefully robbed his grandma of her innocence. The same man who hated his skin color so much that he stood him out in the midst of the sun and watched as the sun scorched him in an attempt to undo the light skin color that he had introduced to his family's bloodline. It was without a doubt,

Cooper's grandfather. Around seventy-years-old, he was still raping women.

Cooper's thoughts returned to him when his grandfather tried to make it to his feet. The high raised stick came down, pounding hard, connecting with the top of Roy's head, splitting his skull. Blood gushed out, energizing Cooper's hatred, his anger, and the efforts to redeem all the pain he'd caused.

Pow, pow, pow. With every blow, an old memory was revenged.
Slave women whose purity he'd confiscated. POW!
Every woman he'd cut. POW!
Every woman he'd killed. POW!
Nina's attack. POW! POW! POW! POW!
His grandmother's rape. POW! POW! PLOW! POW! POW! POW!

Blood splashed out onto the walls, the floors, Cooper's face, his clothes. He thought of Rosa's words. POW! POW! POW! POW!

A loud rumbling grunt from Cooper accompanied every blow. The thick bloody log continued beating, pounding what was left of his grandfather's head. Cooper continued bashing until nothing was left but thick gushy blood matter in the socket of a deep dent.

"Jesse." Nina's weakened voice stopped him. Throwing the stick aside, Cooper rushed over and lifted her in his arms. She tried to smile, but her swollen mouth and jaw had imprisoned her happiness to see him. She rested her head on his chest. "Jesse." As she lay wrapped in the strength of his arms, her head remained pinned to his chest, listening to his strong heartbeat while hers weakened.

Cooper exited the shack carrying Nina. He was met by a crowd of obedient slaves. Never minding their stares, he crossed the field, blood dripped from her wounds with every step he made.

The sea of slaves watched and parted like the Red Sea, allowing him to pass as he walked to his horse, leaving a trail of blood behind.

Cooper turned to one of the young slave women whose dark beauty had been blemished by a thick, long scar that ran horizontally from her hairline to her chin, barely missing her eye. It deeply scarred the beauty that still showed through. Hanging off her legs were three small girls that looked to be around ages *1 to 3*, all mixed with a white man's blood.

"Do you have a blanket?"

"Yes, sar'." She left and like ducklings, her 'babies' followed suit. Soon after, she returned carrying a beautiful hand stitched quilt that looked to never have been used. Two of her babies each carried a flask of water. "This blanket was started by the first woman who was abused by Massa. Every woman he brought here since the first added a new patch. After today, no more patches will be added." She smiled. "Thanks to you. Bertha wanted you to have this."

"Bertha?" He was reminded of his sister-in-law.

"Yes, sar'." She looked back at an old matriarch figure sitting in a rocker on a porch of an aged shack. Cooper smiled at the woman who slightly nodded.

The girl helped Cooper wrap Nina and secure her on the horse. She took the two flasks from the babies and handed them to him. He jumped on the horse, secured the flask and left. He had a half of a day's ride ahead of him. And believing that the authorities would soon be on his trail, he went as fast as he could while minding the precious cargo on the horse he pulled. His measured trip back to the farm took almost a full day just before dark. During the ride there, he stopped to check on Nina and to give her water.

Nina's weakened voice murmured, "The baby."

"The baby is fine. The girl they brought to replace you is taking good care of her."

"No, our baby." She tried to rub her stomach, but she could barely move a limb.

"The baby is fine and you will be too. The moment I get you back on the farm, all will be well and so will you. I need you to hold on. Can you do that for me—"

Her eyes lowered; her head fell to the side.

"I love you, Nina. My precious, sweet wife. I love you dearly." He rubbed her face. "Just rest now. You'll be fine. I just have to get you back to the farm." He put her back on the horse, got on the other and rode off.

Now that they were back on the farm, he sat by the well with Nina's limp body resting on his lap. Her head wrapped in his arm. No breaths coming from her lungs, no beat of her heart, her beautiful smile and deep dimples never to be seen again.

"I love you." He kissed her forehead. "I love you so much." He pulled her into his chest and rocked his wife with falling tears, looking at her and smiling. "At first I marveled at your beauty from the outside, but you showed me that it came from within." He kissed her again and looked up to the heavens, staring as if he was witnessing her spirit ascend.

Life for her had been so unfair. A lost child, a man who left her with no explanation. She bore the marks on her back, the imprints of faithfulness and a forever reminder of pain. He'd brought her to live in a difficult situation, forcing her to quietly watch as he openly loved another. Submissively becoming his secret lover, and now, she'd paid for his sins with her life.

A lantern that had been left on the well by Remy, who was the last to come to the scene accompanied the moon's glow, giving Cooper visibility as he gazed upon his wife. He applied light strokes to her hair and kissed her forehead once more.

Looking up the road, time was of the essence. The authorities could be on their way at any time. Pain and sadness had to be postponed, at least for now. He closed his eyes, took in a deep breath and summoned up enough peace to push sorrow aside.

Cooper had killed a white man and as kind as the slaves on that plantation had been, there were no guarantees of a slave's loyalty. Afraid of being beaten, family separation, torture, and death had ripped slaves of their alliance to one another. One question by the authorities, and in fear, they might lead them directly to him. To include in the threat, he'd stopped in town to ask for directions to the plantation. People had seen him, people who knew where he was going. And he had left a dead white man behind.

Cooper looked as far up the road as he could see, but saw no men, horses or dogs. No threat of death was on the empty road. Being careful to place Nina aside, he looked at her. One final enduring kiss brought his grieving to a temporary end. Sadness turned into survival. Cooper grabbed the lantern and left her at the well.

Sixty-eight

*T*he family of slaves sat futilely, waiting for Cooper and mentally preparing for the fear that lay ahead of them. They decided amongst themselves that no matter what the cost, they would stand by their brother's side, even if all of them had to lose their own lives to do so.

Micah saw the lantern coming towards them. He stood and stepped off the porch, jogging to meet Cooper. "You be alright?"

"Yes."

The two walked back to the porch. The family rushed to comfort him, but he broke up the lovefest. It had to wait. "We have to leave. Tonight!" Things had changed and so had his plans. He pulled Micah aside and told him everything. Sarah watched from a distance as Micah bent over and rested his hands on his knees to support himself.

"What now?" she said to herself. With all that was unfolding seemingly by the hour, she suspected the worst.

"Mother, Father, May, all the kids and Nina's and Bertha's mother are well and waiting for us on the land I've purchased for our family. We have to hurry to get to them. I've drawn up two maps. The first can no longer be used as it may lead the authorities in our direction. The second one will take longer to get you all up north—"

"Us? What about you?"

"I will join you later. The information that I am about to give you will be overwhelming—"

"Over, overwhelming?" Micah asked.

"Meaning, a lot to take in at once, but I need you to listen carefully. Once you get a distance away from the farm, tell Reah and Thomas all that I have told you. We can't leave anything to chance. You all must stay on course at all times. I've planned this path for a while and people are set in place to help you all. You should be safe until you make it to the train station where I will meet you." Cooper went inside his vest pocket and pulled out a pocket watch. "If I'm not there when this hand reaches that number, pay for your fares and leave without me."

"We can't leave you."

"You have to. Remember, the family is waiting for you. They need you. They are what's important now. Often times when I said I was going into town for business, I was using the time to plan this route, assuring the safest paths. I have faith that if you all stay on the course I've outlined, markers I've made on trees, roads I've coded with rocks, like the ones I've indicated on this map, you will reach the train station without any problems. The paths are all wide and solid enough for wagons and horses. You should be fine."

"Okay." Micah was excited, afraid, but he had to be brave for his family.

"Micah, it's very important to follow these instructions exactly as I have written them. Any straying from them and all could go horribly wrong."

Micah gave his brother a manly look. "You can depend on me, and we'll see you again."

"Of course, you will."

The brothers hugged and departed. Micah went to the family and Cooper headed to the main house.

Walking across the lawn, Cooper was still stricken with grief, fighting against its control and pushing aside self-pity that was grasping every part of his thought. He took a deep breath and grabbed hold of focus while heading to the house.

A distance away, a figure emerged from the darkness, fuming with erupting rage, an ax in hand, waiting to attack its prey.

Sixty-nine

*T*he night prior...

"You be alright?"

She didn't answer.

While sitting on the floor, Cecil reached over in the dark and felt for Suzanna's face. It was full of moistened tears, all caused by Cooper after learning that she'd sold Nina. Suzanna was not able to see the fury that grew in Cecil's eyes.

He turned in her direction and as soft as possible, caressed the white beauty, remembering every freckle on her face. Touching her momentarily removed his anger that gave into a smile that she could not see.

He gently wiped her tears. A quick brush to his clothes to dry his hand and he returned it to her face, wiping any moisture that remained and all that was new. Drying his hand one final time, he lifted her chin.

He was so gentle. The moment melted her heart. She raised her face and became aware of the close proximity of his lips. She puckered in compliance, knowing that his lips wanted her to.

Cecil's body burned all over when her lips pressed against his. Both his hands went to her face, one on each side as he embraced their softness. *What else will she let me do?*

He hated his brother, but his deeds had given him the chance to be with the woman he loved. Through her tears and pain, she allowed him to comfort her.

The kiss ended. "It's dark, I can't see you. Did he hurt you?" He carefully arranged his words to sound as proper as possible.

She imagined his face from the gloom of what was visible. She took a hard swallow. "He beat and choked me," she half lied. "Because..."

"Why?"

"Because...I confessed to him that I was in love with you."

Cecil stared at her. He couldn't believe it. She, a white woman was in love with him? He knew he was precise in his thinking that she had craved him. That she wanted to be with him and not his brother. His heart felt funny. A feeling he'd experienced from years past on the night he and Bertha as young teenagers made love for the first time. The muscle between his thighs grew stiff while going back to Suzanna's lips. Everything in him wanted to show her *exactly* how much of him loved her.

His hands moved from her face and found her breast, squeezing its firmness, he imagined doing so much more. Her loose gown allowed him to explore and that he did. Sliding his hand underneath it. He smiled when he realized that the gown was the only thing she wore. Continuing to its destiny, his hand found the most graceful thing he'd ever touched in all his days of living. And she welcomed his touch with spread legs. He slowly caressed while trying to control a premature eruption. She made the task all the more difficult when she pressed her lips against his and moaned. Moving her hips, she complied to every caress and finger stroke, moaning with enjoyment.

Suddenly, she closed her legs, clamping his hand still.

He became dumb, at a loss for words, and completely unaware of her devious smile. His weakness was perfect for preying.

"I love you, Cecil. But we can never be together."

He could still feel the warm wet moisture that covered his fingers and all of her that surrounded it. "Why?" He sounded like a weak, confused boy.

She smiled and opened her legs, granting him resumption.

"Mmmm. Awmmm. Yesss…" She couldn't deny the feeling of his hand that was about to make her melt.

Cecil's ears went up. He heard something outside the window that momentarily took away his concentration, but only for a moment. His thoughts returned. His motion decreased. No need for speed, he knew the right spot to tease, to deliver complete satisfaction. He balled in his lips and took her to task. Making her huff and puff, moan and groan, raise her hips, ascend and descend, trembling, she clamped his hand again. She could take no more.

He smiled. "And that's just my hand. There be so much more waiting for you."

She smiled. "And I want it. I want all of you, but it can never be. Cooper will never allow it. As long as he lives, we will have to love each other from afar. He controls us both. After all, he is your master, and I am his wife."

"You are mine."

"Not as long as he's alive. I am his and we can never be together. He will never allow me to return to the field now that he's back. Never will our lips kiss again…never will our bodies join in love. Oh, Cecil, I want so much of you. I want all of you, but it's not to be. Not while Cooper lives. I love you so much. We could be so happy together, so in love. But it will always be but a dream as long as there is breath in Cooper's body."

"I won't let 'em come between us."

"How can you stop him?"

He was quiet. The thought that came to mind became too serious to fathom.

"You have to leave now, and you can never return. You can never touch me ever again. She released her legs. He tried to caress her again, but she pushed his hand away. You have to leave. Because of our love, Cooper will sell you from me."

"Can't you stop him?"

"No one can stop him. He owns you. And I'm his wife, a powerless woman. Only death can stop him."

"Then so be it."

"What do you mean?"

"He gotta die!"

She allowed his words to simmer, to settle in his heart.

"It be, I mean, it's the only way we can be together."

"It would be the only way." She turned to him. "Oh, darling, I love you so. I just want to be with you." Putting her hands on his expanded muscle, she squeezed. "All of you," She opened her legs.

He rubbed.

She purred.

His manhood throbbed for attention.

"I can't wait to celebrate his death with you in my bed."

In the darkness, he gazed upon her. "I'll do anything to be the only man in your bed."

"Kill Cooper and we can be together. Forever."

"Okay. I'll do it. Then we celebrate right after."

She smiled. "With his blood still on your hands, smearing it all over my body. I can't wait."

He left out the back door and the moment he crossed the door's threshold, every step that followed moved him towards the barn, closer to his new life, further away from his former self. He was a new creature, Suzanna's man, and her happiness was now his responsibility.

Cecil put his hand to his nose and smelt with blinking eyes. The smell of her sweet juices excited him so that he rubbed his genitals with the same hand. It was late. He sat in the barn unable to uproot the premeditated plan to murder his eldest brother.

Cooper had abused the love of his life after she'd confessed to loving him. He had to pay him for the pain he caused her. "And I'll be the new Massa of the farm. The first thing um'ma do is get rid of Sam. He gots to go."

Cecil sat for a while, planning his attack until his eyes grew heavy. He leaned over on the hay. It could never compare to the bed he would be sharing with Suzanna. He thought of them in bed together. "Ain't gone be much sleeping." He laughed.

He tried to get comfortable. This darn hay too hard." He sat up. "Where they room be? I know it's in here sum' where. Cheatin' on Miss Suzanna wit' Nina." He searched for the private room that Cooper and Nina shared. Throwing things aside, moving things around. "There it be." A door behind a stack of hay. He entered the secret room and saw a full-size bed blanketed in the softest linens he'd ever felt. "Almost like sleeping on a cloud." He looked around. A lantern sat on a table. The room was so cozy, surprisingly cool, the perfect hideaway love nest. In there, he was finally able to rest.

The next day, he emerged from the barn starving.

Remy had no idea that he was missing from the fields when he opened the back door. She looked him over. He had on the clothes she saw him wearing from the night before. "Why you here and not in the field. I already sent breakfast. Lunch got a ways to go."

"Yeah, 'um. I know. And that breakfast was sum'thin good," he lied. "I just need a few more biscuits to hold me over till lunchtime."

"Hmp... I don't have anymore. But you welcome to have what Miss Suzanna didn't eat. It sittin' over there." She nodded towards a full plate of cold breakfast.

Cecil wanted to inquire about Suzanna. Her leftovers meant she didn't have an appetite. *She still be sad.* He'd taken on the responsibility of making her happy and knew exactly what would put a smile on her face. He quickly demolished her leftovers and headed back to the barn.

Laying on the bed, Cecil fell into a deep sleep, lost in a dreaming world, he had no idea that Cooper had returned to the farm. Stretching, it took a moment to discover his location, but looking around the private room, he remembered where he was and why he was there. Recalling his mission, he sat up on the side of the bed. "It's time!"

Seventy

Aggressively pulling, yanking and tossing things aside, Cecil stopped when he saw the perfect weapon. A Viking shaped ax that had a deadly hook. He sized it up and imagined the damage it would cause, the death it would render, the life it would take. He headed to the barn door and pulled it back, watching as Cooper walked towards the main house *to hurt my Suzanna.*

Countering his conscience, Cecil denied his heart's reasoning. *How you gone kill your blood for a white woman?* "Cause she loves me, and I love her."

Suzanna was all that matter to him. Not his wife or his family, nor his three children he'd left behind. He would start a new life with the woman who accepted him as a slave in a time when the world viewed their type of love as a disgrace. "I'll never be as dumb as Cooper, mistreating her, choosing a slave over her. Beating her up. Now he gone pay."

Cecil stood in the center of the barn's door watching Cooper walking across the field. "There he be. The man who beat my woman." *But that's your brother, your blood.* "And she be my woman. How um'ma be her man if I don't protect her?" He made a step forward to meet Cooper but stopped.

"Hey, Cooper." Micah ran out.

Cooper turned around.

"Listen. I know you hurtin', but you done killed a white man. Now, they don't know you a slave, but they do know you a murderer. Don't be so angry that you leave two bodies behind. They may not come after you for killin' that white man 'cause them slaves probably can't send them to fine' you. But they'll surely come after you if you kill a white woman."

"Thank you for your concern, but you have no need to worry. I don't know what I'm going to say to Suzanna, but I could never take the life of the mother of my only son. Enough time has passed, you all need to start your journey as soon as possible."

Both men stood face-to-face, no height difference, same body structure, both with hazel eyes, wavy dark hair, one silkier than the other. Their skin color was similar, but Micah was a little darker. They both shared the same mother but had different fathers. Yet, Micah loved his brother dearly no matter what variations separated them. It frightened him to leave his brother behind knowing the danger that awaited. "Please come wit' us."

Cooper's hand went to Micah's shoulder. "You will see me soon, I promise. I have to finalize some things here and say goodbye to my son."

Micah grabbed Cooper and hugging him, he held tight.

Their meeting lasted longer than Cecil wanted to wait. In anger, he charged toward the two, overtaken by malice and determination that fought against the morality of reasoning. He sprinted, his body propelled with vengeance, lifting the ax above his head as far back as his limb would bend. A growling grunt got Micah's and Cooper's attention, but it was too late, the ax was coming down, too fast, too soon for them to move.

An unexpected dive and three men hit the ground. Sam, who'd curiously watched the family's interaction from afar had noticed Cecil standing in the barn's doorway. "Where 'dis fool runnin' to?" Seeing Cecil sprinting out of the barn, his eyes widened. "What he got in his hand? What?" With old injuries limiting his speed, Sam jumped on his horse and pushed it to its fullest, trying to make it to Cooper and Micah before Cecil.

The ax went up before he was there and came down just as Sam dived off the horse, his body landing on Cooper and Micah just in time. They all hit the ground and turned to see Cecil fighting to pull the deadly hook from the wild grass weeds that tangled it.

"Cecil! Stop, please, stop!" Bertha begged from the porch while witnessing her husband's crazed attack.

Cecil struggled to untangle the ax from the grass.

Bertha ran in the house. "Mark! Thomas! Cecil's attacking Cooper and Micah. Come out here, quick. Come stop Cecil!"

Mark and Thomas dashed out the house, zooming toward harm's way just as Cecil unplanted his weapon and was going for a second attack.

"Cecil, put that ax down!" Mark shouted.

"Come on, brother, we can talk about this," Thomas begged.

Holding up two calming hands, Micah pleaded, "Come on, now. Put that ax down. You don't wanna do this."

Cecil swiped. The blade came within inches of Cooper's face.

"Cecil! Cecil, put down 'dat ax! 'Dis not cause for!" Sam fussed.

Like an uncaged animal, Cecil let out a loud growl and attacked with a wild strike, forcing everyone to retreat, warning them of his intent. He turned, planting his attention solely on Cooper. The death of the others meant nothing to him, but Cooper's death was imminent. It had to be. His blood shed was the pledge that Suzanna required.

Cooper saw the rage in this brother's eyes. His unforgiving state said only death would stop him.

The others noticed Cecil's real target. They shouted, they pleaded.

Thomas even dropped to his knees. "Take it out on me, brother. I won't try to stop you. Let Cooper live. He gone give us our freedom. We gone' be wit' our fam'ly, man. Your childrun, Micah and Sarah gone be wit' they childrun. You gotta let 'em live, so we can all be free. Take it out on me instead!"

"What he talkin' 'bout?" Sam was confused.

"That's your blood you tryin' to kill. For what, a white woman?" Mark yelled. "Come on, Cecil, this ain't you. You gotta a wife. You got three childrun. What we gone tell your childrun, yo' ma and pa? Look how yo' fam'ly lookin' at you, man. You don't want this on your conscience. Come on, Cecil, don't do this."

Their pleas crowded Cecil's mind. He couldn't think. He needed to quiet their petitions, the guilt they put on him... The ax went up.

Thomas, who was still on his knees, saw the blade blending with the moon. It came down, a powerful swipe powered by evil.

"Noooo..." Bertha yelled from afar.

Sarah covered her face. Reah and John stared in fear. Jalean dashed off the porch, screaming, crying, running towards Thomas, her twin brother who'd humbly submitted his sacrificial body as Cecil's ax came down and made contact.

Cooper could not stop it from happening. He fell back, hitting the ground. His hand rushed to his stomach, passing through the open cut of his shirt, stopping on his bloody skin that was scrapped by the ax. His hand came up to his face, he saw blood, but not enough to take his life. He looked at Thomas, who was still on his knees, his eyes drenched in tears. "I'm alright," he said to relieve him of his sorrow.

Ignoring Thomas, who was willing to give his life, Cecil's attack had remained steadfast on Cooper, whose feet scurried against the grass, trying to gain enough traction to escape the blade that was on its way at him again. This time aiming for his head.

The blade came down, but its destination cut off by a powerful sideswipe. Micah rammed into Cecil, forcefully knocking him to the ground. The ax knocked out of his hand. He was quickly surrounded by a group of able body angry farm men who were all fed up.

Witnessing it all was Suzanna who stood in the doorway, watching her wild animal growling, trying to escape the bodies of men who circled him.

Cecil quickly reached over and grabbed the ax. Making it to his feet, he danced from side to side, violently swinging the ax, trying to force his way out of the circle. But they stood strong, Micah, Thomas, Mark, Sam, Yes'sa Man, all willing to protect Cooper, even if it meant being struck down by the deadly weapon that Cecil wildly swung.

"Put the ax down, Cecil!" Thomas yelled.

"Drop it, Cecil!" Reah pleaded, standing behind the circle of men.

"Cecil, baby, please put the ax down!" Bertha implored. "Me and you can work this thang out, and make thangs better between us again!"

Cecil turned in every direction, looking between Thomas and Mark, he saw Cooper making it to his feet. He tried to break the circle, but they quickly clamped hands, locking in the out of control wild beast he'd become.

Cecil looked around. His crazed look concerned everyone. His loud, angry words hosted their attention. "Cooper... He ain't nothang! He ain't no better than us. He just got white skin, but he black as the rest of us! He just be a black runaway slave pretendin' he white! And his name ain't no Cooper. He be Jesse, a runaway slave from the Hartford's Plantation!"

Looks of shock filled their faces. Sam, Yes'sa Man, and Remy...Suzanna!

"He ain't married to Miss Suzanna 'cause he loves her...he married her to use her money to buy us, his fam'ly. That's why he gets so mad 'bout Nina. She ain't our cousin, she be his wife, and we be his brothers and sisters. We his blood! Y'all look at me like 'um wrong, when he the one. He the one who wrong. He gets mad at Miss Suzanna 'cause she tell 'em she loves me and want to be wit' me."

"You're a fool!" Mark shouted.

Cooper was in shock. He looked back and saw Suzanna on the porch, an earshot away.

"She told 'em she loves me, and he gets mad and beat her."

Cooper understood Cecil's attack and was furious. It was Suzanna's lie that had driven Cecil mad.

Cecil continued, "He the one who beat and tried to kill her 'cause she in love wit' me. I love Miss Suzanna, and she loves me and after I kill him, we gone be d'gather."

Shocked by his admittance, Reah's hand went to her forehead, the other to her hip. "Cecil, you can't be that foolish to believe her?"

Sarah looked over at Bertha, who was releasing thick tears. "Bertha, give me your hand." Bertha did so. "Reah," Sarah reached for her hand as well. Their hands met, Reah took John's hand. Jalean walked over and took John's hand, and they squeezed in between the men and took their hands, forming a wider circle. "Cecil, if you wanna get to Cooper, you gotta come through us," Reah said. "Now, put down that ax and act like you gots some sense. Like you our brother. That white woman don't care nothin' 'bout you. She usin' you to kill Cooper and you a fool to believe her."

"Me. I got more sense than all of y'all. Y'all the fool to let Cooper trick you. Well, I ain't gone let him trick me. And if he ever put another hand on Suzanna, 'um gone kill 'em." He turned to Cooper. "And come sunup, if you be here, it gone be the last sun you'll ever see and ain't nobody gone stop me 'dis time!"

No one moved as Cecil's words sent waves of threat not only to Cooper but to them all. His actions had consequences for everyone. He'd told a vengeful white woman that she'd been deceived by a black runaway slave. He included the plantation where he'd run from. Only tomorrow's light would determine the outcome of the damage Cecil had caused. But they had no plans to be there when morning came.

Sam and Micah released their hands, making a path for Cecil to exit. He retreated back to the barn.

Stunned and in shock, Suzanna doubted the ability of her ears. "Cooper's a slave? Never! How could that be? He's white! White men aren't slaves. Cecil was talking nonsense, mad out of his mind. It was all a tale. Horrible lies to hurt Cooper. A fabrication to justify his attack. If Cooper was a slave, that would mean he's black and that I was married to a nig—that my son is a...lies. All lies!"

In denial, she went into the house and headed for the kitchen. A crazed look dressed her face as she grabbed a knife and went to the dining table. She stabbed the knife into it and sat quietly while Cecil's words endangered her sanity.

"He a slave!" She snatched the knife from the handmade wooden table that was given to them as a wedding gift by her youngest sister and brother-in-law. Placing her arm on the table, palm up, she fixated on her pumping vein.

"He ain't married Miss Suzanna 'cause he loves her. He married her to use her money to buy us."

With eyes filled with tears, she put the knife to her wrist and pressed softly, then harder and harder until the blade edge faded into her skin.

"...Nina, she ain't our cousin, she be his wife."

Pressing down, the knife buried in her skin, turning it red. And with one sideswipe, her skin opened, blood spewed, traveling down the side of her wrist. Suzanna watched the flow of blood from the cut that stung.

"We his blood!"

Lifting the knife, she placed it on a different area.

Nina be his wife.

Folding her lips in, tears rushed down her face, she sliced again, making another line of ill-channeled pain, but only a little blood emerged. She put the blade in a different location and sliced again. Blood seeped down the sides of her arm. Not enough to bleed to death, just enough to reassign her pain.

Weakened by the thought of his words, Suzanna dropped the knife on the table, cupped her face and cried. Her unfiltered tears came rushing down the sides of her face as blood streamed down her arm. Drying her tears with her arms, blood smeared on her face. She went to her bedroom, dripping blood from her fingertips along the way.

In her room, she drank herself to sleep.

⁜⁜⁜

The family waited until Cecil closed the barn door before returning to their cabins where they finished packing and loaded the two large wagons.

Remy ran to Cooper. "Are you alright? Where did he cut you?" She examined him.

"I'm fine. It only scraped me. Just shaken. Thank you for caring. I'm so sorry for my deceit—"

"You don't owe me no explanation. I'm just glad you alright."

"I am. I need you to go into the house. On the parlor floor, near the fireplace, you will find my satchel. Can you retrieve it for me?"

"Yes. I'll be right back."

"If you're confronted by Miss Suzanna, tell her—"

"I know how to handle Miss Suzanna. I'll be back shortly." She jogged away.

Cooper looked towards the family cabin. They were all getting on the wagons. He walked over and was met by Bertha. "I'm glad he didn't hurt you."

Cooper slightly smiled. "Me too."

To fight off tears, Bertha dropped her head.

"Bertha what has happened to your husband is not your fault. He's just confused, mixed up."

"I know...I know." She sighed. "Mister Cooper."

"It's just Cooper."

She smiled. "Cooper. I don't know if I should tell you this."

"Tell me what?"

"Nina was pregnant. I think she would've wanted you to know. I'm so sorry."

Cooper stared off. "She kept saying, 'the baby.' That's what she was talking about."

"I'm so sorry."

"I know. I just..." He sighed. "You all need to get moving."

"Yeah." She gave him a hug, and he helped her get on the wagon.

"Micah! Micah, where you goin'?" Thomas called out while climbing onto the wagon. He was the last of the family members to do so except for Micah.

"I'll be right back," Micah answered, barely looking behind him as he headed for the barn.

"Go wit' 'em, Thomas," Reah said.

"I'll be alright. Stay wit' the fam'ly," Micah shouted.

"I'll go with him," Cooper said.

"No, Mister Cooper. He'll be alright. You goin' will only cause problems," Sarah said, trusting that her husband had things under control.

Cecil sat up on the bed in the private room when he heard the barn's door open. Before he could rise to his feet, Micah was standing in the doorway of the private room. "I'on wanna talk about it, Micah. I don't need yo' preachin'."

"Cecil, what's gotten into you? This woman ain't yo' fam'ly. Your babies, Ma, Pa, Bertha's ma, our baby sister, May, they all waitin' for us."

"On the Hartford's Plantation. 'Um not goin' back there—"

"No, they're..." Micah hesitated. Cecil had betrayed the whole family for a woman. Trusting him with the family's whereabouts would not be wise. "No, they free, Cecil. They all free. Cooper done bought everybody's freedom, including yours."

Suzanna had told him that Cooper was going to sell him. Cecil looked down, thinking for a moment, feeling convicted, feeling like a fool, but foolishly in love. "It don't matter. Miss Suzanna's my world now. Nobody else matters."

Micah stared into Cecil's eyes and shook his head knowing there was nothing he could do or say to convince him to think rationally. He went towards Cecil, who jumped in defense. He reached over by the wall and picked up the ax.

Micah continued walking towards him. He slowly wrapped his arms around his brother's neck. "I love you, man." Micah released him and walked away.

Tears filled Cecil's eyes. He'd been wrong about Cooper. What if he was wrong about Suzanna? He closed the door to the private room, turned off the lantern, and sat in the dark.

‡‡‡‡‡‡

Remy came out of the kitchen house with Yes'sa Man following her, both carrying crates of food. She held Cooper's satchel beneath the crate she was holding. "Here you go, Mister Cooper."

"Here, let me help you." He reached for the crate.

"No, I got it. You take care of your business. Just take the satchel."

He took it. "Did she give you any problems?"

"I didn't see her. I think she's in her room."

"Thomas, come get this," Remy called.

Thomas jumped off the wagon and taking both crates, he placed one on each wagon.

"I don't know how long ya'll have to travel, but this should hold you over a bit. Make it last as long as you can."

They thanked her.

Micah returned, walking up to Cooper, whose hand reached out waiting for a handshake. The two hugged. Cooper went into the satchel and took out papers. "Here's the map. Protect it with your life." Then reaching back into the satchel, he pulled out a thick envelope. "If you follow the map correctly, you will need money at these locations." He pointed on the map. "Here, this should be plenty." He went back into the satchel and pulled out papers. "These are all of your freedom papers and a letter signed by me authorizing your permission to travel. I've included two copies of each should something happen to one. Keep them separate, one on each wagon" He turned to his family who was sitting on the wagons. "You are all free men and women now. Micah will further direct you until you reach your new home. I need each of you to trust him with your lives. I will meet you all later."

Thinking about their freedom, many of them cried, others praised God.

As soon as Micah got on the wagon, Cooper looked up at him. "Micah, if I'm not there by—"

"No, brother. You will, and we'll be waiting," Micah's authoritarian voice ended the conversation.

Rosa rushed out of the house. "Wait." She opened her fist and dropped Nina's ring into Cooper's hand. "I found 'dis on the flo' the other day. I don't know how to read, but it got some writing on the inside. I figure it belonged to her."

Cooper took the ring, kissed it and balled it up in Bertha's hand. He looked at his daughter, Alexandria who sat in her lap. "It's the ring I gave to Nina. It will belong to Alex once she becomes of age. Please hold onto it for me."

Bertha took the ring and tucked it into her pouch.

Cooper took Alexandria's small hand and kissed it. "Father loves you dearly." He waved as the wagons pulled away, his eyes full of tears.

Sam watched from the main house porch as the family's wagons rode away into the night.

Cooper didn't move until they were no longer in sight. He dropped his head and went to the main house. Sam was still standing on the porch. "I'll be right back." Cooper returned with a thicker satchel.

Sam noticed that he was covered in blood. " 'Dat be Nina's blood or the white man's?"

"Both."

"You should go. The law maybe come at you soon."

"I know. I have to say goodbye to my son."

"Make it quick and get. Clean up first. He don't need to see you like 'dat."

Cooper looked directly in Sam's eyes. "I want you to know that I did love her. And although I'm taking my family—"

"So 'dey really be yo' fam'ly?"

"Yes. And Nina was my wife. I'm a passer. A man stained with the white man's color and cursed by the black man's fate. Growing up, I hated my skin color. Looking like them, white on the outside, thinking I was black on the inside. But now I know that we're no different. We all bleed red blood. It's not what's on the outside that makes us human, it's what's in our hearts."

"I never saw nobody like you."

"How do you know?"

"Hmp." Sam smirked.

"Suzanna was good to me when I arrived. I had to make sure that all that I've built, what we worked so hard for continues. Over the next few weeks, expect the arrival of new slaves and all the inventory needed to continue the productivity of the farm. Orders have been made, everything is in her name. I've removed my name from all that she owns, making her and CJ the sole proprietors of everything." Cooper held the briefcase up in front of Sam who took it.

"What 'dis? It's heavy."

"That it is. It's your freedom papers, Sam. And those of Remy and Yes'sa Man."

Sam's eyes grew. Tears fell without warning. "I...I'on know what to say."

"Your tears are understandable. But there's more. Included in that brief is a land deed. Sitting on the property is a five-bedroom two-story house and enough money to purchase all the inventory you all need to grow your own land. I've arranged for a carriage to pick you all up in exactly two months."

"Miss Suzanna, know?"

"No. It will be at your discretion, your judgment, to tell her when you feel she's ready to hear it. Use it wisely. She's no longer the person she once was."

"But, Mister Cooper, I'on how to—"

"To read. Remy does. And I've allowed you to run the farm to prepare you to run your own. It is why I took you into town with me when I did business and taught you everything I know. You are very capable of running a farm, Sam. Remy caught on impressively as a student. With your farm knowledge and her education, and Yes'sa Man's strength, you all should do well. I've included my contact information. Please stay in touch. And if you need anything… anything at all, please let me know. I may not be able to return because of all that has happened, but I will make a way to see you if you ever need me. Also, I hired a white man to help you all out in the field. He'll be your cover to help you deal with those who look like him."

"How you know we can trust 'em?"

"He came recommended by a friend who helped me purchase my family. I will see to it that he is always paid well for helping you all." Cooper patted Sam on the shoulder and went into the house.

Sam rushed off the porch on his way to his cabin to share the news with the others.

Cooper cleaned up and changed clothes before going into his son's room. Despite all that had happened around him, he lay peacefully, innocent of life's problems and nothing like the people who caused them.

Cooper picked up the sleeping child. He felt so warm, so cuddly. Squeezing him gently, he placed several kisses on his thick red cheeks, hating to return him to his bed. As soon as he laid him back down, CJ curled up.

Cooper went into the bedroom. He lit it and saw Suzanna laying across the bed sound asleep. An empty bottle of wine sat on the table nearby.

His eyes reasoned with the stained bedspread. Taking a closer look, he found his assumption to be correct. "Blood. What have you done, Suzanna?" He searched, following the trails from the bed to the floor on one end and Suzanna's wrist that was full of dried blood on the other. Remembering the former conversation he had with Remy, he believed the lacerations to be self-inflicted. Superficial wounds that were of no deadly threat to her.

Cooper left the room and returned with supplies to clean and dress her wounds. He sat next to her, propped up a leg, took her arm and began.

She moved. Her eyes opened. "Cooper. I knew you would come back."

He didn't respond but continued cleaning her wounds.

"We can get past this...We just had a husband and wife spat, that's all."

He could smell the alcohol on her breath. "It's much more serious than that, Suzanna, I think you know that."

She closed her eyes and went back to sleep.

Cooper finished dressing her wounds, laid her arm on her stomach and looked at her. He'd blamed her for Nina's death and the death of his unborn child. Staring at her, he wanted to hate her for it. He tried to find every reason to, but he was just as guilty. He knew that now. No matter how much he wanted to assign blame outside of his own actions, each reason returned with a *but I did...if it wasn't for me...because of what I've done...I, me, I've...It's me.*

He went to the chair where the breakfast table once was and sat by the broken window nursing his conscience. His mind refusing to grant him pity while he thought about the last time he spoke to Nina. He'd broken her heart that day, and death stripped him of begging for her forgiveness.

He went over to Suzanna and whispered in her sleeping ears. "This is not your fault. I'm sorry for every pain I caused you. I allowed you to fall in love with me knowing that my heart would always belong to Nina. Never telling you who I was, lying about where I came from, and the black blood that ran through my veins." He caressed her face with the back of his hand. "I deceived you. From the moment I met you, I was dishonest. To force my family and my wife on you, I—I was wrong."

The guilt that he'd charged to Suzanna was slowly being paid by his admissions. "It was never fair to you. How did I expect you to deal with this? To handle it?"

He'd created the perfect storm that had come and destroyed lives. It was him. He was the catalyst. He had injected the virus and formed the disease that caused hate, malice, and the pain that led to the death of his unborn child and the woman he truly loved. Suzanna's actions, the person she'd become were born out of the pain he'd caused.

"I do hope you find it in your heart to forgive me. I hope that forgiveness brings you the peace that guilt shall never grant me." He kissed her on the forehead. "Please return to the loving and kind woman I knew and not the bitter woman I created. Goodbye, dear heart. I will always love you."

The anger he'd harvested against her faded away with every step that moved him further away from her presence. She quickly became a part of his past. Going inside one of his traveling bags, he took out a thick envelope full of money. Funds he needed to travel with. Turning off the lantern, he walked to the front porch where all three helpers were waiting for him.

Yes'sa Man dived into his arms, burying his face into his chest. "Take me wit' you."

Patting his back, Cooper had forgotten how attached Yes'sa Man was to him. "Remy needs you and so does Sam. What will they do without you? You'll have to show them how to work the fields. Can you do that for me?"

"Yes'sa, I'll do it." Yes'sa Man turned to Remy, falling into her arms.

"Mister Cooper need for you to be strong, okay?" she told him.

"Yes'sa." Saddened, Yes'sa Man sat on the edge of the porch, head down, legs bouncing wildly with tears falling slowly.

"Remy. I'll need you to look after Suzanna."

"You know I will."

"I gave Sam everything you all will need to start your new lives."

"I got it back at the cabin," Sam said.

Understanding, Remy shook her head. She reached for Cooper's hand and walked him away from the others. "Mister Cooper, I don't want you holding no guilt about what happened here. You know life is hard for us slaves. All we can do is be our best and give our best. You've been a blessing to every one of us, no matter how it ended. Your family is happy. You brought Suzanna back to life when she wanted to hand her life over to death. And you're leaving her with a son to love. That's plenty of reason to live. She didn't have that before you came. Now she got somebody to live for. And Nina, well, like I said, life is hard for a slave. But I talked to Nina. She was in love with you. And when we find love, real love, it beats never knowing it on any day."

"Hurry up, woman, fo' daylight come. He gotta go," Sam fussed.

Still holding Cooper's hand, Remy gave Sam the mean-eyes. She continued, "Ain't nothing you can do 'bout the road behind you, but you got a long road before you. And you gonna be alright. Just don't look behind you and don't ever stop moving cause when you do, you give life a chance to catch up with you. Don't dwell on death, Mister Cooper, dwell on living. You have to live life instead of letting life live you."

Cooper pulled out an envelope and papers and gave them to Remy.

Taking them, she looked at him curiously.

"This is for Cecil. It's his freedom papers. Make sure he gets it."

"I will. And this?" She held up the envelope.

"Open it."

She dug inside the envelope and pulled out a business card. "Da-Dar-well, La-ing-ston?"

"That's right, Darwell Lingston, He can help you find your family."

She rushed Cooper with a hug so hard that it pushed him back. Releasing him, she wiped tears.

He reached into his waistcoat pocket and took out a letter and gave it to Remy. "This is for my son. Please give it to him when he becomes of age."

"What age is that?"

"When you feel he is ready to know."

She tucked the letter in her pocket.

Sam walked over. "Well, 'dis be it. I sho' gone miss you. And if the authorities come, they'll have to kill us buh'fo we breave' a word."

"That's right," Remy said.

Yes'sa Man came over. Cooper hugged them all, stepped off the porch, and climbed onto his horse that Sam had ready for him. Before leaving, he took a separate horse and loaded Nina's wrapped body onto it and pulled it behind him.

Stopping by the river at the spot where he and Nina had created wonderful memories, he took her body from the horse, and carried her to the river. He made a fire and burned her body in the quilt she was wrapped in. He smacked the horse that had carried her body. It raced off in the opposite direction.

Cooper climbed onto his horse. "CLCK, CLCK." The horse sped off, carrying Cooper Edwards, the slave named Jesse, who became *The Passer*.

Jesse, The Passer

That which he hated,
He learned to embrace.
That which he embraced,
Gave him freedom,
That which gave him freedom,
Put him in bondage.
That which put him in bondage,
Set him free.

÷÷÷÷÷÷

For my grandfather...

His name was Edward Cooper and he was my grandfather. Not by blood, but by marriage. Never knowing my biological grandfathers due to death, he took that role, cloaked himself in it and wore it with honor. Although he is totally and completely unrelated to the character, I named my character for him. My love for my grandfather will always be. May he rest in God's care for all eternity.

Share Your Thoughts

Hope you enjoyed *The Passer*. If so, please take a few seconds to write a positive review. Love you for it!

C. Yvette Spencer, Drama Novelist on Amazon, Facebook, Twitter, and Goodreads
C. Yvette Spencer, Drama Novelist's newsletter: c.yvettespencer@gmail.com

Scan to grab your next favorite C. Yvette Spencer book

C. Yvette Spencer's Series
Desperate Struggles Trilogy
Book 1: "Mama Ain't Dead Yet!"
Book 2: By Any Means Necessary!
Book 3: The Struggle Just Got Real!
Khonnie & Khyle Chronicles (2021)
Book 1: Uncharted Territory
Book 2: Enjoying the Ride
Book 3: Climatic High
Book 4: From Dusk to Dawn

Twisted Lessons Collection
Be Careful What You Pray For
Confessions in the Dark
Untimely Death
Devil's Prey

African American Historical Novels
The Passer
The Story of Gloria & Sadie
The Life Alterer (2021)

PENT Up Freedom Collection
Life's Reflections from a Broken Mirror (2021)

This is a:

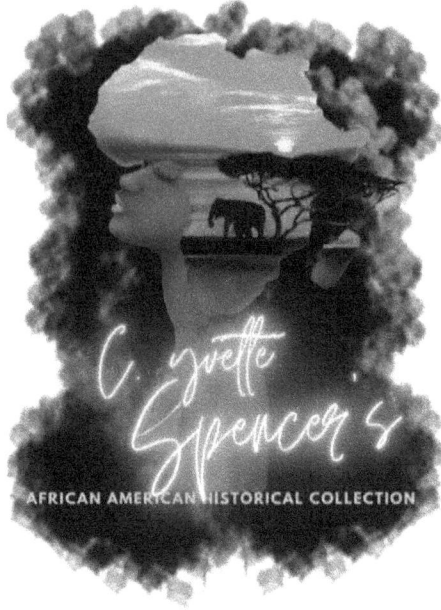

C. Yvette Spencer's

AFRICAN AMERICAN HISTORICAL COLLECTION

From the collection of:

C. Yvette Spencer's Books

GIVING YOU WHAT I LOVE TO WRITE

C. YVETTE SPENCER

Drama Novelist

www.ingramcontent.com/pod-product-compliance
Lightning Source LLC
Chambersburg PA
CBHW020905100426
42737CB00043B/141